Pre-trial Detention in 20th and 21st Century Common Law and Civil Law Systems

Pre-trial Detention in 20th and 21st Century Common Law and Civil Law Systems

Edited by

Marion Charret-Del Bove and Fabrice Mourlon

CAMBRIDGE SCHOLARS PUBLISHING

Pre-trial Detention in 20th and 21st Century Common Law and Civil Law Systems,
Edited by Marion Charret-Del Bove and Fabrice Mourlon

This book first published 2014

Cambridge Scholars Publishing

12 Back Chapman Street, Newcastle upon Tyne, NE6 2XX, UK

British Library Cataloguing in Publication Data
A catalogue record for this book is available from the British Library

ISBN (10): 1-4438-5991-5, ISBN (13): 978-1-4438-5991-2

TABLE OF CONTENTS

INTRODUCTION

Now limbo will be
A cold glitter of souls
Through some far briny zone.
—Seamus Heaney, Limbo

Although written to describe the state of limbo in which the population of Northern Ireland were in during the conflict and the failure by the Catholic Church to acknowledge its illegitimate children, the extract of the poem by Seamus Heaney reminds us of the conditions and special legislation under which individuals or groups are detained. The floating legality that hinders their freedom might often be seen to be a "far briny zone" to which our attention should be drawn.

Since the last quarter of the 20th century detention centres keeping alleged terrorists or immigrants have caught the public eye through large media coverage and NGO's scrutiny. With increasing flows of immigrants leaving their country for economic or political reasons, whose mobility has been eased by globalisation; with the changing nature of terrorism and the rise of inter-ethnic and intra-state conflicts, governments have used detention centres as a way to contain these phenomena.

On 13 and 14 December 2012, the *Centre de Recherches Interculturelles sur les Domaines Anglophones et Francophones* (CRIDAF), a research centre at the University of Paris 13 organised a symposium to debate these issues focusing on principles and modalities of pre-trial detention in common law and civil law countries in the 20th and 21st centuries. The international and interdisciplinary approach was one of the main features of the centre. This approach has been prolonged since then by the integration of the centre into a larger research unit, *Pléiade*, gathering specialists from other disciplines including history, literature and linguistics. One of the core values and *raison d'être* of the new unit is to consider and analyse research objects through a multi-faceted and multi-disciplinary prism, making the symposium on pre-trial detention a timely event.

This book contains a selection of papers derived from presentations made at the conference by academics specialized in law and comparative criminal procedure, political science, history sociology, linguistics, and legal translation offering a comparative analysis of countries with differing legal traditions. Its aim is to make a contribution to the newly-researched topic of pre-trial detention from a theoretical and empirical point of view. Papers alternatively consider various issues: they analyse the philosophical principles and policies underlying pre-trial detention and look at the different forms it takes according to several countries; on a more technical and pragmatic level they raise the question of the use of an appropriate terminology and the problem of translation that may arise from the differences between the studied legal systems. Finally, they consider the checks and balances mechanisms put in place to limit the negative effects of the measures restricting liberty.

Detention is commonly regarded as a form of punishment resulting from a criminal act and often means the deprivation of a person's liberty after judgment. The history of imprisonment as a sanction for criminal offences has been well documented. This form of punishment became widely used at the end of the 18th century to put an end to public sanctions and acts of torture and was also spurred by the abolitionist movement initiated by Cesare Beccaria in *On Crimes and Punishments*. Penal reformers such as John Howard and Jeremy Bentham organised the prison system which in the 19th century served either as a deterrent to criminal offences or as a place deemed to rehabilitate convicts.

However, incarceration as a sentence after trial overlooks other forms of detention. The legal definition of the term implies "the action to hold a person against his will" (Cornu 304) which as a result infringes upon his/her freedom to come and go. This broader meaning covers a large array of legislation and places pending trial, which have attracted growing interest among academics, NGOs and International Organisations. In recent years, the Guantanamo Bay Detention Camp has come to epitomize such pre-trial places and legal arrangements with principles often tainted with being arbitrary. In the mid-1980s, the United Nations Commission on Human Rights acknowledged the need to address the expanding phenomenon of arbitrary detention, leading to the setting up of the Working Group on Arbitrary Detention in 1991.

The exceptional arrangements that are more or less detrimental to human rights have appeared in times of crisis, conflict or facing particularly serious offences. Systems of administrative detentions have had several avatars. For instance, Great Britain and Northern Ireland introduced Prevention of Terrorism Acts in the early 1970s to tackle the rise in political violence, continuing a long tradition of measures aimed at curbing Irish rebellions since the 19th century. (See Paddy Hillyard) Other examples can be drawn from Latin America dictatorships in the 1970s, from France during the Algerian war, or more recently with the provisions of anti-terrorist legislation in the United Kingdom and the United States—*Terrorism Act 2000, Patriot Act 2001*. Immigration Detention Camps have been a feature of contemporary states, i.e. the migrant camps of Calais in France, the reinforcement of such places in the US in 1981 onwards (see Daniel Wilsher) or the Immigration Removal Centres in the UK (Home Office, UK Border Agency) and its Immigration Detention Centres representing one of the largest estates in Europe. (The Migration Observatory)

Pre-trial detention is also an arrangement belonging to general schemes of the legal system. Michel Foucault, in *Discipline and Punish: The Birth of the Prison*, argued that if surveillance is usually meant to prevent crime, it also lies at the heart of the punitive scheme, and is used by political power as a way of controlling individuals through the prison system. Pre-trial detention appears to be at the crossroads of these principles. It is both part and parcel of the legal proceedings of the criminal investigation and aims at striking a fragile balance between protecting the State and respecting individual freedoms. Pre-charge detention corresponds to the period when a person, after being arrested is detained so as to determine the nature of the offences and the characterization of the charges. We are not short of examples to illustrate the variety of pre-trial detention modalities in common law and civil law traditions: the duration of custody, custody rights, right to silence, right to the presence of a lawyer, modalities and control of pre-trial detention, procedures in case of wrongful detention.

The present collection of papers starts with an invaluable contribution by Kenneth O. Morgan who is both a distinguished scholar and a member of the House of Lords. In "The Politics of Pre-trial Detention in the United Kingdom since 2000" he analyses how the ideal of liberty in a country celebrated as the "mother of the free" since Magna Carta has come under severe attack since the 2001 Anti-Terrorism Act. The terrorist threats to British citizens since the 9/11 attacks, the fear of immigration, the rise in Euro-scepticism and Europhobia and the erosion of the libertarian tradition within the Labour party have contributed to the passing of a series of laws concerning pre-trial detention that have curtailed the civil liberties of non-British and then British citizens. This system of detention relies on control orders, thus providing the executive with extensive powers over the normal judicial process, which is reminiscent of legislation passed for Northern Ireland in the 1970s. However, as Kenneth O. Morgan points out, the House of Lords besides pressure groups and a few legal and political figures, has played a significant role in upholding civil liberties issues and challenging the various anti-terrorism legislation until the present day. According to him, the role of Parliament should be re-affirmed in the re-examination of pre-trial detention legal arrangements.

Restrictions of people's rights and freedoms by the State are further explored in the context of public protests. In "Preventive Interventions and the Right to Protest," Neil Jarman argues that governments and police in Europe and North America are increasingly using preventive interventions as a way to prevent individuals and groups from exercising their right to protest, which major human rights instruments guarantee as a form of peaceful assembly. Although the State may impose restrictions on such rights, it should not undermine the essence of the fundamental right to assemble, nor should it prevent the assembly from achieving its aim. However, the author points out that governments are more and more concerned about security, order and control over protests and have used their police force to arrest and detain individuals or groups on the suspicion that they may commit an offence or an act of violence. Three main forms of preventive interventions are considered: preventing people from reaching the protest; containing people in a defined area and mass detentions or arrests of protesters; finally preventive detention of targeted individuals. Although these new instruments of State repression are being challenged in courts and by international organisations' recommendations, Neil Jarman maintains that preventive interventions should be monitored and questioned to ensure that citizens have the right to voice their opinions.

Striking a balance between concerns for collective security and individual rights is addressed by Roy Carpenter in his paper on the specific context of pre-trial detention in Guantamo Bay: "Habeas, Hamdan and History: Separation of Powers and Pre-trial Detention in Guantanamo Bay." Sometimes referred to as a "legal black hole," this detention facility and the rights of its detainees are also part of a long tradition of policy influenced by political institutions in the US, namely the separation of powers. The author contends that constants can be identified in the history of the country in wartime and exceptional situations. The executive takes action in response to a national security crisis and individuals identified as the enemy are taken into custody and denied their basic legal rights; then the judiciary questions the validity of such decisions; finally the executive seeks legislative approval, which is usually granted. The detainee has the right to call into question the legitimacy of his/her detention before a neutral judge —*habeas corpus*. Assessing these mechanisms in the case of Guantamo Bay and in the light of other historical developments, Roy Carpenter shows that the doctrine of the separation of powers has been beneficial in the pre-trial detention policy since it has enabled procedures to be publicly debated through institutional challenges.

In her paper "Crime and punishment in the 20th Century Brazilian War Navy: the punishment of rebellious and insubordinate seamen," Silvia Capanema relates the story of two rebellions organised by seamen in 1910 and 1964 in Brazil. She explains the specificity of judgement and punishment in the Brazilian War Navy which accounts for the subsequent revolts. The life experience of Joâo Cândido (the leader of the 1910 uprising) while he was detained without trial for two years is analysed through his memoirs written and artefacts made during his imprisonment. The second uprising (1964) is considered in relation to the memorial references to the 1910 revolt. Joâo Cândido's figure, which became part of the collective memory, was used by the new group of rebellious seamen who were acting in a highly politicized context leading to a dictatorship. The comparative study of these two revolts help understand the relationships between power and law in a military context between ordinary seamen and their hierarchy as well as the response of the State in different political regimes.

Marie Marty's paper "The right to a lawyer: the first of the Europeanisation of procedural guarantees in pre-trial detention" examines the influence of European institutions on guaranteeing access to a lawyer for suspects during police custody, which can be regarded as a form of pre-trial detention. The author takes the example of two European countries, France and Belgium as they have similar definitions of police custody and have the same inquisitorial tradition in their legal systems. Although both countries are parties to the European Convention on Human Rights which ensures the protection of defence rights including the right to access to a lawyer, they did not comply with those rights until the *Salduz* decision that led to major reforms. The European influence on these two legal systems is a starting point to consider whether the pre-trial detention regime could be harmonised throughout all Member States. After analysing the already existing mechanisms of judicial cooperation between States, Marie Marty contends that the strengthening of fundamental rights in the pre-trial phase is a way forward towards harmonisation. She then explains how legal instruments emanating from various European institutions have had a limited impact on national legislation. In turn, Member States have been reluctant in implementing the right to access to a lawyer as national legislations are still incomplete in this matter and as abuse of process can be used to circumvent legislation itself. The author concludes that even if her analysis of the convergence of national legislations is limited to two Member States, the impact of the *Salduz* jurisprudence in other States is a sign towards the building up of harmonisation in the EU.

Elizabeth Gibson-Morgan's paper "Police Custody in England and France: a Lawful Deprivation of Liberty?"constitutes another major contribution to comparative legal studies. It focuses on the evolution of police custody in England and France while comparing the legal rules applied during the few hours or days spent by a person taken into police custody on suspicion of his/ her having committed an offence. The analysis of this evolution underscores the past and present flaws of both police custody regimes. Firstly, the most striking feature of the English situation is the absence of proportionality of the custodial measure. As a matter of fact, since 1 January, 2006, the notion of arrestable offence has been abolished, thus making the decision to take someone into custody possible whatever the seriousness of the allegedly committed offence. On the opposite, the 2011 French police custody reform introduced an enhancement of suspects' rights, as the author has it. It aims at preserving the principle of proportionality by linking the custodial measure to the seriousness of the alleged offence and extending the right to legal counsel. Indeed, French lawyers are now allowed to be present from the outset of the police custody even during police interviews even if they still have no access to the file itself. The author raises the tricky issue of the respect of the rule of the law during this crucial investigating period. Due to recent cuts in legal aid in England and the poor legal aid funding in France, there is an urgent need in both countries for clear and accessible rules regarding police custody to achieve "legal security."

Common law and civil law systems have traditionally been opposed. Alika Taleb, in her paper "The Pre-trial detention in the French and the English Criminal Justice Systems: towards a balance between Security and Liberty," convincingly demonstrates how English and French justice systems are based on different legal cultures. Nevertheless, what is striking, according to Mrs Taleb, is the process of convergence between French and English justice systems regarding police custody rules. The author examines two topical issues from a comparative point of view: the question of the effective legal assistance when defence counsel has limited access to the case file; on the other hand, the controversial issue of the lack of independence of the French public prosecutor. Mrs Taleb even considers a possible conviction of France should the French current legislation be reviewed by the European Court of Human Rights (EctHR) for non-compliance with the European Convention on Human Rights. Indeed, she analyses the case *Moulin v. France* that dealt with the ambiguous status of the French prosecutor connected both to the executive and judicial powers. For the author, the decision highlighted the flaws in the French prosecuting system: the prosecutor as he stands is not considered as an independent judicial authority from case parties. As a conclusion, the paper focuses on two possible solutions to solve this tricky matter: either greater autonomy of the French prosecutor from the executive, or the removal of all detention powers from this function.

Thanks to Celine Chassang's contribution, "Detention on remand and the presumption of innocence principle: the French pattern of a tricky conciliation," another aspect of pre-trial detention is thoroughly examined: detention on remand or *detention provisoire* in French. Mrs. Chassang highlights the apparent contradiction that lies between the deprivation of liberty of someone detained pending trial and his/her right to be presumed innocent until proven guilty. The analysis of the legal modalities of this form of pre-trial detention lays the emphasis on the exceptional nature of the measure—it is sometimes replaced by judicial supervision or house arrest—that needs to be duly justified. However, the justifications of detention on remand set out in Article 144 of the French Code of Criminal Procedure (CCP) do not fully respect of the presumption of innocence, the author argues. Indeed, they designate the person charged with an offence as already guilty, thus re-enforcing the pre-judgment of the suspect. The contribution is all the more relevant as it points to a double-checking principle embodied by the French liberty and custody judge, who, according to the Mrs. Chassang, is not necessarily the best person to asses if detention on remand is useful or not. Furthermore, an absence of conciliation between the presumption of innocence and detention on remand is even more obvious when the person is actually detained pending trial. First of all, the possible length of such a detention is far too excessive. Second of all, it constitutes a burdensome measure that imposes rigorous detention conditions, even more rigorous than for prison detention. Eventually, to attenuate the ambiguous position prisoners on remand are, Mrs. Chassang, along with other colleagues, advocates the creation of separate facilities especially designed for persons remanded in custody as a way to reach the tricky conciliation between detention on remand and the presumption of innocence.

To take the matter one step further, Sacha Raoult, in "The Functional Ambiguities of Pre-Trial Detention in France," presents the three ambiguous social functions fulfilled by pre-trial detention : governing social marginality, punishing guilt after the fact and presenting a bargaining tool to the defendant while hoping to get a confession. Firstly, the author recalls the traditional differences between punishment and pre-trial detention but to challenge this over-simplified opposition. In order to emphasize the ambiguously disturbing similarities between pre-trial detention and post-sentence detention, Mr. Raoult dwells on the practical modalities of the two forms of detention. Safety and guilt are in fact involved in the detention decision. The author efficiently demonstrates how pre and post-trial detention in fact overlap. The originality of the paper lies in the exploratory empirical research conducted into pre-trial detention decisions collected from judges and lawyers. By way of conclusion, Mr. Raoult concludes that pre-trial detention, as it is currently used in France, is a punitive practice, an emergency judgment revised ex post, revealing the multi-functional ambiguity of detention on remand.

There is another aspect of detention that requires further examination: the detention of illegal immigrants. Géraldine Gadbin-George analyses immigration policies and detention centres in France and the UK in her contribution "Detention Centres in France and the United Kingdom and the Criminalisation of Migrants: the Reality of Access to Justice?" The author provides us with a brief reminder of both countries' respective immigration policies, highlighting the periods when immigration was either encouraged or discouraged because of economic factors. She starts by defining who an illegal migrant is: any person who entered the territory without prior authorisation. To detain such people is a purely administrative decision which should not be assimilated to a prison sentence. When arrested, unauthorised migrants are invited to return to their countries. In case of refusal, Mrs Gadbin-George explains, they are detained or placed under house arrest. Illegal migrants are momentarily deprived of their freedom of movement in French *Centres de Rétention Administrative* or English Immigration Removal Centres. And yet, they are not deprived of their rights to access legal services if necessary. As a matter of fact, the comparative description of the detention process in both countries helps us understand the context in which non-European migrants are detained. Detention procedures are complex enough to make legal assistance necessary, which is the reason why France and the UK seem to provide adequate ways of accessing law, Mrs. Gadbin-George argues. Nevertheless, the author does not forget to mention the phenomenon of "crimmigration" (Stumpf) through which migrants, whether authorised or not, are sometimes treated as criminals.

Detention of illegal migrants can also be used as a technique of migration and border control, as argued by Catherine Puzzo in "Immigration Detention in the UK: the Role of Oversight Mechanisms and Constricting Rules to Raise Standards." Her contribution presents the recent evolution of immigration detention and how it has gradually criminalized migrants. For instance, the Nationality, Immigration and Asylum Act 2000 leaves the onus to make a bail application on the representative of the migrant detainee.

Mrs Puzzo questions the proportionality of the use and continuation of detention measures justified by the government for the sake of public protection. Her analysis of current detention practices raises controversial questions such as how the State seems more concerned with the maintenance of controls than with the psychological costs of detainees and the financial costs of the government. Nevertheless, Mrs Puzzo also points to the efforts made to improve and guarantee optimal detention conditions in face of problems of mismanagement of Immigration Removal Centres by private providers. In her article, she examines the gradual implementation of standard regulations and their effectiveness thanks to the role of field charities and institutional watchdogs. They have been closely monitoring detention centres to detect and prevent abuses as well as to promote better practices more respectful of migrants' rights. Even though migrants' detaining conditions have been improved over the past 15 years, some progress still has to be made particularly regarding the way migrants are sometimes (mis)considered.

Last, but not least, this book addresses the tricky question of legal translation thanks to Georges Fournier's paper which tackles the general topic of the translation of laws of exception, and more particularly specific counter-terrorism measures of arrest and detention of alleged terrorists such as Control Orders in Great Britain. The author adopts a diachronic approach justified by the extended period covered by the counter-terrorism legislation under consideration, between the Prevention of Terrorism Act 2005 and the Terrorism Prevention and Investigation Measure Act 2011. He first points out the controversial nature of these measures, especially the preventive and indefinite detention of supposed terrorists (nationals or foreigners) without prior appearance before a judge or any legal representative. By way of illustration, Mr. Fournier uses Peter Kosminsky's film *Blitz*, a well-documented fiction film on the jihad in Great Britain. The paper starts with a comparative linguistic analysis of the 2005 and 2011 Acts of Parliament, highlighting an increased inflation in words and a sharp decrease in the repetition of Control Order. Then, the author turns to possible ways of translating laws of exception and the multiple pitfalls the translator may fall into. For instance, one major obstacle is the "uncertainty as to whether the terminology applies to the judicial or administrative domain, keeping in mind that, under normal circumstances, measures designed to restrict freedom result from a judiciary and not an administrative decision." The article lays the emphasis on the use of equivalences and calques. The former is used "to avoid coining words and phrases which would be meaningless in the target language" while the latter is resorted to by translators to "underline [...] the foreign dimension of laws which require to be explained from a different perspective." Mr. Fournier takes great care to explain how the impossibility to find exact equivalences between different legal systems leads to the choice of hyperonyms, explanatory statements or even periphrastic structures designed to avoid mistakes. He examines several possible translations of Control Order from English into French using equivalences, calques or even neologism such as *contrôle judiciaire. mesures de police*, *detention préventive*, *détention provisoire rétention* or *assignation à residence*, *tutelle pénale*, *mesure de sûreté*, *ordre de contrôle*, *ordonnance de contrôle.* As a conclusion, Mr. Fournier presents two translating solutions, *contrôle judiciaire* for linguists and legal experts, *ordonnance de contrôle* for the general public, bearing in mind that translating legal measures evolving over a period of several years requires to take into account the period at which a text is issued.

All things considered, whatever the legal system under scrutiny —common law or civil law—the different authors convincingly demonstrated throughout their contributions that pre-trial detention is a legal reality that challenges several fundamental issues: the balance between individual rights (right to legal counsel, right to legal assistance....) and the protection of public order and security; the proportionality of custodial measures for persons suspected of an offence, or detention measures for unauthorized migrants; the preservation of the presumption of innocence as well as the difficulties in translating legal terminologies specific to common law or civil law. This proves how legal and linguistic matters are constantly intertwined and need to be examined in an interdisciplinary way.

Works Cited

BECCARIA Cesare. *On Crimes and Punishments.* 1764. Empire Books, 2012.

CORNU, Gérard. *Vocabulaire juridique*. Paris: PUF, 2008.

Find an immigration removal centre. Home Office, UK Border Agency. Accessed March 2014. URL: <http://www.ukba.homeoffice.gov.uk/aboutus/organisation/immigrationremovalcentres/>.

FOUCAULT, Michel, translated by Alan SHERIDAN. *Discipline and Punish: The Birth of the Prison.* Vintage Books, 1995, second edition.

HEANEY, Seamus. "Limbo" in *Wintering Out,* London: Faber&Faber, 1972.

HILLYARD, Paddy. *Suspect Community*, London: Pluto Press, 1993.

Immigration Detention in the UK. URL: <http://migrationobservatory.ox.ac.uk/briefings/immigration-detention-uk>. Accessed March 2014.

STUMPF, Juliet. "The Crimmigration Crisis: Immigrants, Crime, and Sovereign Power." *American University Law Review* 56 (2006): 367-419.

WILSHER, Daniel. *Immigration Detention: Law, History, Politics*, Cambridge: Cambridge University Press, 2012.

THE POLITICS OF PRE-TRIAL DETENTION IN THE UNITED KINGDOM SINCE 2000

KENNETH O. MORGAN
KING'S COLLEGE, LONDON

As every French schoolboy knows, the three great ideals of modern France are liberty, equality and fraternity. In Great Britain, political argument in the last hundred years has been largely over the last two, equality above all. Liberty has not seemed to be a contentious issue in a country where the patriotic song "Land of Hope and Glory" celebrates the land as "mother of the free." Civil and political liberty has apparently been enshrined in Great Britain for many centuries. Back in 1215, King John was forced to accept *Magna Carta*, embodying personal liberty and freedom from arbitrary arrest by the forces of the state. There has also been since the Middle Ages the great principle of open liberty endorsed in the legal doctrine of *Habeas Corpus*, given statutory force in the Habeas Corpus Act of 1679, while the seventeenth-century civil war resulted in the victory of Parliament and the common law over arbitrary rule and royalist tyranny. In the twentieth century there were few great political arguments over issues of liberty after the end of the second world war in 1945. Nor was there any detention before charge or trial other than in the tragic exception of Northern Ireland in the 1970s which somehow seemed to be quite distinct in its political experience from the rest of the British Isles. Detention or custody by the police was carefully defined in the 1984 Police and Criminal Evidence Act, with pre-trial detention in custody limited to just 48 hours at most.

Personal liberty seemed even more entrenched after 1997 with a series of New Labour legal and constitutional reforms enacted by the Blair government—the Human Rights Act of 1998 incorporating the European Convention of Human Rights into British law, followed by devolution for Scotland and Wales, the establishment of a new Supreme Court and a reinforced separation of the executive and the judiciary with the changed role of the Lord Chancellor who had previously straddled legislative, executive and the judiciary. No longer would this constitutional anomaly occur. The new view of the uncodified British constitution was that it was rights-based, with a clear and fair balance apparently struck between considerations of national security and the protection of citizens from outside threat, and the underpinning of personal liberty. There appeared to be no political problem.

Yet in fact the new century was to produce a series of major political conflicts over liberty issues. A steady series of invasions of personal liberty by the government was now to follow. It began with the 2001 Anti-Terrorism Act, which was whisked through the House of Commons after a mere 16 hours of debate. It applied only to non-British residents in the first instance. A process of pre-trial internment of much personal harshness was conducted in detention centres, of which Belmarsh prison became the most notorious. As we shall see, particularly significant arguments were to build up over a growing tendency to pre-trial custody. High Court judges became more and more outspoken, seeing it as disproportionate and discriminatory, notably Lord Hoffman who condemned the process and declared parts of the Act of 2001 to be illegal. As Anti-Terrorism Acts mounted up, political conflict and tension built up also. So why should this change in the atmosphere in public discussions of liberty be now occurring?

A primary reason, of course, was that the Anti-Terrorist measures were a result of a clear and visible terrorist threat to British citizens, a factor often under-estimated by critics of recent British legal processes. The attack on the twin towers in New York in 2001 on 9/11 had a massive impact on Britain. After all, it was a major tragedy for British as well as American citizens, with 67 British people killed, the worst such atrocity to befall Britain since 1945. On home soil, on 7 July 2005 a series of terrorist attacks on public transport in London killed 56 people (four of them bombers) and maimed or injured another 700. Four Muslim men were convicted and sentenced to 40 years' imprisonment. Another two potentially very serious terrorist attacks in London and Glasgow were narrowly averted in June 2007. Britain seemed under threat as never before, and a whole raft of new security measures were undertaken to protect citizens and buildings from attack. The government was under pressure from press and public to use wider coercive powers. This point was absorbed especially by the Home Office which recalled the techniques against terrorism, real or alleged, used in Northern Ireland in the 1970s such as the Diplock courts and detention without trial. The bureaucratic memory was a long one, and Northern Ireland became a template for future procedures in Great Britain generally.

Secondly, a background issue was widespread fear of immigration into Britain, as a threat not only to social services and provision but perhaps to national security. At least a million and a half people entered Britain, many of them from Eastern Europe and the Middle East between 1997 and 2007. The 2011 population census showed that the British population contained seven and a half million people born outside the United Kingdom, 13% of the total population, and a radical shift since the 2001 census. This fanned some popular concern—not necessarily racial since the older post-1960 immigration from the black and brown population had been absorbed into the community, while many of the new immigrants were white, from Eastern Europe, Poles above all, the second largest group of new migrants identified in the 2011 census.

A third, subsidiary issue was the linking of security issues with some animus towards Europe. Euro-scepticism or Europhobia, never far from the surface in England especially, was stirred up when the European court at Strasbourg appeared to be overruling British common law by making contentious calls for the free rights of entry for immigrants and asylum-seekers. Here, it seemed, was another threat to domestic safety, coming from an alien court overseas. There were calls in return for a British Bill of Rights to be framed to discriminate in favour of the native-born.

Finally, in the political aspects, it was noticeable that New Labour under Tony Blair, in its zeal to occupy the centre ground and reject the frequent anti-police attitudes of socialist militants in the 1980s, was far less libertarian than its Labour predecessors. "Toughness on crime" as well as on the causes of crime was now paramount, with much talk of "zero tolerance." Labour, with a series of hard-line Home Secretaries such as David Blunkett, Charles Clarke and John Reid, seemed to have forgotten its old zeal for personal freedom. Major Labour figures like Clement Attlee, Stafford Cripps, Aneurin Bevan and Harold Laski had been prominent in the founding of the National Council of Civil Liberties under Ronald Kidd in 1934. In the 1950s, Hugh Gaitskell and Aneurin Bevan, greatly at odds on foreign and defence issues, stood shoulder to shoulder in defence of civil liberties, but those libertarian traditions seemed in the era of New Labour, so-called, to be set aside.

At first, in the period from 2001 to 2004, the emphasis was on detaining suspected aliens, immigrants and asylum seekers. Belmarsh was used widely and controversially: it was compared by human rights lawyers to the illegalities of American practices in Guantanamo Bay. Pressure built up relentlessly now to extending the legal period of pre-trial detention. In 2001 it was raised to seven days, in 2003 it went up to 14 days, and in 2005 Tony Blair proposed raising the limit to no less than 90 days. As detention centres came to be followed by control orders drastically limiting the personal freedom of movement and communication of the people involved, a South African High Court judge, Lord Steyn, compared the situation in Britain as comparable to house arrest in South Africa during the era of apartheid. The suspension of Article 5 of the European Convention on Human Rights so that "people can be locked up without trial when there is no evidence on which they could be prosecuted" was not justified. The British government, citing a state of national emergency in the face of terrorist threats, was derogating from the European Convention on Human Rights and in effect from its own Human Rights Act of 1998. Finally in 2004, on somewhat restricted grounds, the Law Lords declared the Anti-Terrorist Act of 2001 to be illegal as being incompatible with the European Convention of Human Rights.

The arguments had been marked by vigorous campaigning by libertarian pressure-groups such as Liberty, Justice and Amnesty International. Shami Chakrabarti, the able young Indian woman lawyer appointed director of Liberty in 2003, became something of a celebrity on the media. The Bar Council, under the chairmanship of a progressive barrister, Matt Kelly, became outspoken in denouncing the illegal features of pre-trial procedures. There was much political protest from the Liberal Democrats and also from a number of Labour legal figures such as Helena Kennedy, a Labour peer. Lady Manningham-Buller, former Director-General of MI5 and Stella Rimmington, her predecessor, were also remarkably critical of the coercive measures used. They pointed out that the recent legislation was actually damaging to acquiring information about terrorists since its counter-productive effect was to alienate young Muslims and discourage them from providing useful evidence. Another, more surprising, critic came from within the police service: he was Andy Hayman, the former Assistant Commissioner for Special Operations at Scotland Yard. There was a call for more use of intercept evidence in open court as occurred in France and other countries. The House of Lords Constitution Committee was also very vocal along these lines. The Bill, it said, risked "conflating the roles of Parliament and the judiciary which would be quite inappropriate."

Politically, a striking feature was the growing involvement of the House of Lords on civil liberties issues. Under the British constitutional system, and in contrast to the role of the Supreme Court in the United States, only Parliament could strike down legislation, and this gave authority to the non-elected House which was nevertheless freer from control of the party whips and more guided by a sense of independence of judgement. Traditionally, since the passage of the 1911 Parliament Act, the

House of Lords had been chary of challenging government and Commons over legislation. But civil liberties proved to be something of an exception, especially with many distinguished lawyers, including former Law Lords like Lords Woolf and Lloyd of Berwick, active in the upper House. The Lords, therefore, with Liberal Democrat lawyers to the fore, began to take the lead after 2000 in the debate over detention issues, and offered a series of searching and fundamental criticisms.

First, it was argued that a system of detention where the key decisions rested not with the law but with the executive was inherently unconstitutional and indeed unfair. Fundamental liberties were being curtailed not by the police or the courts, but by the state without formulation of any legal charge. Here was a British version of the *raison d'état* France had experienced before 1789. Further it was based on subjective belief not on evidential proof. There was also grave doubt that existed about the predictive accuracy of charges made against detainees, who had committed no offence and were innocent in the eyes of the law. In 2011 the terms of the law were changed from being defined as a basis of "reasonable suspicion" to "reasonable belief" but this was a semantic distinction without a difference. The state, therefore, was acting in a coercive fashion. It was quite contrary to what had been laid down by Churchill, prime minister during the supreme security emergency of the second world war, when he declared that confining or incarcerating people who had committed no offence for an indefinite period in detention was "in the highest degree odious." It was also at variance with the famous wartime libertarian judgement in the case of *Liversidge v. Anderson* in 1942 delivered by Lord Atkin of Aberdyfi, "In times of war, the laws are not silent."

Secondly, the courts proved to have only limited control over the actions of the executive. The system of detention or control orders, after all, lay outside the normal judicial process. Hearing could be held private without the suspect not being present. The process in practice had become a rubber-stamp for the decisions of the minister. The Home Secretary was being elevated above the law, in defiance of the famous dictum of Sir Edward Coke in the seventeenth century "Be you ever so mighty, the law is above you." There was also serious accompanying doubt as to whether the process of pre-trial detention was intended to be preventive or punitive.

Thirdly, individuals were unable to find out in detail the case against them. They could not discover the whole range of evidence that would be deployed by the government and could not communicate freely on these matters with the Special Advocates appointed to give them legal guidance.

The Courts were thus able to accept evidence normally inadmissible. Individuals charged with no offence did not, therefore, have the same rights as criminal defendants who had defending lawyers to act in their interests whom they could freely instruct, and were told all the details of the evidence to be used against them. There was an air of secrecy involved, under which detainees, many of them of humble background or from ethnic minorities with language difficulties perhaps, did not have access to a lawyer in the normal way.

Fourthly, the restrictions imposed on detainees under control orders were exceptionally severe and punitive. They could lead nothing like a normal life before trial—if, indeed, they were to be tried at all, since most of them were not. Their freedom of movement was greatly curtailed, as if they were under curfew, and their social and private life made virtually impossible in every respect. The European Court of Human Rights condemned the misleading re-labelling of detention under the guise of control orders, and involving processes that were imprisonment in every respect save the name. These detainees were treated like common criminals. Yet they had had no trial and had been charged with no offence. Most commonly, no prosecutions would ultimately follow. It was a clear abuse of legal processes, the rule of law and the doctrine of human rights and the European Court was vocal in its response.

Fifthly and finally, pre-trial detention under control orders was manifestly becoming the norm, built into legal processes over the years as an inherent part of the legal response to terrorism. Despite sunset clauses galore, the temporary remorselessly became permanent. It seemed that it could be extended almost indefinitely. There was minimal supervision or controls by the courts, far less so than in other jurisdictions. While an independent Reviewer of the Anti-Terrorist Acts was appointed to monitor the operation of the system, there was no annual renewal. The aberration had been incorporated into the operation of the common law, one of the historic glories of England.

Politically, there were two major crises, in 2005 and 2008. Following the Law Lords' declaration that the act of 2001 was illegal, the Blair government introduced a new Prevention of Terrorism Bill in 2005. To avoid accusations of racism, it now extended powers of pre-trial detention not simply to aliens and immigrants but to British citizens as well—to every citizen. As before, the Commons offered little debate, let along resistance, and the Bill was whisked through there. But in the House of Lords, the outcome in March 2005 was an immense political battle between the two Houses of Parliament. There was much time-pressure since previous orders might otherwise expire. There was a tense all-night session in the Lords on 9 March with Conservative and Liberal Democrat, plus a few Labour peers, adamant in resisting the government. Significantly, for the first time, Lord Irvine, the former Lord Chancellor, voted against the government on libertarian grounds. In the end, as they invariably did, the Lords yielded to government pressure in the inter-house "ping-pong" (*lutte à la corde* in French) that followed the Lords debate, but they did gain important concessions on a sunset clause and the monitoring of the pre-trial process by ensuring that judges, rather than the Home Secretary, should decide on all categories of control orders. Tony Blair, angry with the outcome, argued against any "signal of weakness" being shown to terrorist threats. Shortly after, on 7 July, there came the terrorist outrages mentioned above, with serious loss of life and hundreds of injured, innocent victims on buses and the underground system. Obviously the security debate intensified as a result. Thus the government came forward with new legislation that autumn, with the proposal now that pre-trial detention be extended from 14 to 90 days.

This resulted in a far bigger political row. The Blair government's majority was now smaller, since the overall majority had fallen by a hundred in the general election that June, while the prime minister's prestige had suffered from the invasion of Iraq. On 28 November, in the most serious revolt by Labour backbenchers since the invasion of Iraq in 2003, a Labour amendment to reduce the period of 90 days to 28 days for pre-trial detention was carried with the aid of 51 Labour rebels, headed by the veteran backbencher, David Winnick. This was a notable political event—the first time that Tony Blair had been defeated in the House of Commons during ten years in office. The defeat was reinforced by caustic criticism of the legislation by the judiciary. Mr. Justice Sullivan in April 2006 attacked the whole idea of pre-trial detention as incompatible both with the right to fair proceeding under Article 6 of the European Convention and with natural justice. It was said, he declared, "conspicuously unfair," despite the "thin veneer of legality." The Court of Appeal, however, was to reverse this judgement that August. There now came a new, tense political phase. Gordon Brown succeeded Tony Blair as prime minister in June 2007, with a keen sense that he wished to exert himself and to show that he could win tactical victories in Parliament where Tony Blair had failed.

There followed the still greater crisis over the 2008 Counter-Terrorism Bill. This suggested raising the pre-trial detention period significantly, from 28 days to 42 days. Immense protests followed, notably from many distinguished figures in the arts world such as the designer Vivienne Westwood, the actor Colin Firth, the film producer Ken Loach, the playwright David Hare, and the novelist John le Carre. Gordon Brown meanwhile indicated that he favoured an even longer period, up to 56 days. But now his authority as prime minister was in some decline. The period of 42 days scraped through the Commons by just 11 votes on 11 June. This was despite the fact that Brown had made several concessions to placate Labour critics thought to number at least 60, and much internal party rancour was thereby caused.

At this stage, developments in the Conservative Party took centre stage. David Davis, a prominent MP who had been a government minister and runner-up to David Cameron in the 2005 leadership election in the Conservative Party, staged his own protest by resigning his Parliamentary seat at Haltemprice and Howden and thus forcing a by-election to be fought on civil liberties issues. Davis, as he told me in an interview (November 6, 2012), feared that Brown might introduce a new Terrorism bill before the 2010 general election and that populist pressure would force Cameron to accept it. Davis thus engaged in a rare and remarkable "sacrificial gamble," which exacerbated an already touchy relationship with his party leader. Close to Remembrance Sunday he had made a notable speech in which he reminded his audience of the traditional liberties for which British servicemen had gallantly given their lives, whereas they now being thrown away wantonly under the plea of defending national security. The by-election was a distinctly odd affair. It was contested by a variety of frivolous candidates. There were 23 Independents including Gemma Garrett, a former Miss Great Britain, who had come in third in an earlier contest for "Britain's sexiest blonde," a better result than she was to achieve in the Haltemprice and Howden by-election. Other candidates stood for the Church of the Militant Elvis Party and the Official Monster Raving Loony Party. Labour and the Liberal Democrats declined to contest the by-election, the Greens came second, and all candidates save Davis, who won easily with 72% of the vote, lost their deposits. On the other hand, Davis's stand received wide cross-party backing including from Shami Chakrabarti of Liberty and the veteran socialist Tony Benn, and public attention was undeniably focused for a time on the pre-trial detention question and personal freedoms in general. There was much media commentary and a stir was caused in Conservative ranks. Davis Davis's unusual and gallant gesture showed that the political ramifications of pre-trial detention were far from being confined to Labour.

That autumn, the Brown government's Counter-Terrorism Bill met with a huge defeat in the House of Lords. On October 13, 2008, in a remarkably assertive gesture, the Bill was lost by 307 votes to 116.

Conservatives, Liberal Democrats and cross-bench peers were, of course, the main opponents, but there were also 24 Labour dissentients whose composition is of some interest. They included Lord Irvine again, Lord Falconer, another former Lord Chancellor and a one-time intimate of Tony Blair's whose flat-mate he had once been. The other Labour opponents were a few legal peers and a number of middle-class professionals, including the present writer. Revealingly, none of the trade unionist or working-class Labour peers opposed the government. For Gordon Brown, whose authority was already in question, it was manifestly a severe setback, as his bill lapsed.

The issue of civil liberties played some part in the June 2010 general election. The Liberal Democrats distinguished themselves by having a strong civil liberties platform, including reducing pre-trial detention to 14 days, ending control orders altogether and ending the production of ID cards. The Conservatives had a very brief civil liberties platform which laid some emphasis on the threat to freedom posed by the ending of fox hunting. Labour did not mention civil liberties at all in their manifesto, a significant comment on 13 years of their party's illiberalism.

After the general election, the subsequent Coalition Agreement between Conservatives and Liberal Democrats somewhat soft-pedalled the Lib-Dem manifesto commitments. It states that control orders would be "urgently reviewed" and a way found "to allow intercept evidence to be used in court." However, change of a reformist kind did follow nevertheless. The annual report in 2011 by the Independent Reviewer of Terrorist Legislation, Sir David Anderson, called for some re-balancing between security considerations and personal liberty over issues such as the proscription of organizations, the storage of personal data, and especially pre-trial detention. He followed the Parliamentary Joint Committee report which argued that the period of detention should be cut from 28 days to 14. As a result, the government's Anti-Terrorism Act of 2011 did introduce several more liberal aspects, cutting back the storage of personal data, ending ID cards, and reducing the pre-trial detention to 14 days. It did however retain, as critics in the Lords pointed out, the more objectionable features of the control process, and orders would remain. Even with the reduction to 14 days the British time-limit was excessive compared, say, with France (nominally two days, which could be extended to six) and the United States (two days, but capable of much extension under executive order). So Britain's period remained well above the norm in western countries.

Where does the issue of pre-trial detention stand in December 2012? Civil liberties remain one of the most hallowed of British values, despite all the conflicts since 2000. The opening ceremony of the London Olympic Games in July 2012 was libertarian in tone: it laid emphasis on successful struggles for liberty in the past by such groups as the women suffragettes or the hunger-strikers of the 1930s. Amongst the political parties, Labour remained slow to shift from the outlook of the Blair years, and re-iterated its passionate support for the police; its views on immigrants and attitudes to Europe also became less favourable. On the other hand, the internal review of Labour party policy and strategy initiated by Ed Miliband as leader, with Jon Cruddas MP as its leading operator, along with the need to appeal to voters who had switched from Labour to Lib. Dem. in 2010 but were now disenchanted by the governing Coalition, could produce a significant shift of approach. Miliband called for Labour's attitude on the 2012 Justice Bill to be based on grounds of principle, apparently a banal change but a significant one. For the Conservatives, by contrast, the liberal-minded veteran Kenneth Clarke was replaced as Justice Minister by the apparently more hard-line Chris Grayling, remarkably not a lawyer himself. The Home Office's Justice and Security Bill in 2012 set up secret courts in which defendants would be subjected to much the same restriction and injustices as under the pre-trial detention regime before. In a further flurry of political conflict, the House of Lords defeated the government three times on key amendments on the processes involved, twice by over 100 votes with several Conservative peers voting against their own party. It looked immediately afterwards as if David Cameron's government were going to give way and accept, with modifications, at least some of the Lords' amendments.

There is now some poll evidence that public opinion may be swinging somewhat against pre-trial detention compared with 2008. In any case, the decline of civil liberties in Britain, while very serious, can be overdone. Some defenders of our liberties do not help their cause with exaggerated comparisons with justice in Ceaucescu's Roumania or Mugabe's Zimbabwe. The United States' record has been distinctly worse. President Bush passed the intrusive Patriot Act. President Obama signed, somewhat apologetically, the National Defence Authorization Act, allowing the presidential powers of detention without trial for almost an indefinite period. Guantanamo Bay remains as an affront to humanitarian and legal principles. The American mind, it seems, remains understandably deeply permeated by the trauma of 9/11 and the new-found sense of vulnerability in the homeland not experienced since Pearl Harbour in 1941. Change here seems unlikely.

In Britain any remedy over pre-trial detention must lie in Parliament. For all its past weaknesses, only Parliament can overturn statute. Judges have rejected any role that can be considered even remotely legislative; even liberal figures like Lord Bingham or Baroness Hale have taken this view. In Parliament, the Lords can usually only suggest revision and amendment, while the Commons has seldom been able to check a powerful executive. But it is in Parliament, as Lord Bingham has said, that the democratic solution has to lie. Parliament at the very least can articulate concern with aspects of the detention process that are disagreeably distinctive to the United Kindgom. It could declare that pre-trial detention here is a disproportionate policy and not obviously a tool of last resort. There is no recognition that detention is used when all other possible remedies have manifestly failed. Also no distinction is commonly made over the gravity of the offence, and pre-trial detention is thus the crudest and bluntest of instruments. Again, many flaws lie in the conditions under which alleged suspects are detained in custody, and legal aspects of the process such as the problems of material witnesses. These points could be taken up, and the whole rationale of pre-trial detention be subjected to fundamental re-examination as public priorities move on and the immediate threat of terrorist outrages in Britain appears to recede. Some of us will fight on determinedly over these issues in Parliament and in the press. Perhaps, it may be hoped, in 2015, when the eight hundredth anniversary of the signing of *Magna Carta* will be celebrated, opinion might tilt back to endorsing that liberty which captured the imagination of our forefathers, and to condemn and countermand recent injustices. It could make Great Britain once again, as in the olden time, "the mother of the free."

PREVENTIVE INTERVENTIONS AND THE RIGHT TO PROTEST

NEIL JARMAN
INSTITUTE FOR CONFLICT RESEARCH, BELFAST

The outcome of the 2003 presidential elections in Armenia had been strongly contested by the opposition parties and one year on they planned a series of protest rallies in early April 2004 to mark the anniversary of their challenge to the results in the Constitutional Court. In the days leading up to the rallies, three activists in the Armavir Region, who were each planning to attend the protests in the capital, Yerevan, were separately detained by the police. Each was accused of relatively minor offences, which were not related to any political activity, and were subjected to an administrative detention of up to seven days. At the end of the initial detention period they were each accused of other offences and subjected to a further period of administrative detention. Each of the three men was released once the cycle of protests had ended.[1]

The 2007 G8 summit in Heiligendamm, Germany, attracted a large number of protesters. The area was subjected to a major security operation and on 2 June, four days before the summit was to begin, there was rioting and clashes between police and protesters in nearby Rostock. The day after the rioting the police searched a vehicle in a car park in front of a local prison and found banners bearing the words "freedom for all prisoners" and "free all now." Two of the occupants of the vehicle were arrested and the Rostock District Court ordered that they be detained until 9 June, when the summit would have ended, because it was argued they intended to commit a criminal offence. No charges were subsequently pressed against either person.[2]

These are two of a growing number of cases that have been highlighted in the media or that have come before the courts in recent years and which

---

[1] *Hakobyan and Others v Armenia* (2012). Application no. 34320/04.
[2] *Schwabe and M.G. v Germany* (2011). Application nos. 8080/08 and 8566/08.

have focused on a diverse array of practices whereby the state has intervened to detain people, either individually or in a group, to prevent them from participating in a public protest. In other examples, the authorities have stopped people travelling in cars or buses, imposed border restrictions, denied people entry to a country to prevent them from reaching the site of a protest; they have contained people in a public area in freezing conditions for several hours; they have made mass "preventive" arrests in the days before an event or at the beginning of a protest; (Hudig) they have used under-cover police officers to work with those organising protest actions and then used the information to charge people with forms of conspiracy. (Home Affairs Committee) In some cases they have changed laws and regulations to enable preventive interventions to take place legally. (Hudig; Starr *et al* 68-71) As the two initial case studies indicate, such practices are not just the responses of perceived authoritarian regimes but rather have become part of the armoury of government and police across Europe and North America, as well as among the countries of the former Soviet Union, over recent years. Preventive interventions have increasingly been accepted as part of the visible routine repertoire of state responses to public protest.

In the examples cited above the individuals were detained or prevented from participating in a protest not because they have acted violently or because they have committed an offence, but because there was a suspicion, fear or concern by the police and other authority that they might commit an offence. In many cases the state intervention has taken place in the context of one of the regular global summit events and which have been subject to heightened security provisions since fears about the impact of protests at such events increased following those at Seattle in 1999 (Cockburn et al) and Genoa in July 2001 (Neale) and as a consequence of the 9/11 attacks a few months later. But such preventive interventions did not begin with the global summit protests nor are confined to them. The history of the use of preventive interventions is not well documented, although they were certainly used to disrupt the activities of striking miners in Britain during the 1984-85 strike, but preventive interventions appear to have escalated in scale and frequency over the past decade and have increasingly been used, developed and adapted as a normative response to a variety of forms of protests.

This paper reviews some of the current forms of preventive intervention by state authorities that have been utilised in relation to various forms of protest in recent years. It questions how far it is legitimate for the state to be pro-active in arresting or detaining people simply because of the possibility that doing so may serve to prevent crime or disorder, rather than adopting other measures that may serve to deter or prevent disorder occurring. It also considers what level of evidence should be required of the likelihood of crime or disorder taking place to justify such interventions. The paper draws on a relatively small (but growing) number of court cases where the actions have been challenged by those who have been subjected to detention, restraint or other forms of restriction and through which the courts have begun to outline some of the formal boundaries to preventive interventions and clarify the contexts in which such intervention may be considered legitimate within the framework of international human rights law. It begins with a brief review of human rights standards relating to the right to protest and limits of state action to limit or intervene in protests and other forms of public assembly. It then briefly outlines the broad approaches to the policing of protest before reviewing a number of examples of different style of preventative intervention that have been used in recent years.

The Right to Protest

The right to protest is guaranteed as a form of peaceful assembly and as such is included in all major human rights instruments including the International Covenant on Civil and Political Rights (Article 21) and the European Convention on Human Rights. (Article 11) However, as with most fundamental rights and freedoms the right to assemble is not an unlimited right and the state may impose restrictions under certain conditions. The primary limitation is that the right only extends to peaceful assembly, use of violence or force or the threat of the use of force (by carrying weapons or similar) are not included in the right to assembly. Furthermore, the ICCPR sets out a number of other grounds which may serve as a justification for restricting a protest. No restrictions may be placed on the exercise of this right other than those imposed in conformity with the law and which are necessary in a democratic society in the interests of national security or public safety, public order (*ordre public*) as well as the protection of public health or morals or the protections of the rights and freedoms of others.

Manfred Nowak's commentary on Article 21 of the ICCPR emphasises the state's positive obligation to protect the right to assemble from interference or attack from opponents (Nowak 487-488) and also the role of the police to both protect assemblies from aggression and the wider society from violence that might result from the actions of those protesting. In order to respond to such obligations it is generally accepted that the state may require the organisers to provide prior notification of planned assemblies both to enable it to put in place the necessary resources to ensure the event can take place safely, and also to reduce the possibility of disruption to other users of public space. While advance notification may be considered as a form of preventive intervention, Nowak notes that the use of such notification as a basis for prohibiting an assembly "must [...] always remain the exception." (Nowak 493)

Any restrictions that might be imposed in advance of the assembly must always be proportionate and thus the minimum necessary to achieve the desired aims, and must always be done in a way that does not serve to undermine the essence of the fundamental right that is being exercised in the first place. Thus, it may be legitimate to impose restrictions on the time, the place, or the manner of the assembly, but not so that it means that the assembly is unable to achieve its aim of conveying a particular message to a particular group of people or section of society. Furthermore, restrictions should not be imposed in an arbitrary and unaccountable manner and they should be able to be challenged by the organisers in advance of the event actually taking place, either by appeal to the relevant authorities or through the court system.

Most attention, in the literature and various court cases, has focused on the nature and legality of different forms of restrictions that have been imposed as a result of a notification system, or that have occurred in the course of the assembly or protest. (OSCE/ODIHR) Little attention has been paid to forms of preventive interventions that occur outside the notification process, or that have been applied to individuals or small groups of people in the run up to an assembly. Such interventions are important in so far as they indicate an increasing disregard for the broad principles underpinning the fundamental freedoms and human rights and a growing focus on concerns for security, order and control over protests, even while a state may be asserting its respect for human rights in general. Arbitrary and unaccountable preventive restrictions are part of a wider body of actions that may serve as "chill factors" that may discourage people from exercising their rights, or may enable them to do so, but only in a manner which effectively reduces the power of the protest or marginalises the actions of protesters physically and socially. These chill factors also include such things as the increasing privatisation of public space that reduces the number and location of sites that protesters may utilise; (Mitchell; Shiffman *et al.*; Zick) the presentation of police in highly militarised "robo-cop" style protective uniforms; and the use of diverse forms of surveillance, among other things. (Starr *et al.* chapter 4)

European Court Judgements

The European Court of Human Rights has dealt with a number of cases that have considered the state's responsibility with regard to taking preventive action to ensure an assembly can take place rather than simply invoking the possibility of disorder as a justification for preventing an assembly from taking place. In general the Court has highlighted the positive obligations of the state to protect and facilitate the right to assemble, which has been interpreted to mean that the authorities should put in place adequate policing measures to counter any threat of violence and disorder, either from those engaging in protest or from those confronting the protesters, rather than use the threat or risk of violence or disruption to public order to ban an assembly.[3] The Court has also ruled, on more than one occasion, that the state should also protect and facilitate peaceful assemblies, even if they are technically illegal because they have failed to comply with notification requirements or other formalities,[4] rather than detaining or arresting people on the grounds of participating in an unlawful assembly. Furthermore, the Court has highlighted the responsibility of the state authorities to make a proper assessment of risk and to put in place the appropriate resources to ensure that the event can take place with a minimum amount of risk of violence or disruption to others, whilst also acknowledging the impossibility of guaranteeing absolute order and absence of violence.[5]

The appropriate form of preventive intervention is thus considered to be designed to protect and facilitate access to rights for all, rather than as a means of restricting rights. Of course the cases cited above deal with instances where the state has focused on the overall assembly as an entity, rather than more specifically on the rights of particular individuals, and it may be argued that some forms of preventive intervention and detention of selected individuals may be justified on the grounds that it may reduce the risk of violence and disorder and thus enable others to exercise their rights in a more peaceful and safe manner. A question that is raised in such a case, and which will be considered in the various examples that will be discussed below, is whether the state has sufficient evidence of the intent to commit an act of violence, or whether the mere possibility of some form

---

[3] See for example *Guneri and Others v Turkey* (2005). Application nos. 42853/98, 43609/98, 44291/98); *Öllinger v Austria* (2006). Application no. 76900/01.

[4] *Oya Ataman v Turkey* (2007). Application no. 74552/01; *Balçik v Turkey* (2007). Application no. 25/01; *Akgöl and Göl v Turkey* (2011). Application nos. 28495/06 and 28516/06.

[5] *Plattform "Ärzte für das Leben" v Austria* (1988). Application no. 10126/82.

of violence occurring is sufficient to justify such an intervention or if the possibility of violence is being used as an excuse to legitimise a preventive intervention. This in turn raises the question of whether preventive detentions should ever be legitimately justified within a human rights framework (except where the threat of violence meets the imminence test,) but rather should be seen as part of a broader strategy to restrain and limit the scale and impact of protests more generally. Article 5.1 of the European Convention of Human Rights states that "everyone has the right to liberty and security of the person" and the article also sets out six contexts under which a person may be "deprived of his liberty." In cases relating to preventive detention related to public protests the state authorities generally cite Article 5.1.(c) which states that:

> The lawful arrest or detention of a person effected for the purpose of bringing him before the competent legal authority on reasonable suspicion of having committed an offence or when it is reasonably considered necessary to prevent his committing an offence or fleeing after having done so;

The two cases cited at the beginning of this paper both focused on the states' justification of a legitimate detention. In one of the examples the authorities accused the detainees of having committed various offences but which were unrelated to any protests; in the other they claimed a likelihood that an offence would be committed if the individual was not detained. It is this latter rationale that is invoked most readily in the cases that will be considered below, a form of direct preventive detention, rather than a more indirect form of preventive work whereby a spurious offence was invoked simply to prevent the individuals from participating in a protest.

These examples also highlight the central role of the police in preventive interventions. The facilitation and regulation of assemblies generally involves two levels of state authority. Usually the municipality or similar body is responsible for dealing with advance notifications of assemblies, and thus of formal prior restrictions, while the police have responsibility for the events on the ground and the management of public order. Obviously the police and the municipality will liaise in advance of an assembly and the police may well influence any prior restrictions that may be imposed, but the two bodies remain relatively autonomous over their respective domains. The police's responsibility for upholding the law and maintaining public order also means that they will take a lead role in intelligence gathering, overt and covert surveillance, and planning and preparation for public events. However, issues of police independence, direction by the political authorities, and a multiplicity of policing agencies, with at times secretive and competing agendas, means that the exact rationale for and expectation of preventive interventions remain obscured and subject to obfuscation and lack of any real accountability.

Policing Protest

In the late 1990s it was argued that there were two broad approaches to the policing of protest and other public assemblies. The Escalated Force model was the dominant approach to policing protest in the 1960s and 1970s. It was viewed as an authoritarian approach whereby the police aimed to remain in control, prioritised order management and sought to determine the nature and scale of public protests, with limited scope for dialogue with the organisers or participants in an assembly and through use of force where necessary. The alternative Negotiated Management model was focused on a more liberal approach that respected human rights and utilised discussions with the organisers to achieve a consensus that would facilitate the effective management of an assembly with minimum disruption to public order. It was argued that it had been the dominant approach in western democracies, at least, since the late 1980s. (Della Porta and Reiter 1998) In reality both options remained open to the police and their approach could oscillate between the hard line "do as we say" approach of the escalated force model and the softer "let's work together" approach of negotiated management.

However, since the turn of the millennium there is an argument that policing has shifted away from a more open engagement with protesters and back to a more confrontational approach, this new approach has variously been termed "command and control" (Vitale) or "strategic incapacitation." (Gillham) These changes have coincided with developing responses to the large globalisation protests, which have been directed at the major summits that brought world leaders together and which have been increasingly confrontational and challenging to host nations since the Seattle protests of 1999. But this more assertive, interventionist and militarised style of policing has also developed at a time of heightened security concerns that have dominated many states approach to protests generally the since the 9/11 attacks of 2001 and other violent incidents associated with extreme Islamic groups. If radical Muslim groups have often been conceptualised as the enemy without, so some of the new social movements been characterised as the enemy within. (Starr *et al.*) And just as preventive detentions and other extreme forms of security and control measures have been imposed on some radicalised Muslims who are perceived as a threat or as a potential threat to public safety and security, so too have forms of surveillance, intelligence gathering and control been extended over those involved in public protest. In particular since the late 1990s there has been an increasing recourse to forms of preventive intervention in response to the mobilisations of new social movements. (Davenport *et al.*; Della Porta *et al.* 2006) And while state authorities have generally justified these as necessary responses to counter threats of violence and public disorder, they have been seen by those in the movement as an excessive and illegal intervention that has violated peoples' rights to assemble, to protest and to express their opinions, and have been designed to act as "chill factors" that deter people from participating in public protests.

The remainder of this paper discusses some of the forms of preventive intervention that have been developed and used towards those involved in, or who desired to participate in, peaceful protests. I broadly consider three main forms of preventive activity: interventions that prevent people from reaching the site of a protest or other form of assembly; forms of control or containment of people who are part of a protest and who may be effectively detained and restrained from leaving an area; and finally I will discuss the response of the European Court of Human Rights to cases where people have been preventively detained in advance of an assembly.

Preventing Participation

Most studies of protest and in particular the policing of protests focus on the activities and interactions that take place at the site of the immediate vicinity of a public assembly. They consider how the police approach the assembly, in terms of numbers of officers, styles of uniform and types of equipment made available, how they engage with participants and how they provoke or respond to acts of provocation and disorder. Much less consideration has been paid to police interventions that focus on limiting access to the site of a protest and on the ways that the police and other state authorities may limit people's freedom of movement in order to stop them getting to the location of a protest.

One of the first examples of where this process was reasonably documented was during the coalminers strike in the United Kingdom in 1984-85 when the police blocked roads, stopped cars and buses, and turned back miners who were planning to participate in pickets of coal mines in other parts of the country and which were part of a wider range of police interventions as they confronted the striking miners:

> But nothing had happened in the disputes of the early 1970s [...] to prepare the Yorkshire pickets for the uses and abuses of the law which greeted them in Nottinghamshire in March 1984: road block (systematically set up along the boundaries of Nottinghamshire and Derbyshire as well as briefly in the Dartford Tunnel); mass arrests (often under vague charges such as 'threatening behaviour', 'obstructing the police' and 'breach of the peace'); restrictive bail conditions; tight control over the number and behaviour of 'official' pickets; [...] and sometimes physical assault. (Field 206)

It is unclear how far the practice of preventing the movements of protesters during the miners' strike was actually a new innovation and how far it was merely the large scale and systematic use of the tactic in relation to a long running and high-profile industrial dispute that brought it to greater public attention. However, it is worth noting that the use of road blocks was but one of a number of police interventions (mass arrests, use of bail conditions, limits to the numbers of protesters, use of force) that were considered to be on the boundaries of legality and which have since become more widely utilised in the policing of public protests.

A more recent example of the police intervening to stop people travelling to a protest actually reaching their destination occurred in March 2003 when the police stopped three coaches carrying some 120 people who planned to participate in a protest at RAF Fairford in Gloucestershire, some 100 miles west of London, as part of a campaign of protests against the Iraq war.[6] The police, acting on intelligence, searched the coaches and found various helmets and masks, plus a tin of spray paint and a safety flare. Although they allowed a small number of those they had stopped to continue to the protest site, most were held on the coaches, which were ordered to return to London. The coaches were escorted by police motorcycle outriders and were not allowed to stop until they arrived in London, which they did some four hours after they had initially been stopped. One of those held on the coaches challenged the police action in the courts and eventually the House of Lords ruled that the police action had been unlawful since there had been no "imminent" risk of a breach of the peace, and in the judgement it was noted "civil rights must be jealously guarded […] prior restraint (pre-emptive action) needs the fullest justification."[7] David Mead concluded his analysis of the case by stating that:

---

[6] *R (Laporte) v Chief Constable of Gloucestershire* (2006) UKHL 55.
[7] *Ibid.*, 114-115.

> The case sends out a strong message to the police that the officers should properly police protests, giving full recognition to the rights of protesters to be present and to the public role such protests can play [...] the police should allow protesters to proceed and then arrest (or divert) at the site only those who present an immediate threat and only then when they do so. (348)

A similar tactic of preventing people from reaching the site of a protest was documented in Armenia in 2009 as members of opposition parties organised a big protest in the capital Yerevan to mark the first anniversary of the deaths of ten people (eight protesters and two police officers) in the protests that followed the 2008 presidential elections. Rumours spread in advance of the protest that roads into the capital would be closed and although in the end the roads remained open, a heavy police presence was deployed to stop cars and question drivers. Furthermore many people would have used public transport to access the capital from the provinces but in some locations the regular mini-buses servicing the capital simply did not operate. (Helsinki Committee of Armenia 50-54)

A variation on this approach has been the suspension of the Schengen Agreement among certain European Union member states (and which allowed free movement across international borders) in the run up to major international summit events. Schengen was first suspended prior to the G8 summit in Genoa in 2001 and some 2,093 people were subsequently denied access to Italy to attend the protests in the city. Drivers heading for Genoa were required to queue in separate queues at the border, the airport and two train stations in Genoa were closed and at least one ferry carrying protesters from Greece was not allowed to dock in Ancona. (Starr *et al.* 42) The Schengen Agreement has also been suspended in advance of many subsequent major events: in Germany (G8, 2007) Italy (G8, 2009) Denmark (COP15, 2009) Portugal (NATO 2010) and Spain (ECB, 2012) as new norms had been established for limiting the right to protest. However, the French government appears not to have requested the suspension of the Schengen Agreement for the November 2012 G20 Summit in Cannes, but instead deployed some 12,000 police to provide security, while confining protesters to the city of Nice some 30 kilometres away. Thus, France constructed an extreme version of the exclusion zone that has become the norm for summits, and restricted the right of protesters by keeping them well away from the summit venue itself preventing them from expressing their views to the world leaders.

In general the Schengen Agreement has been suspended due to concerns over internal security or public order, which are always relatively open and broad terms usually invoked by the police on the basis of "intelligence," which is not based on public information. It is a form of justification which is difficult to challenge, particularly in the run up to an event and in particular to a type of event that is increasingly dominated by concerns for security rather than by the need to protect and facilitate human rights. And if such restrictions are not challenged, then they can quickly become established as the norm, or at least as an obvious option, as the suspension of the Schengen Agreement appears to have become in the run up to any major summit event in Europe.

Indiscriminate Detentions and Containment

The previous section discussed policing strategies that were designed to stop people participating in a protest by limiting their freedom of movement to actually reach the site of the assembly, but the police have also developed new approaches to control people who are at the protest, to limit their movements or to prevent their active participation in a public assembly. The two strategies that the police have used have been containing people in a tightly defined area (often referred to as "kettling") until the police decide they can leave, and mass detentions or arrests of protesters. Both strategies involve the containment and control of protesters by police officers, but "kettling" does not usually involve mass arrests, although some of those contained may be arrested. The significant feature of both approaches is that these forms of detention have been applied to peaceful protesters on the grounds that they might cause disorder, rather than be applied to already disorderly or violent crowds.

Mass detentions and arrests of protesters have been used on a number of occasions in recent years, particularly in relation to major summit events that attract often large and diverse groups of protesters. In 2009 in advance of the climate change summit (COP15) in Copenhagen the Danish government passed legislation that gave the police powers to pre-emptively detain people for up to 12 hours on the grounds that they might break the law in the near future, while the new law also increased the penalty for hindering the police from a fine to 40 days in jail.[8] During the summit nearly 2,000 people were subjected to preventative arrest, most were subsequently released without charge, although a few were charged with relatively minor offences. A similar approach was taken by the Belgian police the following year when they arrested up to 300 people from the "noborder" camp to stop then participating in a European wide

---

[8] See <http://www.guardian.co.uk/environment/2009/nov/26/denmark-police-powers-copenhagen>.

trade union protest, the police used a law that allows them to detain people for up to 12 hours in order to protect public order in an "absolute emergency." (Hudig) Although some objections were raised at the approach taken by the Belgian police, in Copenhagen 250 of those detained took a more radical approach and sued the police for unlawful arrest, and in December 2010 the City Court of Copenhagen ruled that the mass arrests had been illegal and ordered the police to pay 9,000 DKK (about €1200) in damages to each of the protesters.[9]

The police were also criticised for their use of mass arrests in relation to the G20 summit in Toronto in 2010. A review of the policing of the G20 event by the Office of the Independent Police Review Director (McNeilly) noted how the police had used containment on a number of occasions during the summit and on one occasion detained 400 people in pouring rain for four hours, while they were being processed for charges of "conspiracy to commit mischief," an offence that actually amounted to participating in a march that had caused some disruption to traffic in the vicinity but which had always remained peaceful. Although the report was limited in its criticism of the police use of containment and preventive detentions, and focused more on the need for greater selectivity in detaining people and greater planning for such eventualities, the Canadian government was later challenged on its use of mass detentions by the Inter-American Commission on Human Rights who argued that only those who had committed an offence during a demonstration should be arrested (however there is no record of any active response by the Canadian authorities).[10] This highlights the contrast between the expectations of a human rights approach, whereby people should face sanctions for what they have done, rather than for what they might do and state authorities who are increasingly developing more assertive forms of intervention in order to reduce the possibility of violence or disorder. While there is clearly a need for the authorities to have the right to intervene in order to prevent a crime, the threshold for detaining people in these cases appears to have been very low. In none of these examples were those arrested involved in acts of disorder beyond the type of disruption to daily routines that may legitimately result from any large protest. Rather the police seem to be increasingly planning their approach on an assessment of what had happened at previous summit events and on stereotypical views of protesters as being bent on violence, and with views of a crowd that owe

---

9 See <http://www.climate-justice-news.org/news/2010/12/16/all-mass-arrests-during-cop-15-last-year-declared-illegal-by-copenhagen-city-court/>.

10 See <http://www.quebecprotest.com/post/24963724249/is-there-a-reason-for-preventive-arrests-barreau-du>.

more to Le Bon's nineteenth century notions of the "irrational mob" than more sophisticated contemporary understanding of police crowd interactions. (Le Bon; Reicher and Stott)

In the Canadian example the police action also resulted in a number of people who were not actually part of the protests being detained. These included members of the media and onlookers who just happened to be in the wrong place when the containment was put in place. This highlights something of the indiscriminate and arbitrary nature of the use of containment as a tactic, which means that all those in a specific place are treated the same as a potential threat. This factor was pointed out in the case of *Austin and Others v the UK* before the European Court of Human Rights in 2012,[11] which focused on the use of kettling by the Metropolitan Police who contained people in a small area albeit without arresting them. The first use of kettling had been recorded in Hamburg in 1986 when some 800 people were held for 13 hours when protesting about the policing of another protest the day before. However, in this case the police action was subsequently declared illegal and compensation awarded to those who had been contained. Nevertheless, the use of kettling has since become widespread in Germany, and since the early 2000s it has also been increasingly used by the police in England.

The practice of containment was challenged by Lois Austin and three others who had been caught in a kettle in central London in May 2001. While Austin herself was participating in the May Day protests against globalisation the other three applicants were not, but rather were caught up in the kettle whilst shopping or on their lunch break from work. In total up to 2,000 people were held in the kettle for more than seven hours, with no access to food, water or toilet facilities. Initially the police refused to allow anyone to leave, but over the course of the afternoon and early evening people were allowed to leave the kettle in small groups. (Mead 349-356) The applicants complained that their containment amounted to a deprivation of liberty under Article 5.1 of the ECHR, while the British government argued that the police decision to impose a temporary restraint on freedom of movement was necessary to prevent serious public disorder, which in turn might have required a more assertive police response. The European Court found that while the nature of the containment could be considered to fall within the bounds of a deprivation of liberty, in the wider context of ongoing protests and disorder in the city this was probably the "least intrusive and most effective means" of preventing

---

[11] *Austin and Others v United Kingdom* (2012). Application nos. 39692/09, 40713/09 and 41008/09.

more serious disorder from occurring and therefore the police action did not amount to a breach of Article 5.1. Thus while the European Court of Human Rights found that in this case the use of kettling was legitimate, it was only so because of the specific context at the time and the Court warned that "measures of crowd control should not be used by the national authorities directly or indirectly to stifle or discourage protest." (*Austin* para. 68)

These different examples of the use of mass detention and containment illustrate how "measures of crowd control" have become increasingly adopted by police in a number of countries to limit the scope for protesters to voice their opinions and express their views. While these tactics have been developed and widely used in the context of major summit events (and the heightened concerns for security that such events generate,) they have also come to be used as a more general form of crowd control in some countries, for example in London where kettling has been used widely in recent years (Netpol)[12] and in the USA where it was used in response to the Occupy protests. (Knuckey *et al.*) While kettling has been found to be lawful, albeit within a relatively narrow context, the use of mass detentions and arrests has proved more problematic for the state, and although few courts have gone so far as the Copenhagen court cited above, in most cases the mass arrest of protesters does not result in a mass of convictions in court. Rather the failure to secure convictions of those arrested for participating in peaceful assemblies suggests that often the practice is focused on control movement of participants in a protest rather than as a legitimate response to any real or imminent threat of disorder.

Selective Preventive Detention

The use of road blocks, the suspension of the Schengen Agreement, and the use of containment and mass arrests at protests are all very general and indiscriminate responses to protests in which anyone travelling to or participating in an event may be affected, as well as some people who happen to be in the wrong place at the wrong time. However, the third and final category of preventive interventions may be more discriminating in approach, with particular individuals being targeted with the specific aim of preventing them from being able to participate in a protest. It can be difficult to assess the scale of such interventions as they do not occur in the public eye in the way that mass detentions or acts of kettling do, but a

---

[12] See for example *McClure and Moos v the Commissioner of the Police of the Metropolis* (2011) Case no C1/2011/1253.

number of cases have come before the ECtHR in recent years that suggest that the arrest of individuals as a preventive act should be considered as part of the wider panoply of state options that are being utilised in response to acts of protest.

In the run up to the EU-Russia Summit in May 2007, the international media carried reports that a number of leading opposition activists had been arrested in various locations as they attempted to make their way to the summit location in Samara,[13] a pattern of behaviour that had also been documented for the previous years' G8 summit in St Petersburg.[14] One of those who the authorities tried to detain was Sergey Shimovolos, a human rights activist, who travelled to Samara but planned to leave before the summit was due to start. He was stopped and questioned and had his documents checked three times during his train journey, on one occasion he was asked to go with the police to a police station, but he refused. However, when the train arrived in Samara he was threatened with force if he refused to go with the police to the police station, where he was questioned for 45 minutes before he was allowed to leave. Shimovolos subsequently complained to the ECtHR that his arrest and detention had been unlawful and amounted to a breach of Article 5.1 of the ECHR.[15] The Court found that there had been a violation of Article 5.1 even though he had only been detained for a short time, because the authorities had no evidence of any specific offences that the applicant had either committed or might be about to commit; the Interior Department was simply trying "to stop members of certain opposition organisations from taking part in (a) rally" against the summit and from committing unspecified "unlawful and extremist acts." (*Shimovolos* para. 55) The case highlights the potential for the use of targeted, rather than indiscriminate, preventive detention to intimidate and harass activists and stop them from attending protests, while the media reports of such detentions may also impact on others from even trying to join the protest. Such practices have been reported in a number of countries and in advance of diverse forms of protests. (Netpol 7-10; Starr *et al.* 43)

The Russian examples illustrate how the state targeted the leadership of the opposition movement and prominent activists with preventive detentions, but the two cases cited at the outset of this paper show that such an approach may also be used on less prominent protesters. The

---

13 <http://www.guardian.co.uk/world/2007/may/18/russia.lukeharding> and <http://www.spiegel.de/international/world/wave-of-arrests-prior-to-summit-kremlin-clamps-down-on-protests-a-483515.html>.

14 <htpp://www.humaniteinenglish.com/ship.php?article220>.

15 *Shimovolos v Russia* (2011). Application no. 30194/09.

ECtHR also found that the state had violated the rights of the protesters in each of the two cases described at the beginning of this paper. In the case of *Hakobyan v Armenia* the Court found that the detention had been arbitrary and there had been "an element of bad faith or deception" by the authorities (para 122) that breached the applicants' Article 5 rights, while in the *Schwabe* case the Court found a violation of the applicants' right to peaceful assembly, since the authorities had over-reacted to the situation and could have taken less intrusive and more proportionate steps to address any risk to disorder and which did not involve the detention of the individuals, who should have remained free to participate in the protests.

The three cases highlight differing perspectives on the use of preventive detention of people intending to participate in protests. The *Shomovolos* case highlights the use of background surveillance of activists and opposition leaders to enable the state to target specific individuals and detain them in order to undermine their credibility or to reduce their impact on the protests. The *Hakobyan* case also relies on a degree of local knowledge of specific political activists but focuses on the use of spurious charges as a rationale for detaining people (a practice also cited in Russian responses to opposition protests at the G8 and EU summits) and thus preventing them from attending the rallies, while the *Schwabe* case illustrates the disproportionate nature of the responses that states may take to the potential for disorder, a factor that has previously been noted in relation to the use of mass arrests, containments and the limitations on freedom of movement. Notably in each case none of those charged had committed acts of violence, nor was there any substantive evidence that they intended to commit acts of violence, but rather they had intended to participate in peaceful and legitimate forms of protests.

These elements also featured in a recent high-profile case in the UK which involved the pre-emptive arrest in April 2009 of 114 people who had been planning to protest at the Ratcliffe-on-Soar power station. The case also raised another issue in relation to how the state may aim to undermine the right to protest. 26 of those who were arrested were charged with conspiracy to commit aggravated trespass, 20 admitted the charge and were convicted, but the case against the six who denied the charges collapsed in January 2011 when it was revealed that one of the protesters (who had been arrested but not charged) was a police officer who had been working undercover in the environmental movement for some seven years. It was suggested that the police officer had gone beyond mere intelligence gathering and had also acted as an agent *provocateur*. (Home Affairs Committee; Rose) As the story emerged in the media it soon became evident that this was not an isolated example, but rather part of a wider and more systematic use of uncover police officers to infiltrate different sections of the protest movement in the UK and who also worked in a covert fashion in a number of countries across Europe as well as in the UK.[16]

Each of these instances of preventive intervention also took place in the context where the state had previously been criticised for the use of excessive force in the policing or dispersal of protests, and which is often the primary focus of critical analysis of the policing of protest. But whereas the use of force by the police on protesters will usually take place in a public arena and under the eye of professional and citizen journalists, the preventive arrest of individual citizens is a more discrete form of intervention, albeit one that may still serve as an effective means of undermining the scale and form of a public assembly and the capacity to exercise the right to assemble.

Conclusions

The use of preventive intervention as a response by state authorities to reduce the potential for violence and disorder to public assemblies and protests appears to have increased over the past decade and is now a standard element of the repertoire of the police in diverse countries. On the one hand, such interventions may be seen as necessary and legitimate response to increasing confrontations at a range of high-profile events and which have been more readily adopted in the context of a culture of securitisation that have been implemented since 2001. On the other hand, the use of preventive interventions is regarded as part of wider culture of state repression which involves arresting and detaining people for what they may possibly do, rather than for what they have done. Such an approach serves as a means of limiting people's rights to legitimate protest and in fact undermines the basic right to protest for all, by creating the risk and fear that people may be arrested and detained for greater or lesser periods for simply being in the wrong place at the wrong time.

The use of preventive interventions have been under criticism in the literature on protest, in large part because it is still a developing process and emerging patterns of a diversity of preventive practices are only beginning to be acknowledged and recognised. The use of mass detentions

[16] See for example <http://www.guardian.co.uk/undercover-with-paul-lewis-and-rob-evans/2012/aug/31/international-undercover-work-still-secret> and <http://www.terminalx.org/2013/03/new-twists-in-british-spy-mark-kennedys-case-unravels-in-the-us.htlm>.

and mass arrests, forms of containment or kettling of peaceful protesters, restrictions on freedom of movement within and between countries, the targeted detentions of protest leaders and human rights activists, the use of deep-entry undercover police activities and surveillance are all now part of the regular state response to protests. When these are linked to the increasing privatisation of erstwhile public state, ever extensive means of broad-sweep intelligence gathering, prohibitions on the right to protest in key strategic locations and the use of blanket bans of all assemblies, they indicate a declining tolerance of and growing constraint on the lawful parameters of peaceful protest in Eurasia and North America.

The nature and timing of the preventive interventions increasingly presents protesters with a *fait accompli*, a situation that cannot be challenged in a way that prevents from occurring and impacting on a protest, but rather the state can only be retrospectively criticised by the courts. But equally in the absence of precedent and past experience the courts are struggling to set out clear boundaries for such preventive interventions. Some examples have been ruled as unlawful interventions that impede people's legitimate right to protests, others have been deemed acceptable, albeit within a specific context. And while individual preventive arrests may well continue to prove difficult for the state to justify with any legitimacy, containments and mass detentions are being more widely used and police rationalisations accepted by the courts.

Research on protests and the policing of protests has emphasised the dynamic interactions that exist at such events between the participants and the police and in which can be recognised both short term adjustments to tactics and longer-term cycles that are dominated by norms of confrontation and violence or of tolerance and dialogue. The current cycle, stretching back from the late 1990s, appears to be one which is dominated by confrontation and a tightening of the boundaries in which legitimate protest may take place. It also suggests that there is a commonality of approach among Eastern and Western states that has rarely been noted in the past. However, the use of preventive interventions to limit the right to protest is not the whole story. People are challenging the restrictions, the courts have not tolerated all such interventions and there is a counter process that has highlighted the importance of the right to freedom of peaceful assembly and the right to protest and has sought defend and promote such rights. The European Court of Human Rights has issued a growing number of judgements relating to state restrictions on public assemblies; the OSCE has developed a body of work to increase understanding of the positive obligations that states have to actively protect and facilitate human rights and the United Nations appointed its first Special Rapporteur on Freedom of Peaceful Assembly and Association in May 2011.

The right to assembly peacefully and to protest in public places remains one of the fundamental rights and freedoms and one of a number of related rights central to a functioning democracy where citizens have the right to voice their opinions collectively without the risk of arbitrary intervention by the state. The increasing use of a broad repertoire of preventive interventions risks undermining these rights. There is therefore a need to monitor and challenge such developments to ensure that the right to protest and hold the authorities accountable remains a viable and active human right rather than merely a paper right.

Works cited

Cases

Plattform "Ärtze für das Leben" v Austria (1988).
Guneri and Others v Turkey (2005).
R (Laporte) v Chief Constable of Gloucestershire (2006).
Öllinger v Austria (2006).
Oya Ataman v Turkey (2007).
Balçik v Turkey (2007).
McClure and Moos v the Commissioner of the Police of the Metropolis (2011).
Schwabe and M.G. v Germany (2011).
Akgöl and Göl v Turkey (2011).
Shimovolos v Russia (2012).
Hakobyan and Others v Armenia (2012).
Austin and Others v United Kingdom (2012).

Secondary sources

COCKBURN, A., J. Saint Clair, and A. Sekula. *5 Days that Shook the World: Seattle and Beyond*. London and New York: Verso Books, 2005.
DAVENPORT, C., H. Johnston, and C. Mueller (eds). *Repression and Mobilization*. Minneapolis: University of Minnesota Press, 2005.
DELLA PORTA, D., and H. Reiter (eds). *Policing Protest: The Control of Mass Demonstrations in Western Democracies*. Minneapolis: University of Minnesota Press, 1998.
DELLA PORTA, D., A. Peterson, and H. Reiter (eds). *The Policing of*

Transnational Protest. Aldershot: Ashgate, 2006.

FIELD, J. "Police Monitoring: The Sheffield Experience," in FINE B., and R. Millar (eds). *Policing the Miners' Strike*. London: Lawrence and Wishart, 1985: 204-216.

GILLHAM, P. "Securitizing America: strategic incapacitation and the policing of protest since the 11 September 2001 terrorist attacks." *Sociology Compass* 5.7 (2011): 636-652.

Helsinki Committee of Armenia. 2009.

Home Affairs Committee. *Undercover Policing: Interim Report*. London: House of Commons, 2013.

HUDIG, K. "The Growing Use of "Preventative" Arrests." *Statewatch Journal* 20. 3/4. (2010) Available at <http://www.statewatch.org/analyses/no-121-preventative-arrests.pdf>. Accessed 3.4.13.

KNUCKEY, S., K. Glenn, and E. Maclean. *Suppressing Protest: Human Rights Violations in the U.S. Response to Occupy Wall Street*. New York: Global Justice Clinic and Walter Leitner International Human Rights Clinic, 2012.

LE BON, G. *The Crowd: A Study of the Popular Mind*. London: Fisher Unwin, 1896.

MEAD, D. *The New Law of Peaceful Protest: Rights and Regulation in the Human Rights Act Era*. Oxford: Hart Publishing, 2010.

MCNEILLY, G. *Policing the Right to Protest: G20 Systemic Review Report*. Toronto: Office of the Independent Review Director, 2012 Available at <https://www.oiprd.on.ca/CMS/getattachment/Publications/Reports/G20_Reports_Eng.pdf.aspx>. Accessed 9.3.13.

MITCHELL, D. *The Right to the City: Social Justice and the Fight for Public Space*. New York: Guildford Press, 2003.

NEALE, J. *You Are G8, We Are 6 Billion: The Truth Behind the Genoa Protests*. London: Vision Publications, 2002.

Netpol. Report into the Policing of Protest in 2010/2011. 2012. Available at <http://netpol.files.wordpress.com/2012/07/wainwright-report-finall.pdf>. Accessed 16.4.2013.

NOWAK, M. *UN Covenant on Civil and political Rights: CCPR Commentary*. Kehl am Rheim: NP Engel Publisher, 2005.

OSCE/ODIHR. *Guidelines on Freedom of Peaceful Assembly*. Warsaw: OSCE/ODIHR, 2010.

REICHER, S., and C. Stott. *Mad Mobs and Englishmen: Myths and Realities of the 2011 Riots*. London: Constable and Robinson, 2011.

ROSE, C. *Ratcliffe-on-Soar Power Station Protest: Inquiry into*

Disclosure. London: Crown Prosecution Service, 2011. Available at <http://www.cps.gov.uk/news/assets/upload/files/rose_report_on_ratcliffe_on_Soar_case.pdf>. Accessed 11.4.13.

SHIFFMAN, R. *et al. Beyond Zuccotti Park: Freedom of Assembly and the Occupation of Public Space*. Oakland, CA: New Village Press, 2012.

STARR, A., L Fernandez, and C. Scholl. *Shutting Down the Street: Political Violence and Social control in the Global Era*. New York: New York University Press, 2011.

VITALE. A. "From Negotiated Management to Command and Control: How the New York Police Department Policies Protests." *Policing and Society* 15.3 (2005): 283-304.

ZICK, T. *Speech Out of Doors: Preserving First Amendment Liberties in Public Places.* Cambridge: Cambridge University Press, 2009.

HABEAS, *HAMDAN* AND HISTORY: SEPARATION OF POWERS AND PRE-TRIAL DETENTION IN GUANTANAMO BAY

ROY CARPENTER
UNIVERSITY LYON 3, FRANCE

At the time of this writing, the American legal community is commemorating the fiftieth anniversary of the landmark Supreme Court decision, *Gideon v. Wainwright*, which affirmed the right of the accused in all criminal cases to have access to counsel, even if they cannot afford it. Justice Black, writing the unanimous opinion, declared:

> [...] reason and reflection require us to recognize that, in our adversary system of criminal justice, any person haled into court, who is too poor to hire a lawyer, cannot be assured a fair trial unless counsel is provided for him. This seems to us to be an obvious truth. (*Gideon* 344)

The obviousness of the truth had been lost in the complex, multi-tiered federal structure of the United States legal system, in which some states provided publicly funded legal assistance while others did not. Nevertheless, the notion of a fair trial, it was finally recognized, began at the moment of arrest, when the accused was formally deprived of his or her liberty. Three years later, in *Miranda v. Arizona*, Chief Justice Earl Warren would reassert this same principle, underlining the need "to make the individual more acutely aware that he is faced with a phase of the adversary system -- that he is not in the presence of persons acting solely in his interest." (*Miranda* 469) The Anglo-Saxon legal tradition, the judge was arguing, is based on the idea of a free and fair fight between opposing points of view, out of which the truth is supposed to emerge. But for the system to work, both parties must understand that it is, in fact, a struggle between adversaries, and be prepared to defend themselves.

Of course, the American Constitution had already enshrined the basic tenets of a fair trial in the 1791 Bill of Rights, including the right to know what one is being accused of, so as to be able to mount a credible defense, and to be judged by an impartial decision-maker. (Amendment VI) Nevertheless, law, tradition and common sense all acknowledge the existence of certain exceptional conditions under which the rights of the accused during the period of pre-trial detention can legitimately be suspended. The most obvious is wartime or other situations of threat to the general security. Clearly the United States found itself in one such situation during the immediate aftermath of the 9-11 attacks. And yet, questions inevitably arise as to when the (presumably) temporary suspension of normal legal procedure should expire and democratic safeguards against the abuse of executive power be restored. The confinement of prisoners captured during the American-led invasion of Afghanistan brought this point home dramatically.

After years of detention in the U.S. Naval facility at Guantanamo Bay, Cuba, legal challenges were mounted on behalf of inmates, claiming that the prisoners had been deprived entirely of all rights with no prospect whatsoever of seeing them restored. The situations and statuses of the parties seeking relief through the courts varied widely, but the gist of their claims was that they were given no sign of being part of a clear legal process, either as prisoners of war or as defendants in criminal cases. The American administration responded with surprising glibness that the indefinite detention of some 800 persons was justified by the extraordinary nature of the so-called war on terror and that they were under no obligation whatsoever to clarify the situation, either in terms of the potential duration of detention or in terms of the legal status of the detainees, including the identification of the kind of illegal conduct that had justified the initial deprivation of freedom.[1] The situation at Guantanamo Bay prompted some commentators to refer to it as a "legal black hole."

Then, in 2002, the father of one inmate, Yaser Hamdi, an American citizen who had grown up in Saudi Arabia, filed a petition for a writ of *habeas corpus*, claiming that his son's detention was illegal because all of the above mentioned basic rights of the accused granted to citizens of the United States were being infringed. The case demanded that the courts evaluate whether the government had struck a fair balance between collective security concerns and individual rights: the state's legitimate interest in both detaining enemies who would otherwise engage in

[1] See <http://projects.nytimes.com/guantanamo> for more detailed information about the population of the detention center and a timeline of events surrounding their incarceration.

belligerent activities against the country and in obtaining intelligence information from such individuals would have to be weighed against the basic protections afforded to citizens against abuses of executive power leading to unjustified limitations of personal freedom. After two years of shuffling back and forth between the district and circuit courts, during which time Hamdi remained in prison, the case was finally heard by the Supreme Court in 2004. Relying on both Blackstone and the American *Federalist* papers, Justice Sandra Day O'Connor stated in the majority opinion: "Due process demands that a citizen held in the United States as an enemy combatant be given a meaningful opportunity to contest the factual basis for that detention before a neutral decisionmaker." (*Hamdi* 1)

This simple formula—the right to have a meaningful opportunity to contest the factual basis of one's detention before a neutral decisionmaker —would appear to be a fair starting point for extending some form of due process to all detainees at Guantanamo Bay. O'Connor's description of what constitutes fair legal treatment of a detainee allows for the possibility that the unique aspects of the "war on terror" may require adjustments in the traditional temporal and administrative framework of the trial, but at the same time it grants prisoners the right to contest the legality of their detention in a way that may, if successful, lead to their release. If, for example, civil courts are deemed inappropriate because of concerns over the sensitivity of the information that would be discussed, military tribunals would provide a reasonable alternative so long as they provided a real opportunity to contest the basis of arrest, not just a formality designed to assuage the public conscience. Indeed, the uniqueness of the present conflict can easily be overstated and has in fact become a convenient excuse for executive usurpations of authority.

As a matter of fact, although the legal conundrums involved in processing hundreds of captives from some 50 different countries are formidable, the challenge posed by wartime security imperatives, jurisdictional ambiguities and questions of nationality has arisen in almost every war that the United States has been involved in. The case of Major André during the American Revolutionary War, for example, was referred to by former Solicitor General Paul Clement during the oral argument of *Hamdan v. Rumsfeld*. Clement claimed it was an example of the executive privilege to convene military tribunals and try captured enemy combatants without specific authorization from Congress. This historical point was hotly contested in 2006, but even in 1780, the British prisoner who was caught out of uniform behind enemy lines rejected the illegal status of spy, demanding instead to be treated as a legal prisoner of war. Even the method of execution was to be a point of contention, as George

Washington sentenced him to death by hanging instead of firing squad, which would have been more becoming to an officer of his social rank.

The predicament of foreign individuals, or combatants in foreign territory, captured during military operations did not therefore rise out of a legal vacuum. A brief review of historical precedents reveals that while the individual personalities of persons occupying the executive office do influence the kind of policy adopted, there are certain constants, determined mainly by political institutions, which remain. It is in this light that the present essay will examine the questions concerning pre-trial detention in Guantanamo Bay. It will attempt to show the extent to which the doctrine of the separation of powers has influenced the formulation of policy in this domain, assessing the amount of progress which has been made towards affirming "the right to have a meaningful opportunity to contest the factual basis of one's detention before a neutral decisionmaker," and finally taking stock of the present situation.

Habeas in time of war: an historical perspective

Guantanamo Bay has been a public relations disaster for the United States government. The photographs of abuses committed at Abu Graib prison in Iraq combined with the debate around "enhanced interrogation" techniques approved by the Bush administration have contributed to the general impression that U.S. military detention centers are zones of lawlessness where the ends of obtaining intelligence justify the means of torture. This is "the direct consequence of an administration ready to bargain away the rule of law." (Lithwick) The Bush administration's earlier declarations of its intention to "treat detainees humanely and […] in a manner consistent with the principles of Geneva" only added to the impression of hypocrisy as stories of acts of humiliation accumulated. (Schlesinger 7) The foreign press understandably condemned U.S. policy and the American press, while remaining highly critical of the administration, seemed, by and large, to believe that the solution lay either in convincing them of the error of their ways or in replacing key officials with others more receptive to the appeals of the international community. It was no surprise, therefore, that they both cheered the Obama administration's lofty declarations of good intentions only to be disappointed with the lack of policy change that followed. A more fruitful approach, and one less prone to unrealistic expectations, would have been to examine the forces brought to bear on the various actors through the prism of the political institutions which define their roles. As it turns out, it would appear that certain tendencies are peculiar to the executive branch of government regardless of party or political orientation.

In fact, functionaries of the executive department have routinely been denounced for their suspension of civil liberties during times of conflict. But the argument is far from being one-sided and justifications for ignoring normal legal procedure—various versions of *Inter arma enim silent leges*—are found in numerous legal texts including the U.S. Constitution. Article I, Section 9, § 2 states, somewhat unhelpfully, that "The Privilege of the Writ of Habeas Corpus shall not be suspended [by Congress], unless when in Case of Rebellion or Invasion the public Safety may require it." In other words, *habeas corpus*, or the right to call into question the legitimacy of one's detention before a neutral judge, should not be suspended, though war or other situations of public emergency may in fact require its suspension. So while the roles of the various actors in this domain are quite clear—citizens have the right to apply for *habeas*, the courts have the right to issue the writ, Congress has the right to suspend the people's right, and in emergency situations the executive has the right to ignore it—the way representatives of different branches of government would interpret their prerogatives is predictable enough. Members of Congress, not wishing to appear to be placing members of their constituencies in danger would be unlikely to oppose presidential claims of extraordinary circumstances, while the courts would hardly look favorable upon their exclusion from a legal process.

History has tended to confirm this analysis, though exceptions do exist. General Andrew Jackson's suspension of the writ during his occupation of New Orleans in the War of 1812 would appear to be little more than the application of martial law in a city rumored to be seething with spies on the eve of an enemy attack.[2] This, however, did not prevent the local judge from fining the future president $1,000 for his unlawful suspension of the writ. Jackson responded by requesting Congress to reimburse him and issuing a stern warning as to the message it would send to future generals if his money were not refunded. Congress conceded and the idea that prevailed seemed to be that because the suspension of rights was made in response to a clear and present danger and since its duration was short lived, it fell within the acceptable range of exceptions envisaged by the constitution and common law tradition. The pragmatism of this decision did not, however, directly address the question of how the executive prerogative to declare martial law relates to the exclusively legislative right to suspend the writ of *habeas corpus*. Was Jackson's military

[2] See Matthew Warshauer's discussion of this event and the parallels with Guantanamo Bay. URL: <http://www.c-spanvideo.org/program/196528-1>.

commission in itself an implicit transfer of that power from the legislative to the executive branch?

The same question would be raised in more dramatic circumstances still when during the Civil War Abraham Lincoln took it upon himself to suspend the writ. The president's 1862 declaration was made in reaction to rebel recruiting activity occurring in Maryland, north of Washington, D.C. The logic of Lincoln's order follows closely that of Jackson: given the extreme urgency of the situation, "the ordinary processes of law" are inadequate and therefore martial law must be declared. As a consequence, the writ of *habeas corpus* is perforce suspended. Unfortunately for the president, John Merryman, one of the first confederate recruiters arrested, appealed directly to Chief Justice Roger Taney, who was at the time serving as circuit court judge in Maryland. Taney served a writ to the military commander in Baltimore holding Merryman but was informed that the detainee's right had been suspended *as per* Lincoln's order declaring martial law. Tanney's response has thundered down through time ever since:

> As the case comes before me […] I understand that the President not only claims the right to suspend the writ of Habeas Corpus himself, at his discretion, but to delegate that discretionary power to a military officer, and to leave it to him to determine whether he will or will not obey Judicial process that may be served upon him. No official notice has been given to the courts of justice, or to the public, by proclamation or otherwise, that the President claimed this power, and had exercised it in the manner stated in the return. And I certainly listened to it with some surprise. For I had supposed it to be one of those points of constitutional law upon which there was no difference of opinion, and that it was admitted on all hands that the privilege of the writ could not be suspended, except by act of Congress […]. (*Ex parte Merryman* 148)

Once again, a debate ensued within and among all branches of government as to whether the intensity of the crisis justified the executive's circumventing of normal judicial procedure. And as in the case of General Jackson, Congress belatedly acquiesced and gave the president the authorization that the court claimed he needed, passing the Habeas Corpus Act in 1873.

A pattern begins to emerge. Executive action is taken in response to a national security crisis: individuals identified as participants in enemy actions are taken into custody and denied basic legal rights. Representatives of the judiciary question the validity of the executive suspension of individual rights. The executive retroactively seeks legislative authorization to be able to continue pursuing a policy already in place, which is granted. In fact, the same sequence of events will be followed in the aftermath of the 9-11 attacks. In all cases, Congress finds itself presented with a sort of *fait accompli* accompanied by a request to validate a mechanism that is already functioning and a stern warning of the dire consequences which may result if they do not comply.

Precedents for military commissions

When the Bush administration proposed establishing military commissions for trying prisoners captured in Afghanistan and Iraq, there was in Europe a general suspicion of illegitimacy, no doubt fed by images of third world tribunals handing out summary judgments against political enemies. Given the administration's handling of detention issues in Iraq, such suspicions are entirely understandable. But military commissions were designed to fill a jurisdictional gap that corresponds to enemy combatants who are not prisoners of war, that is to say soldiers captured fighting on behalf of a belligerent foreign state, and citizens of one's own country who have been accused of crimes like aiding the enemy or treason. Basically, they were designed to address clear violations of the laws of war as recognized by both sides of a conflict, often both signatories of the same convention; they allowed a government to render justice to a detainee who could not be held as a prisoner until the end of hostilities because it was suspected that he would not be held accountable for his illegal acts in his home country. The Bush administration's recourse to military commissions for illegal enemy combatants was therefore not entirely without precedent, though it by no means resolved the ambiguities surrounding pre-trial detention in Guantanamo Bay.

By their very nature, military commissions raise questions of justiciability. Indeed, whereas the accused in a normal criminal trial is a citizen being judged by the laws of his own country, and whereas prisoners of war are detained until the end of the conflict then returned to their own country without incurring any risk of responsibility for their actions during the conflict, having been under the command of superior officers, the situation of the accused in a military commission is entirely different. Here, a citizen of one country is accused of breaking either the laws of a second country or some internationally recognized standards, and he is being judged by a court and by the standards of the country against which he is purportedly fighting. Can the accused have a meaningful opportunity to contest the factual basis of his detention before a neutral decisionmaker in these circumstances? While it would be difficult to ignore the inherent contradictions involved in such an endeavor, the history of the Guantanamo detainees and in particular the case of *Hamdan v. Rumsfeld* would suggest that the obstacles are not insurmountable, the key being the attribution of counsel with whom the detainee can establish a reasonable degree of trust.

Historically, however, the obstacles have not always been surmounted. Beginning with the case of Major André, the legitimacy of the venue must be balanced against a whole range of other factors, such as the place of arrest, the place of the alleged criminal act, the legal jurisdiction of the accuser and the nationality and status of the accused. *Ex parte Milligan*, a Supreme Court case from the end of the Civil War, illustrates this point well. Lamdin P. Milligan was accused of belonging to a secret organization that was assisting the Confederacy. He was tried, convicted and sentenced to death by a military commission. However, Milligan was a resident and citizen of Indiana, a state not in rebellion against the union where federal civil courts were still functioning normally. Despite the fact that the accusation involved his participation in what was basically an international conflict, the court ruled that there can be no parallel justice system in an area where the civil system is intact and therefore his conviction was overturned.

A series of cases during World War II wrestled with the same questions of jurisdiction and detainee status which inevitably accompany military commissions. In the 1942 case *Ex parte Quirin*, a group of German spies were captured before they could successfully execute a plan to sabotage a number of targets within the United States. President Roosevelt convened a special military commission, which found them guilty and sentenced them to death. They applied for *habeas*, claiming that the logic of Milligan would require that the military commission be declared illegal since it involved a military and civil court functioning in parallel within the same territorial jurisdiction. The Supreme Court eventually affirmed the validity of the commission on the grounds that the accused were not American citizens and therefore could not be tried in civil court. Moreover, their acts of espionage committed out of uniform were clear violations of the laws of war, the precise reason for which military commissions were conceived in the first place. Nonetheless, the fact that the high court agreed to hear their claim was a tacit acknowledgment that the validity of a military commission could be called into question through an appeal for a writ of *habeas corpus* and that civil courts could then judge whether the commission did indeed provide a fair forum for the accused to be tried in.

In 1946, another case added a twist to the discussion surrounding justiciability when a Japanese general in the Philippines was accused of not stopping his troops from committing war crimes. A Philippine court rejected his request for *habeas*, but the U.S. Supreme agreed to it, though the justices confirmed the legitimacy of the military commission. The commission was harshly criticized for the hastiness of the way the trial was conducted. On the positive side, General Yamashita's lawyers were tenacious in defending their client, while on the negative side, they claimed not to have enough time to prepare the case as thoroughly as they had wanted. Nevertheless, the executive's right to establish commissions for trying war crimes was affirmed while simultaneously asserting the high court's right to oversee that they provide a meaningful opportunity for the detainee to defend himself against the accusations of the government.

Two more cases, *Ahrens v. Clark* (1948) and *Johnson v. Eisentrager* (1950,) raised questions about the geographical dimension of the problem. In the first, 120 Germans were being held on Ellis Island in New York, waiting for deportation. When they filed a writ of *habeas corpus* with the District Court of Washington, D.C., the question as to territorial jurisdiction arose. The detainees claimed that since it was the U.S. Attorney General's order which resulted in their confinement on Ellis Island, the request must be made in Washington, where Attorney General Clark exercised his profession. The problem was whether the detainees needed to be physically present within the jurisdictional territory of the court to which the application for *habeas* was being made. In a narrow construction of constitutional language, which would later be overturned, the Supreme Court affirmed that they did. Nevertheless, the geographical dimension of the problem remained largely unresolved. In *Johnson v. Eisentrager*, this same question was raised in still different terms when a group of Germans arrested by U.S. forces in China were transferred to Germany and tried before an American military commission there. The accused applied for *habeas* in the United States, claiming that the rights granted by the American constitution to its citizens should be accorded to them since they were being tried in a place that was under complete control of the United States government. Once again the court agreed to consider their petition but affirmed the legitimacy of military commissions as forums for trying foreign captives for war crimes.

Most of the issues mentioned above would come back into the light when the Bush administration began processing the prisoners it had captured in various phases of its "war on terror." Clearly, the president was weary of the legal ramifications of bringing suspected terrorists to the territory of the United States, no doubt rightly fearing that their physical presence would increase the chances of the inmates being given greater legal protection and thus interfering with the government's efforts to extract what it considered vital information from them. But the solution of keeping them on a U.S. naval base leased from Cuba did not entirely free them from the sort of judicial interference they were wishing to avoid.

Pre-trial detention in Guantanamo Bay and the separation of powers

In 2003, the Supreme Court heard the first of a series of cases calling into question the fairness of the military commissions established to try prisoners held in Guantanamo Bay. In oral argument for *Rasul v. Bush*, the lawyers for the government and the detainees opened up the proverbial can of worms, rehashing all the issues already raised in both the Civil War and World War II cases: Does the length of detention matter? Can it be considered indefinite just because the end cannot be determined at the present time? Do foreign detainees have the right to *habeas corpus*? If so, at what stage of the procedure can they assert it? Do civilian courts have jurisdiction to consider *habeas* claims against military detention? Do the Geneva conventions apply to combatants for non state organizations? Once a detainee's status has been determined, can it be reviewed? If so, by whom? What is the exact definition of "enemy aliens?" Of "illegal combatants?" Of "enemy combatants?" Do civil courts have "battlefield jurisdiction?" What is the legal status of a U.S. naval base? What if the captured combatant is a U.S. citizen? So many questions the administration had been hoping to avoid addressing when it decided to send prisoners to Guantanamo Bay.

The story of how these issues were addressed follows the same pattern already noted above at the time of Andrew Jackson and Abraham Lincoln. First, executive action is taken in response to a national security crisis; then, individuals identified as participants in enemy actions are taken into custody and denied basic legal rights; next, representatives of the judiciary question the validity of the executive suspension of individual rights; at last, the executive retroactively seeks legislative authorization to be able to continue pursuing a policy already in place, which is granted. Following the narrative through its convoluted developments reveals that the influence of American political institutions is perhaps the single most important and overlooked feature of the way the United States has come to grips with what is at stake in how foreign fighters captured in conflicts linked to the "war on terror" are brought to justice.

After the devastating attacks of 9-11, the U.S. Congress declared:

> [...] that the President is authorized to use all necessary and appropriate force against those nations, organizations, or persons he determines planned, authorized, committed, or aided the terrorist attacks that occurred

> on September 11, 2001, or harbored such organizations or persons, in order to prevent any future acts of international terrorism against the United States by such nations, organizations or persons. (Section 2-a, *Authorization for Use of Military Force*)

Much like the Tonkin Gulf Resolution, which President Lyndon Johnson appreciatively described as being similar to grandma's nightshirt, because it covered everything, the *Authorization for Use of Military Force* (AUMF) gave large sway to the executive to pursue the perpetrators of the largest acts of terrorism ever perpetrated in the United States.

Within a month, plans for invading Afghanistan were well under way and already the question of how best to try suspected terrorists was being raised. In November, an executive order concerning "Detention, Treatment, and Trial of Certain Non-Citizens" was issued. In it the president warned:

> Given the danger to the safety of the United States and the nature of international terrorism, [...] it is not practicable to apply in military commissions under this order the principles of law and the rules of evidence generally recognized in the trial of criminal cases in the United States district courts. (Section 1-f, *Military Order of November 13*)

One is tempted to read in this declaration a sign of things to come: indeed, military commissions, as explained above, do not, by their very definition, apply the principles of law generally recognized in American criminal law. We need to return to the principle laid out by Justice O'Connor, that detainees be given a meaningful opportunity to defend themselves before a neutral decisionmaker in order to conceive of a military commission that, while not following the standards of a civil court, would nonetheless fulfill the basic requirements of fairness. But the order goes on to affirm that the accused will be given a "full and fair trial" (Section 4-c-1) and are to be treated humanely and given the freedoms to practice their religion. (Section 3-b & d)

Four months later, however, the executive branch, through the Department of Defense, began to protect itself from interference by the other branches of government. *Military Commission Order No. 1* reaffirms the basic principles of the executive order, even adding the rights to be defended "zealously" by a lawyer (Section 4.C.2.a,) and for a speedy trial. (Section 6.B.2) But near the end of the order, the impartiality of the tribunals is severely limited if not entirely abrogated when we read:

> A Commission finding as to a charge and any sentence of a Commission becomes final when the President or, if designated by the President, the

> Secretary of Defense makes a final decision thereon [...]. (Section 6.H.2, "Finality of Findings and Sentence")

As a result, all verdicts that may be rendered are really only "recommendations" that "will be forwarded to the President for review and final decision." (Section 6.H.6, "Final Decision") Such assertions would seem to constitute an attempt at pre-empting any judicial interference in the proceedings. However, all the Civil War and World War II decisions, despite the persistence of certain gray areas, affirmed the judicial branch's right and duty both to verify the fairness of military commissions and to confirm the justiciability of the cases before them.

It should be noted that *Military Commission Order No. 1* went into effect just as the invasion of Afghanistan began. Once military operations were under way, the allied forces were flooded with detainees who could potentially be identified as terrorists. The situation was further complicated when the American government offered awards for the capture of members of Al Qaeda, which incited local tribal authorities to bring in persons with dubious connections to terrorism whose real identities would have to be verified later. All in all, it is estimated that some 50,000 people were taken into custody by American forces, a mere 800 of whom ended up in Guantanamo Bay. Initially, little attention was paid to the situation in the Cuban base as the media followed the development of events on the ground in Afghanistan. However, as time went on and information was not forthcoming, the American press began to realize that a policy of secrecy had been adopted by the executive branch regarding the detention center.

The case of *Rasul v. Bush* encapsulates the lack of clarity with which the administration pursued this policy. Four men of British and Australian nationalities were captured by the Northern Alliance in December 2001. Their reasons for being in such a troubled region at that time were variously convincing. According to the petitioners' brief to the Supreme Court, Mr. Rasul was there "to visit relatives in Pakistan, explore his culture, and continue his computer studies." (*Rasul*, Petitioners' Brief 3) Another petitioner was looking for a school for his daughter while a third claimed he had gone to get married. According to the father of David Hicks, one of the two Australian nationals, his son had joined the Taliban forces in Afghanistan, a story that seemed to have been corroborated by now famous photographs of Hicks holding a rocket launcher (which he claims was actually taken in Albania.) After capture, all four men were transferred to Guantanamo where they claimed that their detention was without basis. The situation provides a neat summary of the difficulties involved for both parties: on one side, the prisoners basically claim that they were simply innocent bystanders caught in the wrong place at the wrong time, whereas the government wonders, with a certain level of legitimacy, what they were doing in a war zone on the Taliban side of the battle lines. The main point of *Rasul v. Bush*, however, was not the merits but the jurisdictional claim.

Rasul *et al.*, through their families who were managing their legal struggle, demanded above all the right to make their cases before a neutral decisionmaker with the assistance of counsel. The administration claimed that non-citizens have no right to *habeas corpus* in American civilian courts when they have not been detained within the territorial confines of the United States. Certainly the government's argument raises legitimate questions about the case's justiciability, but after two years of detainment without accusation, the basic right to know clearly what one's status is, be it prisoner of war or that of the accused in a criminal proceeding, had been blatantly flaunted. As John J. Gibbons, the lawyer for petitioners put it in his opening statement:

> What is at stake in this case is the authority of the Federal courts to uphold the rule of law. Respondents assert that their actions are absolutely immune from judicial examination whenever they elect to detain foreign nationals outside our borders. Under this theory, neither the length of the detention, the conditions of their confinement, nor the fact that they have been wrongfully detained makes the slightest difference. Respondents would create a lawless enclave insulating the executive branch from any judicial scrutiny now or in the future. (*Rasul* "Proceedings")

In a 6-3 decision, the high court agreed with Mr. Gibbons that the executive's assurances of fair treatment and warnings of potential threats to homeland security should a public trial be held were insufficient to overcome the challenge posed by the four petitioners. While the notion that Guantanamo Bay may constitute a unique legal situation was not entirely debunked, the idea that there could be in fact no judicial oversight whatsoever was firmly rejected.

Eight days after *Rasul*, the Supreme Court heard oral argument in *Hamdi v. Rumsfeld*, to which we have already alluded above. Hamdi's case rounded out the discussion over basic rights and jurisdictions insofar as he was an American citizen and thus both possible kinds of citizenship status were examined. The decision began to define the legal framework in which the government needed to work mainly by pointing out the imbalance of the present relation between executive prerogatives and due process. Justice O'Connor first identified the issue in question, namely the right to make the claim of "you've got the wrong guy":

> Even in cases in which the detention of enemy combatants is legally authorized, there remains the question of what process is constitutionally due to a citizen who disputes his enemy-combatant status. (*Hamdi* 17)

Hence, the court wished to make it clear that in the extraordinary situation of combating terrorism during a foreign military intervention, the executive does indeed have the right to establish its own procedures for determining the status of those captured on the field of battle. Nonetheless, despite the great degree of independence with which the president is permitted to act, those detained must have some clear and fair forum in which to make the claim that their arrest was a mistake.

O'Connor continued, "It is beyond question that substantial interests lie on both sides of the scale in this case." (*Ibid.* 22) Yet while detainees must be able to argue against their detention, we must not lose sight, she wrote, of "the weighty and sensitive governmental interests in ensuring that those who have in fact fought with the enemy during a war do not return to battle against the United States." (*Ibid.* 24) But she concluded:

> With due recognition of these competing concerns, we believe that [...] the process proposed by the Government [does not strike] the proper constitutional balance [... A] citizen-detainee seeking to challenge his classification as an enemy combatant must receive notice of the factual basis for his classification, and a fair opportunity to rebut the Government's factual assertions before a neutral decisionmaker. (*Ibid.* 25-26)

A month after the Supreme Court handed down its decision, the administration issued an executive order "establishing combatant status review tribunals" to be "comprised of three neutral officers, none of whom were involved with the detainee." (*Combatant Status Review Tribunal Order* 1-2) A direct response to the court's ruling, the CSRTs incorporated all the procedural safeguards demanded, including the right for detainees "to contest their status as enemy combatants," a promise to begin proceedings "as soon as possible," "the right to seek a writ of *habeas corpus* in the courts of the United States," and "the right to testify before the tribunal, call witnesses and introduce any other evidence." (*Ibid* 3) Perhaps most importantly, they granted the right to have a "personal representative" to assist in the preparation of the detainees' cases.

Hamdi v. Rumsfeld concluded the first phase of the previously mentioned cycle in which the executive takes suspected enemy collaborators into custody before being forced by the judiciary to seek congressional approval for its policy of suspending normal procedural rights. Members of Congress were beginning to feel pressure from constituents concerned, on the one hand, by reports of abuses occurring inside the detention centers, and on the other hand, the prospect of bringing dangerous terrorists to the homeland for trial in civil courts. On Capitol Hill it was clear enough where the impetus for closing down Guantanamo and bringing the prisoners to the U.S. mainland would come from: the Supreme Court. With retrospect, the legislative reaction was predictable enough. The Detainee Treatment Act of 2005 prohibits the "cruel, inhuman, or degrading treatment or punishment" of detainees by providing "uniform standards" for interrogation of prisoners. (DTA § a, Section 2000dd) At the same time, it declared that "no court, justice or judge shall have jurisdiction to hear or consider" applications on behalf of Guantanamo detainees. (§ e (1), Section 2241, 28 USC 153 (2012)) Not wishing to appear soft on matters of national security, the legislative branch was backing up the president, just as it had with Jackson and Lincoln.

The counter-attack from the judiciary would not be long in coming. In fact, one month before Congress passed the Detainee Treatment Act, the Supreme Court accepted the petition of Salim Hamdan, a Yemeni citizen and personal driver of Osama Bin Laden. Hamdan's case involved all the now usual paradoxes surrounding Guantanamo detainees. He was an Al Qaeda employee but his actual involvement in plotting or combating against the United States was relatively limited. Moreover, his detention bore all the hallmarks of the policy of total secrecy and lack of transparency that the Bush administration had put into place in Guantanamo. Ironically, it was the establishment of the CSRTs by the executive which gave Hamdan the opportunity to question the legitimacy of the military commission before which he was to be tried. Charles Swift, the navy lawyer assigned to defend him, contacted Georgetown law professor Neal Katyal and attempted to show that while the military commissions created to try the detainees was a step in the right direction, insofar as they at least provided some forum in which the case could be debated and a judgment rendered, they were still operating within no clearly identifiable legal structure, such as the laws of war, the Geneva conventions, the Uniform Code of Military Justice or normal criminal law. (Malher 2008) The executive branch, it was contended, was basically acting on its own, trying prisoners by its own standards that remained unclear and not subject to any external scrutiny whatsoever.

In *Hamdan v. Rumsfeld*, the court brushed aside Section 2241 of the Detainee Treatment Act forbidding judicial interference, claiming, somewhat disingenuously, that "Congress has not issued the executive a 'blank check'" and thus "the Executive is bound to comply with the Rule of Law that prevails in this jurisdiction." (*Hamdan* 72) So the congressional phase of the cycle was more complicated than in the earlier examples due to the tenacity of the court. But Congress once again came out in support of the President when it enacted the Military Commissions Act of 2006, which addressed the question of just how blank a check it was issuing the president. The law began by explicitly giving the president authorization to set up military commissions, though in a concession to the court it established Common Article 3 of the Geneva Conventions as the standard for the interrogation and prosecution of prisoners. Strangely, however, it denied the accused the right to invoke the Geneva Conventions during trials as well as the right to file *habeas corpus* petitions in federal court. Congress seemed to be positioning itself somewhere between the judiciary, which insisted on clear procedures and respect of the rights of the accused, and the Executive, who was asserting his time-honored claims to exclusive control of national policy during a security crisis. Unfortunately, for the legislative branch, while the court might have accepted congressional permission for the president to establish his own tribunals in a time of war, it could not agree to letting him do so without granting the accused the right to at least claim that his arrest was unfair.

Boumediene v. Bush was the last major challenge to the legitimacy of executive policy in matters of prosecuting Guantanamo detainees outside the normal criminal procedure. Here, the Congress and president essentially fought the courts to a standstill after the justices reaffirmed the right to *habeas corpus*:

> We hold that petitioners may invoke the fundamental procedural protections of habeas corpus. The laws and Constitution are designed to survive, and remain in force, in extraordinary times. Liberty and security can be reconciled; and in our system they are reconciled within the framework of the law. The Framers decided that habeas corpus, a right of first importance, must be a part of that framework. (*Boumediene* 69-70)

While striking down the provision of the law that had suppressed the right to *habeas* reasserts the court's oversight of executive proceedings, the court implicitly concedes that except in cases of actual unconstitutionality, it is Congress which enacts the laws that the court interprets and the president executes. The lofty language belies the fact that a new category of procedure, neither military nor criminal, has come into being. As Jonathan Hafetz comments in the *Columbia Law Review*:

> *Boumediene* does provide some check against arbitrary detention by establishing a constitutional right to judicial review for detainees at Guantánamo. But [...] the *habeas* process it engendered has helped institutionalize the military detention of terrorism suspects by recognizing it as a permissible form of noncriminal detention and by upholding detentions based on evidentiary standards and procedures that deviate substantially from those in the criminal justice system.

The ruling was handed down five months before a presidential election for which the incumbent, George W. Bush, was not eligible, so for those wishing to close the Guantanamo Bay detention center, all hope rested with the new president. When Barrack Obama was elected, his first official act was to issue the order to close the now infamous facility and thus an era had finally come to an end. Or so it seemed.

Conclusion

Closing Gitmo would be harder than expected for the new president. Congress maintained the same policy position it had taken under President Bush, but this time it engaged in some budgetary muscle-flexing by refusing to provide the funding necessary to transfer the prisoners to facilities in the U.S. This effectively rendered moot the promise that the prison "be closed as soon as practicable, and no later than 1year from the date of this order." (*Executive Order - Closure Of Guantanamo Detention Facilities*, Section 3) But President Obama had gone further than just ordering the prison to be shut down; he added an "or else" clause that states:

> If any individuals covered by this order remain in detention at Guantánamo at the time of closure of those detention facilities, they shall be returned to their home country, released, transferred to a third country, or transferred to another United States detention facility. (*Ibid*)

His total failure to make good on this promise raises many questions and one is tempted to read in the chronology of the events a degree of pre-presidential naiveté. Is it the case, in other words, that once the executive has taken the full measure of his responsibilities that he is inexorably drawn towards a policy of accumulating tools by which he can wage a war against those threatening national security with the greatest degree of institutional liberty and the least degree of oversight and restraint by other the other branches of government?

To be fair to Mr. Obama, the process of trying prisoners or transferring them out of Guantánamo has continued. At the same time, his once official intention of transferring inmates to civil courts on the U.S. mainland has quietly been abandoned. The military commissions, in a somewhat improved and more impartial form, nonetheless remain in place. If any progress has been made in clarifying what the appropriate legal procedure for the remaining 166 detainees is (at this writing,) it has been by process of elimination, mainly as a result of the Supreme Court striking down those practices which are not acceptable. Obama's executive order of March 7, 2011 reaffirms the two categories of detainees identified in the original order 2009 that envisaged the final closure of the facility: those "designated for continued law of war detention" and those "referred for prosecution." (*Executive Order 13567*, Section 1. Scope and Purpose) In other words, the prisoners are either subject to the laws of war and hence the Uniform Code of Military Justice, or normal criminal procedure. But references to "continued law of war detention" indicate that no trials are envisaged for certain prisoners, but rather a return to their home countries in the context of a return of prisoners at the end of hostilities. (*Ibid.*, Sec. 2. Standard for Continued Detention) Of course, given the nature of the conflict, the question then arises as to when the conflict will end or what conditions must be met to declare that it is in fact over.

The lack of clear response to such questions has prompted an outpouring of denunciation: "Obama creates indefinite detention system for prisoners at Guantánamo Bay," thundered *The Washington Post* the day after the executive order was issued. In a speech to the Oxford Union in late 2012, Jeh Johnson, General Counsel of the Department of Defense, did his best to shed some light on the underlying principles guiding policy in this area. He began by stating clearly that although the conflict the United States is involved in is entirely "unconventional," the legal principles that the government applies are resolutely "conventional:" "Our efforts remain grounded in the rule of law." (Johnson) Moving forward with what some find to be enervatingly slow caution, the Defense Department lawyer said that policy of detaining members of enemy organizations should be "viewed within the context of conventional armed conflict" in which "capture, detention and lethal force are traditional practices as old as armies." (*Ibid*) He then went on to address the question of when it will end, offering a very disappointing, "we don't really know" as an answer:

> In the current conflict with Al Qaeda, I can offer no prediction about when this conflict will end [...] I do believe that on the present course, there will come a tipping point [...] at which [...] the group is no longer able to [...] launch a strategic attack against the United States, such

> that Al Qaeda as we know it, the organization that our Congress authorized the military to pursue in 2001, has been effectively destroyed. (*Ibid*)

But does it really need to be so vague? In *Hamdi v. Rumsfeld*, Justice O'Connor provided what could be useful guidelines as to how a more definite answer could be reached. Accepting the premise that detention for the duration of a conflict was a time-honored practice for belligerent parties in wartime, she went on to say:

> If the record establishes that United States troops are still involved in active combat in Afghanistan, those detentions are part of the exercise of "necessary and appropriate force," and therefore are authorized. (*Hamdi* 14)

One logical inference from this could be that if the record establishes that United States troops are no longer involved in active combat in Afghanistan, then the detentions are no longer part of the exercise of the "necessary and appropriate force" authorized by Congress and therefore are no longer sanctioned by the law.

On balance, the role that the doctrine of separation of powers has played in the formation of pre-trial detention policy in the U.S. "war on terror" has been, in the opinion of this author, largely beneficial. For whereas the United States has been involved to a far greater extent in the execution of this policy, other Western and non Western countries have also declared "wars on terror" but with far less public debate generated by institutionally generated critique of the new procedures being used to deal with this novel situation. France and Britain, to name only two countries which share America's enlightenment values, are reported to have been involved in similarly shady practices while implementing diverse anti-terror policies, sometimes in collaboration with American agencies. (Cobain) However, without the critical influence of judicial review, criticism is more easily sidelined and attributed to media bias. The public forum of the trial provides the opportunity for public exposition of the different positions on an issue in their most poignant and probing forms of expression. Cases such as *Hamdan v. Rumsfeld* give at least some vindication for the adversarial system, which is rightly criticized for its seemingly excessive emphasis on procedure, and openness to the influence of money. Whereas the heavy responsibility of the executive office opens up the possibility of abuses of power, the balance of powers system at least allows for the exposure of such abuses if not also for their partial correction. One need only imagine how the situation of Guantanamo Bay would have developed without an executive subject to the independent scrutiny of the judiciary.

Works cited

Cases

Ex parte Merryman, 144 C.C.D. Md. (1861).
Gideon v. Wainwright, 372 U.S. 335 (1963).
Miranda v. Arizona, 384 U.S. 436 (1966).
Rasul v. Bush, 542 U.S. 466 (2004).
Rasul v. Bush, 542 U.S. 466 (2004). "Proceedings." Arguments Transcripts. The Supreme Court of the United States. Accessed April 15, 2013, URL: <http://www.supremecourt.gov/oral_arguments/argument_transcripts/03-334.pdf>.
Hamdi et al. v. Rumsfeld, Secretary of Defense, et al, 542 U.S. 507 (2004).
Hamdan v. Rumsfeld 548 U.S. 557 (2006).
Boumediene v. Bush, 553 U.S. 723 (2008).

Primary sources

Authorization for Use of Military Force. Public Law 107-40, 107th Congress. 18 September, 2001. Accessed 9 April, 2013. URL: <http://www.gpo.gov/fdsys/pkg/PLAW-107publ40/html/PLAW-107publ40.htm>.
Combatant Status Review Tribunal Order, 651-04, 7 July, 2004. Accessed 9 April, 2013, URL: <http://www.defense.gov/news/Jul2004/d20040707review.pdf>.
Department of Defense Military Commission Order No. 1. 21 March, 2002.
Executive Order - Closure Of Guantanamo Detention Facilities. Federal Register. 74.16 (27 January, 2009.)
Executive Order 13567--Periodic Review of Individuals Detained at Guantánamo Bay Naval Station Pursuant to the Authorization for Use of Military Force. 7 March, 2011.
Military Order of November 13, 2001--Detention, Treatment, and Trial of Certain Non-Citizens in the War Against Terrorism. Federal Register. 66. 222 (16 November 16, 2001.)
The Detainee Treatment Act (DTA) of 2005, 42 USC 21D (2012.)
SCHLESINGER, James R. *et al. Final Report of the Independent Panel to Review DoD Detention Operations.* Independent Panel to Review DoD Detention Operations. Washington D.C.: Government Printing Office, 2004.

Secondary sources

COBAIN, Ian. *Cruel Britannia: A Secret History of Torture.* London: Portobello Books, 2012.

"France terror removals condemned." BBC News. June 6, 2007. Accessed 15 April, 2013. URL: <http://news.bbc.co. uk/2/hi/europe/6726603.stm>.

HAFETZ, Jonathan. "Military Detention in the 'War on Terrorism': Normalizing the Exceptional After 9/11." *Columbia Law Review* 112 (2012). Accessed 15 April, 2013. URL: <http://papers.ssrn.com/sol3/papers. cfm?abstract_id=2025057>.

JOHNSON, Jeh. "Full Address | Oxford Union." 2012. Accessed 15 April 2013. URL: <http://www. youtube.com/watch?v=cun8o2sDJgE>.

LITHWICK, Dahlia. "No Smoking Gun." *The New York Times.* 26 August, 2004. Accessed 9 April, 2013. URL: <http://www.nytimes.com/2004/08/26/opinion26lit hwick.html>.

MAHLER, Jonathan. *The Challenge: Hamdan v. Rumsfeld and the Fight over Presidential Power*. New York: Farrar, Straus and Giroux, 2008.

Appendix: Chart of Separation of Powers and the Legal Developments Concerning the Detention Center in Guantanamo Bay, Cuba

DATE	NAME OF LEGAL ACTION TAKEN	GOV. BRANCH : EX	LEG	JUD
9/01	Authorization of Use of Military Force Act		✓	
11/01	Ex. ord. "Detention, Treatment, & Trial…"	✓		
3/02	Dept. of Def. Military Commission Order #1	✓		
6/04	*Rasul v. Bush*			✓
6/04	*Hamdi v. Rumsfeld*			✓
7/04	Combatant Status Review Tribunal (CSRT) Order	✓		
12/05	Detainee Treatment Act		✓	
6/06	*Hamdan v. Rumsfeld*			✓
10/06	Military Commissions Act		✓	
6/08	*Boumediene v. Bush*			✓
1/09	Ex. ord. "Closure of Guantanamo Det. Facil."	✓		
3/11	Ex. ord. "Periodic Review of Indiv. Detain."	✓		

CRIME AND PUNISHMENT IN THE 20TH-CENTURY BRAZILIAN WAR NAVY: THE PUNISHMENT OF REBELLIOUS AND INSUBORDINATE SEAMEN (THE 1910 REVOLT AND THE 1964 REBELLION)

SILVIA CAPANEMA
UNIVERSITY PARIS NORD, FRANCE

This article proposes to analyze the repression of two lower rank seamen rebellions in the Brazilian War Navy that took place in Rio de Janeiro in the 20th century. Firstly, the logics of judgment and punishment peculiar to the Brazilian War Navy at the end of the 19th and beginning of the 20th century are studied, particularly the practices and the ways that rendered these corporal punishments legitimate. Then, the revolt of the seamen against these punishments is analysed, as well as the repression of the uprising and the life experience of one of the prisoners detained without trial for almost two years, the leader of the mutiny, the seaman João Cândido. Thirdly, a second uprising of Brazilian military sailors which took place in 1964 is examined, just before a *coup d'état* by the military and civil dictatorship. The study particularly focuses on the repression mechanisms and the prisons within a specific context of *l'état d'exception* from indirect sources, three other studies on the subject (Almeida; Capitani; Rodrigues 2004) and interviews undertaken in order to understand the memorial references of the 1964 rebellion made in connection with the 1910 revolt on the one hand (Capanema 2009) and, on the other hand the relationship between power and the law from these two cases that challenge military practices in Brazil.

Logics of punishment in the War Navy at the end of the 19th and at the beginning of the 20th century

On 21 November, 1910, the whole crew of the biggest battleship of the fleet, named *Minas Gerais*[1], anchored at Rio de Janeiro's Bay, gathered on the deck of the ship to watch the punishment of the sailor Marcelino Rodrigues Menezes. According to the "Book of Punishments" of the ship, the sailor had been punished because he had hit a corporal who had turned him in to the commander for hiding a bottle of *cachaça*, alcohol being forbidden on board. Marcelino Menezes was flogged between 200 and 250 times as ordered by the commander. (Nascimento 2002: 20) The sailor escaped before being taken to the Armada's Infirmary. This punishment was the spark that triggered the November revolt in the same year, organized after some months. According to the testimony of the representative José Carlos de Carvalho, who had come to negotiate an amnesty with the sailors, Marcelino's Rodrigues's back looked like "a fish slashed to be salted." (Morel 82)

The lack of personnel and the pragmatism of the Navy's authorities were at the root of the consolidation of the two instances of punishment: one called "Board Court" and the other "Military Court." The latter was composed of three instances: a Disciplinary Council in charge of gathering evidence and testimonies, the War Council in which the witnesses and defendants were interrogated and where the trial took place, and the Superior Military Court (*Supremo Tribunal Militar)* which affirmed or reinforced the War Council's sentences. (Capanema 2009; Nascimento 2008) The everyday disciplinary faults were most often punished by the "Board Court" which was presided over by the ship's commander himself. Thus, the cases of misbehavior, lack of attention to work, disputes and fights, inebriation, gambling, etc. were usually sentenced to corporal punishment or imprisonment. The penalty was therefore applied immediately on board following the decision and arbitration of the commander, whereas crimes such as physical assault, insubordination, theft, homicide, desertion, uprising, among others, could and should be presented to the War Council or War Court, usually made up by officers from outside the naval unit where the defendant worked. The War Council almost always imposed imprisonment penalties.

The use of the whip had been regulated by the internal disciplinary codes since the imperial times between the independence in 1822 and the

[1] As in the USA, warships are named after the States in the Brazilian Federative Republic.

Proclamation of the Republic in 1889, in conformity with the *Artigos de Guerra* (Articles of War.) A whole range of penalties, including imprisonment, sometimes reinforced by the use of shackles, hard labor and capital punishment. Corporal punishment corresponded to Article 80 and was imposed neither on the pupils of the School of Apprentice Sailors nor sailor officers in general. It determined that :

> All the other faults such as drunkenness, excessive gambling and the like, which the preceding articles may not particularly mention, will be left at the prudent discernment of the superior officer to impose on the delinquents the punishment that may suit them; the use of the iron necklace, imprisonment in the cellar and the loss of the wine ration is what must be imposed on sailor officers, inferior officers and craftsmen; as well as on the sailors in general and soldiers, who may be corrected by means of blows with a sword and whipping, *not exceeding the number of 25 per day*, that is, for guilt that will not demand the War Council. (*Artigos de Guerra*, emphasis added)

Thus, the application of this article dismissed the need for the War Council, the court to which the members of the Army were submitted to whenever necessary, instead of the traditional judgments for civilians. In the War Council, the defendant had the right to an oral or written defence or even to a lawyer when it was possible to have one. However, to call a War Council took time and presupposed the absence of the sailor or member of the crew for up to two years. (Nascimento 2001) Due to the lack of board personnel and the difficulty in recruitment, officers preferred most of the time to execute the penalties on board in case of faults that were not considered as serious crimes.

Most of the sentences of the Superior Military Court were penalties of imprisonment together with the work routine. The other penalties foreseen were capital punishment (in general foreseen in war situations or when facing an enemy), mere imprisonment, the lowering of military rank, destitution, dismissal, deprivation of command, reform. (Title V, Article 39, *Código Penal da Armada dos Estados Unidos do Brasil*) The time spent in prison was not deductible from the sailors' compulsory enlistment time. For instance, if a sailor, coming from the Apprentices School enlisted in the Navy for 15 years and then deserted after 5 years' work, was captured and sentenced to 3 years in prison, at the end of his punishment he should still serve in the Navy for another 10 years. The lack of discipline and other crimes such as desertion were not therefore a good thing for the ones wanting to free themselves from the military institution: not only were crimes and other faults punished, but this punishment itself could also increase one's enlistment time in the Navy. To punish a deserter by granting him a leave would not be, in the Navy's logics, a penalty, but rather a reward.

As for the faults judged and punished by the "Board Court," they did not always appear in the Navy's registers. In the absence of a real court and lawsuits, officers seldom wrote down this kind of punishment in the ship's log. Instead, other punishments were often mentioned, such as solitary prison with bread and water, the obligation to be shackled, etc. as found in the testimony of Raja Gabaglia, a politician, doctor and Navy Officer:

> […] commanders by merit do not feel ashamed to write down in the punishment books conventional signs in order to escape punishment by the law: for instance, where it reads four hours of iron necklace or six hours at the bar a certain number of whiplashes was imposed [...] I witnessed the punishment of a stoker with 800 whiplashes at one time. I know that sailor apprentices were punished with 125 blows, on one occasion. It is trivial to impose three penalties for the same fault: a) to lower one's ranking; b) to be included in the Correctional Company; c) to be whipped. (Correspondências recebidas, CR636/1, 7 dez., 1910)

In a certain way, the silence of the official sources is explained by the embarrassment that this type of individual raised in this context, be it in the civilian environment or the military environment itself. Some cases are known though. Sometimes, the Military Court prosecution mentioned them. Table 1 shows some accessible cases of corporal punishment imposed by the "Board Court."

As one may notice, recidivism was frequent. In addition, two other elements are worth being pointed out. On the one hand, it is necessary to acknowledge the importance of the authority of the commander who decided whether the fault should be presented to the War Council or punished on board. In this case he also decided the conditions of the punishment: the number of whippings, the possibility to be protected with a shirt or not... Even so, the penalties imposed by the "Board Court" were frequently a lot more severe than the 25 whippings prescribed by the military legislation. On the other hand, the fact that the judgment by the "Board Court" was very often preferred by the commander has to be taken into account since this alternative avoided the absence of the sailor or soldier for several months or even years, which was not at all desirable in view of the lack of personnel.

The ritual of punishment by whipping was composed of four stages: firstly, the whole garrison was presented on the deck in uniform, both officers and ordinary sailors; then, the one who suffered the punishment had to walk across the whole deck, through the garrison, feet in chains; thirdly, the commander read the article of the disciplinary code related to the fault committed by the sailor; finally, the whipping started while someone designated beforehand counted them. (Capanema 2009) If one whiplash was not strong enough, the ship's commander did not consider it valid. (Greenhalgh 75) Drums were also used either to pace the screams of pain or to set the pace of the lashes. Some officers and sailors, who could barely stand such a spectacle, looked away. The punished sailor moaned, supplicated, but the punishment did not stop until the commander authorized it to or the board surgeon intervened. (Morel) This kind of punishment was considered to be twice as effective by the officers: it was imposed on board without the need to form a council and keep the sailor away from work when labor was scarce. It set an example to the crew that watched it. It is possible to add a third justification: the expression of power and domination in a country that had recently abolished slavery in 1888.

The revolt of 1910 against the use of the whip

In that atmosphere, on the night of 22 November, 1910, a group of over 2,000 ordinary sailors of the Brazilian War Navy rebels in the Guanabara Bay, took over the main ships of the fleet, especially the three largest battleships, and turned their guns against the federal power's siege. These seamen, most of whom were blacks and browns, demanded in the first place that corporal punishment come to an end and, more specifically, that the whip be suppressed. Their other claims dealt with the replacement of incompetent officers, a pay raise, the improvement of their qualification course and the implementation of a new salary scale for services.

This revolt lasted five days, caused fear and astonishment in the population, especially in the city of Rio de Janeiro, and mobilized the society and the public opinion of that time. Certain newspapers evinced sympathy with the sailors. Others both criticized the act of insubordination and acknowledged the legitimacy of their claim: the end of corporal punishment. According to the conservative paper *O Paiz,* it was about "a fair complaint made in a very strong voice." (11/27/1910) The mutiny also found support with the parliamentary representatives, most of the politicians asking for a quick solution in order to minimize human losses and material damage. In those conditions, the government, threatened, criticized and weakened, granted amnesty to the revolted sailors. The seamen had succeeded in drawing attention to their claims, not only thanks to the press, which covered the rebellion extensively, but also to the discussions established with the authorities. Nevertheless, a few days after signing the amnesty, the State authorized the leave of the individuals harmful to discipline on board.

Close to 1,000 sailors were excluded from the Navy at the beginning of the month of December of the same year. An atmosphere of mistrust between officers and seamen took over the ships, the latter complaining that no concrete measure had been taken in their favor. Rumors concerning future attacks on the ships by the Armada forces circulated, feeding the tensions on board. In this context, a second rebellion started in December among the marines, which was quickly suppressed by the official forces of the Brazilian Republic which declared the state of siege and carried out numerous arrests. A ship was freighted to deport 491 persons in the Amazon Region, so-called "The Brazilian Siberia" according to historians (Menezes) including 105 sailors and other persons from the lower classes identified as "vagabonds, prostitutes, soldiers of the Army."[2] Some among them perished during the voyage, nine were shot dead. In other places, the authorities confined certain members of the 1910 revolt in the prison of the Island of Cobras, in the complex of the Navy in Rio de Janeiro, at Christmas the same year. Most of them died there after three days due to the lack of fresh air and the heat. Only two men survived: the sailor João Cândido, who was the leader of the mutiny, and the marine João Avelino Lira. Then, two years later, a War Council was constituted in order to establish the guilt of the November mutinies within the December rebellion. Among the 70 found guilty, only 10 were present, the others being declared "missing, dead from sunstroke, astray." Those 10 were acquitted, the prosecution process having proved their loyalty to the government after the amnesty. All these events are known in Brazilian historiography as "The Revolt of the Whip," the title of a book by the journalist Edmar Morel published in 1959. (Morel)[3]

The imprisonment without and before judgment experienced by the seaman João Cãndido

The black sailor João Cândido, who became a hero of the uprising due to its reception by the public and the memory of the revolt, was detained in

---

[2] They were "105 former sailors, 292 vagabonds, 44 women and 50 soldiers of the Army." Diretoria do Patrimônio Histórico e Documentação da Marinha, Divisão de Documentos Especiais, Storry, Carlos Brandão, "Relatório da extraordinária viagem do navio Satélite a Santo Antônio do Rio Madeira" 6/03/1911.

[3] A paper on this revolt was published in English by the historian Joseph Love.

two different conditions while waiting for judgment, which took place in December 1912. At first, he was put in a prison cell on the Ilha das Cobras (Snakes Island) in the Navy's complex. Next, between December 1910 and December 1912, he got sick and stayed in the Army's prison, then at the Asylum of the Invalid because, according to himself, "he was considered a fool for not witnessing." (Morel)

On December 24, 1910, João Cândido was put with 17 other sailors in a prison cell which was classified as "solitary" in the complex of the Navy.[4] The food ration was reduced to bread and water. According to several reports, in response to the demand for water on the part of the prisoners, from time to time they threw a solution of water and lime in order to disinfect the prison cell, so to speak. (Smallman & Shawn) The more the prisoners moved inside the cell or asked for water, the more the lime evaporated and came into their noses and lungs. The lack of fresh air and the heat contributed to the death of several among them a few days after their transfer. As the cell was opened, 16 dead were found among the 18 sailors who had been locked inside. The Navy's doctor, Dr. Ferreira de Abreu, attributed their death to sunstroke in their death certificates. (Morel 180-182)

João Cândido retold this episode in his memoirs published in December 1912 and January 1913. In this first testimony, he evoked a larger number of sick sailors, all of them having been treated with the greatest cruelty by the guardians and the authorities of the Navy:

> On the 25th, in the morning, the first cases of sunstroke started taking place. Some men, already hallucinated, others poisoned by the water that shed down their trousers and also by the urine that they drank, showed the first symptoms of mental weakening. I kept my nose in an opening that there was below the door, my body being the floor for the others, thus breathing a little fresh air, because the world belongs to the smart ones. [...] On the same day I asked the sentinel that was farther away, separated from us by two wooden doors and a grate, to tell the jailman that there were already some dead bodies. As the latter one came, accompanied by two other prisoners, he threw under the doors a large quantity of phenic acid, creolin and lime. He asked then whether João Cândido had already died, gettng a negative answer. Then he declared that we were all there to die and that we should not talk much or else he would get a can of kerosene and set fire. ("Memórias de João Cândido, o marinheiro")

After this episode, he was taken to the Navy's Mental Hospital where he stayed nearly two years in the course of which he wrote his memories

[4] About 600 men were enclosed in this Navy's prison at the same time (Morel).

and embroidered two napkins. These were revealed by historian José Murilo de Carvalho and were deposited at the *Museum of Regional Art of São João Del Rey* by an old sergeant of this village who had met João Cândido during that period. (Carvalho)

The napkins (figure 2) are a good example of what the symbolic in the lives of the sailors of that time. The first one entitled "The Sailor's Goodbye" (*O Adeus do Marujo*) represents an anchor made of branches and crossed by handclasping between a Navy Officer and a sailor. One may read the words "order" and "freedom," the initials J.C.F. (after João Cândido Felisberto) and F.D. Martins (Francisco Dias Martins, one of João Cândido's companions during the revolt, the leader in the battleship Bahia,) and the date of 22 November, 1910, the first day of the uprising. The second one represents two pigeons holding a banner in their beaks over which one may read the word "love." Below, a bleeding heart cut through by a sword, above flowers, butterflies and a hummingbird. Without intending to analyze the personal meanings of these embroideries, one may see that these drawings represent a well-known iconography of the sailors: anchors, pierced hearts, branches, handclaspings, birds, initials, words. So many symbols shared by the sailors, Brazilians or foreigners, written on their skin with tattoos (Capanema 2009) The descriptions and drawings present in the identification forms hold a large number of elements similar to the embroidered drawings by João Cândido.

The body speaks when the voices are silenced. It is very likely that what was revealed through João Cândido's points of embroidery was the suffering of the traumas lived after the revolt as well as the fact that he was away from the Navy. The period during which Joâo Cândido stayed in prison waiting for judgment was also a moment of melancholy and reflection on the revolt and its meanings. If the words "order" and "freedom" may seem contradictory at first, they make sense in the context studied. Order, a military value *par excellence*, was not criticized by the sailors and soldiers that identified themselves with that profession or found some personal and professional growth in the Navy. Freedom echoed slavery and its heritage in Brazilian society. In this way, the sailors appropriated the motto of the Brazilian Republic, "order and progress," and João Cândido inscribed it in his embroidery.

As for the memoirs of Joâo Cândido written during his imprisonment, they did not become public before December 1912 and January 1913, when the journalist Paulo Barreto, dubbed João do Rio, decided to publish a series of 12 articles in the newspaper *Gazeta de Notícias* entitled *Memories of João Cândido, the Sailor* after João Cândido left the Mental Hospital and was acquitted by the Military Justice in December 1912. If it is to be believed, João Cãndido was received in the newspaper's headquarters soon after his liberation and on December 31st of that year the *Gazeta de Notícias* posted on the first page: "João Cândido is free at last! The sailor writes in prison his life story till amnesty day. The *Gazeta* begins today to publish this gripping narrative." (12/31/1912) The *Memories* are a whole *feuilleton*. According to the *Gazeta,* "they were not written in a hurry." (*Ibid.*) João Cândido had firstly mentioned them when he was at the Mental Hospital, and a second time at the Navy's Hospital. The paper added to the authenticity of the writings that "Yesterday, despite being very tired, João Cândido read only the first chapters, that we already had in proofs, making their revision." (12/31/1912)

The Memories of João Cândido, the Sailor may be divided into three parts. In the first part, João Cândido retold his first days in the Navy, his international trips and his impressions. In this respect, his memoirs look like travel stories extracted from a journal or a travel diary, a genre of text often found with Navy officers, as their words carried a strong nationalistic feeling. But its specificity lies in the fact that this time the report was written by a sailor, a subordinate, a member of the lower classes to whom the "status of writer" is seldom attributed.

In a second part, *The Memories* retold the sailors' uprising, from its organization to the amnesty. João Cândido emphasized his role in both commanding and making decisions, inviting the reader to look at the facts as they took place on board the ships during the three days of the revolt. João Cândido also provided several details such as precise dates and times, the names of the other commanders of the rebel seamen, the movement of the ships, the plans of attack, the defence and the counterattack. Here, the narrative takes the typical aspect of war stories also generally written by commanders and officers.

Finally, the third moment of João Cândido's story begins after the end of the revolt, from the amnesty to his liberation by the Military Court, passing by the revolt of the Naval Batallion, his imprisonment, his hospitalization and his exclusion from the Navy. The horrors experienced inside the prisons of the Ilha das Cobras are revealed and represent one of the climaxes of his memories. Therefore, the third part of João Cândido's text is interesting for its function of denunciation: it blames the government for having contributed to the preparation of the December uprising and, in order to conclude, the author exposed his feeling of injustice towards his exclusion from the Navy. To retell and to remember are also a way to denounce. This may also be the reason why João Cândido felt the need to dictate his memories to someone when he was hospitalized in the Mental Hospital. The denunciations and revelations of

João Cândido perhaps justify the importance of his *Memories* in the press, beyond its interest as travel or combat stories.

The quality of the text raised a question regarding its authenticity and its author. On 7 January, 1913, an anonymous article published in the Carioca newspaper *O Imparcial* questioned the "literary marriage" of the journalist and editor João do Rio and João Cândido and criticized the director of the *Gazeta* for the publication of the *Memories* recalling the dead officers. A reply from the *Gazeta* was published in an article signed by João do Rio who then explained how his newspaper had access to the manuscripts of the memoirs of João Cândido:

> About a year and a half ago when João Cândido, the Sailor, pretended to be insane in the Mental Hospital, the story that he had dictated to one of the nurses and had been read by the doctor was brought to the *Gazeta.* The one who got this scoop is today, I was told, a member of *O Imparcial's* editorial staff and can testify to that. The story was and is written in foolscap, with a dark paper cover. It is written in pencil on both sides of the paper. It may be seen by anyone who wishes to see it. Its authenticity being verified, the *Gazeta* decided not to publish it at that moment [...] the *Memories*, however, were and are only João Cândido's memories. (*Gazeta de Notícias*, 01/08/1913: 2)

These explanations are coherent insofar as they refer to the existence of a manuscript dictated by João Cândido and are mentioned by other sources. In addition, the information present in the text and its accuracy allow to think that only João Cândido himself (or another sailor) could have known them.

There are therefore vestiges of two copies of manuscripts of João Cândido's memoirs, one written in pencil paper, the other written in ink, both of them lost. (Morel: attachment I) It may have become two different versions, both of them dictated by João Cândido at two different moments: firstly at the Mental Hospital, then at the Navy's Hospital, as written in the *Gazeta de Notícias.* Or there could still have been an original and a copy, given the interest in these documents evinced by different actors: historians, journalists, copyists, the military…

During his stay at the Mental Hospital, while he was waiting for his judgment, João Cândido, who missed a phalanx in his right hand following an amputation caused while charging a canon, refused to write any word or even his name. He was very distrustful and said many times that he had trusted the government once and that now, despite that, he found himself imprisoned. According to his hospitalization records, he repeatedly evoked the massacre of the Ilha das Cobras and behaved as an intelligent person, very sad for Brazil, very lucid yet pessimistic. He refused to write his name because he trembled and feared to be compromised by writing whatever it was. Regarding his memoirs, the director of the hospital reported in his record that:

> He asked me for two reams of foolscap paper to write a novel of his life, wishing to leave here only when this is finished and published. We argued with him that maybe he would not need so much paper, which he agreed with [...] On the 1st of May, no change, the paper was provided to him and he began writing the novel which he dictated for another prisoner to write. It will be titled: 'João Cândido's Life or A Dream of Freedom!'. He formulated several chapters of which one is about the happenings of the *Martyrdom Island* [...]. The 4th of May [...], he spent the day dictating his novel to another patient named Castanhola. ("Ficha de João Cândido Felisberto")

Would the *Memories of João Cândido* be the memories of *The life of João Cândido* or *The Dream of Freedom* dictated to his companion in the Mental Hospital? That is possible. In spite of all the changes that may have been made to the original text—adaptations, new information added by other journalists, such as João do Rio, to the newspaper's management staff responsible for the edition of the texts—the memories are those of João Cândido. The sailor was certainly paid for that publication. (Rodrigues 1996) Whatever it may have been, even if this text was left little known until the present days before being published in the last edition of Morel's book, these memoirs written during the period of waiting for judgment and retrieved in other reports recognized a version of the revolt and helped to form the character named João Cândido in the collective memory, the other leaders starting to fall into oblivion.

The "Revolt of the Whip" and the 1964 Military *Coup d'État*

In the 1960's, João Cândido once again became an important actor in the history of Brazil, a figure particularly exploited by a new group of sailors, the Association of Sailors and Marines of Brazil. (AMFNB) This association was created in 1962 in a context of politicization of society and fear of a *coup d'État*. Between 1961 and 1964, the period that coincided with the presidency of João Goulart, was a moment of radicalization of several movements. As the president attempted to make a series of social reforms called "base reforms," several sectors of the population got organized into associations such as workers, who expanded their strikes, members of the military, the catholic church, students and women. Thus, the social movement was organized between these two poles, conservative and progressive. (Ferreira 2001)

The association of the Brazilian sailors and marines firstly aimed at supporting the military's lives. Next, it got involved in political claims. The sailors and marines at that time often came from the North and the Northeast of the country from poor families, and found in the Navy the hope to get a job and a qualification and be able to travel and discover other places. (Rodrigues 2004; Almeida) However, the naval institution was actually more complex and the sailors were submitted to an authoritarian regime imposed by the officers, in which the everyday treatment was very unequal and studies, although of good quality, did not aim at preparing the sailors for the civilian world, only for the military one.

Therefore, the AMFNB's role consisted in gathering the sailors and marines and helping them to adapt to daily changes: a newspaper was started, courses were offered and some claims came to be accepted such as the revocation of registration booklets, of the prohibition for members of the military below the corporal rank to get married as well as the preservation of their political rights such as the right to vote and to be elected, which was not granted to lower rank military members. Nevertheless, the association quickly displeased the authorities of the Navy which accused it of not respecting military hierarchy and feared that sailors of the association would support the base reforms of Goulart's government. As repression intensified with the imprisonment of the main leaders of the association, the movement became radical. In 1963, the AMFNB gave its support to the Air-Force's and Navy's sergeants movement. This movement questioned the cancellation of political rights of sergeants and non-commissioned officers of these corporations, of whom many had been elected in the regional elections of 1962. From that moment, hostility between the association and the naval authorities became more serious as well as the hostility between the latter and the executive power itself that supported the sergeants. The Press also changed its orientation after the revolt and became largely critical of President João Goulart due to his support to the sergeants and non-commissioned officers. (Abreu)

João Cândido represented a model and a hero to the members of this association. Not only was João Cândido aided financially by the AMFNB, which gave him a pension, but he was also in close contact with several members of the association. On 24 March, 1964, on the two-year anniversary date of the association, the sailors organized a demonstration. At first, it was a festive ball, but, after the imprisonment of several members, the movement became a political protest which took place at the headquarters of the Metallurgical Trade Union, gathering around 5,400 sailors (Capitani). According to the words of the president of the AMFNB, José Anselmo dos Santos, the sailors' movement was obviously two-fold: on the one hand, they demanded a change in the Navy's statutes; on the other hand, they were committed to the wider struggle of the popular leftist movements of their time:

> In our young sailors' hearts, there is the same blood that runs in the veins of the brave sailor João Cândido, the Great Black Admiral, and his battle companions who extinguished whipping in the Navy. We will extinguish the moral whipping [...] We want in practice the application of the constitutional principle: All are equal before the law [...] We, sailors and marines, demand: the reformation of the Navy's Disciplinary Code, an anachronistic regulation that forbids even marriage; no interference of the Admiralty Council with the internal business of the AMFNB; acknowledgment of the AMFNB by the authorities; [...] irrestrict and ample amnesty to the ones involved in the protest movement in Brasilia [...]. So that schools may be built, where our children may learn with pride the history of a new country that we have started building, so that factories and roads may be built on which our richness may be transported. So that our people may find work that is worthwhile, bringing to an end the horde of starving people that die day after day without having where to work or what to eat. (cited by Rodrigues 2004: 1009-110)

The meeting was followed by several arrests. But, as after the 1910 revolt, the sailors and marines arrested were pardoned by President João Goulart. This gesture irritated the military authorities and triggered the decision of the military to take over the power a few days later, the notion of democracy being not very important to either side. (Ferreira 2004) The sailors and rebel marines were expelled from the corporation from which many of the militants of the resistance movements and the subsequent armed fight came. (Rodrigues 2004; Almeida)

On 25 March, João Cândido was present at the meeting. On 27 March, Rio's newspaper *Última Hora* published a cliché (figure 3) of the ex-sailor, aged 84, next to the new leader of the sailors and marines dubbed "Cabo Anselmo" (Corporal Anselmo) under the title "1910 revolt present in 1964." This image was explicit too as it gathered the two leaders of the subordinate military of the Navy, one from the past, another from the present. It also implied the existence of a continuity between both movements, at the same time as it warned the authorities and the conservative sectors about a new revolt. On this cliché, João Cândido is shown the way he loved to appear usually in public whereas Corporal

Anselmo is wearing the sailors' uniform. As for the effective participation of João Cândido, the journalist Araújo Neto wrote:

> [...] sitting on his chair, next to José Anselmo, old João Cândido kept understanding little, things were half understood as José Anselmo went on talking [...]. João Cândido, a man of the times of the whip, asked himself all alone, speaking to within, not to be shameful. (Cited by Rodrigues 2004: 108)

This type of discourse, although published in an inoffensive way at a first look, seems to reinforce—or to be in connection with—other discourses, stemming from the military environment or not, which despises João Cândido's political consciousness. But an interview the former sailor had given to *Jornal do Brasil* a short time before the assembly of the sailors on 25 March reveals the opposite. In spite of his advanced age, João Cândido had a conception that was a little more elaborate regarding the 1964's sailors movement, in particular, and of the Brazilian context of his time, in general. Thus, in his testimony, he is said to have argued that:

> I am totally in favor of the base reforms [...] and I know well that the revolution is in the streets and that nobody can avoid it. Because of this, the expulsion of the sailors represents nothing more than the fear of the admiralty which does not admit that they stand out too much. (Cited by Rodrigues 2004: 108).

Other elements showed that João Cândido and the seamen of 1964 did not completely share the same opinions. Whether João Cândido showed sympathy or not, in a way or another, to the sailors of the association, he was skeptical regarding their movement. On 25 March, 1964, he returned home very demotivated and made a last emblematic remark. According to him, "A sailors' revolt can only work out at sea." (cited by Morel 255) Thus, he appeared to be critical of the sailors and marines' 1964 movement due to the fact that the discourse and acts of the members of the AMFNB were far from the claims stemming from the inside of the Navy to reinforce a struggle that had its place outside. (*João Cândido, o almirante negro* 90)

The movement of the Brazilian Sailors and Marines Association was nevertheless discredited and it is part of a "dark page" of the history of Brazil. A little later, it came to be known that the president of the association, Cabo Anselmo, had changed sides and had become a collaborator of the military and civilian dictatorship by denouncing several individuals to the repression forces. (Almeida) The image of the sailors group is made similar to the figure of its leader and the movement was accused of having triggered the military coup. However, some more recent papers supported other theories: Corporal Anselmo was not alone and not the actual leader; he was a man of communication, while others, such as Marco Antonio da Silva Lima, the vice-president, and Avelino Capitani, the second vice-president, were the "thinkers" of the actions and discourses. (Rodrigues 2004) In addition, the sailors of the association had a legitimate movement and were nothing but the victims of a bigger project, the one of the 1964 military-civilian *coup d'État*. (Reis)

Dictatorship and persecution, 1964's day after

On 31 March, the Army Forces organized themselves and threw over João Goulart's government on 1 April. It was the beginning of the military-civilian dictatorship. On 14 April of the same year, the journalist Edmar Morel said on the radio that the "High Commandment of the Revolution"—this is how the military members of the three armed forces installed in the government called themselves—had suspended all his political rights for ten years.

The *coup d'État* demobilized all the organizations of the social movements at once. Even during its less violent period (before 1968, when repression began to play a major part,) persecutions were constant and political debate was depleted and forbidden. The sailors involved in the AMFNB were put on leave or expelled from the Navy and prosecution started in 1966. 145 of them were found guilty, but only one sailor appeared in court—he was acquitted. The other ones disappeared (Almeida), but were sentenced to different imprisonment penalties. How did they disappear? There is a number of hypotheses: they were hiding, had returned to their families in the countryside, were doing other jobs or even a number of them had become resistance fighters and enlisted in the armed fight. They were hunted down as they were called "communists" and "subversives." After the *coup d'État*, the valid argument presented in discourses to have taken over the power returned: according to the military and civilians that supported the dictatorship, the regime was necessary to prevent Brazil from becoming "a communist country." (Almeida)

Anderson da Silva Almeida argued that several sailors, after the *coup d'État*, did not have many social choices but to become members of clandestine resistance movements and join the armed fight. Several were arrested, tortured and exiled. In spite of the 1979 Political Amnesty Act, the sailors were effectively included in the Political Amnesty Act not until

2002 as the Navy considered that they had not committed political actions but insubordination crimes and did not want to reintegrate them. From 1980 to 2000, they got organized into two organizations, the UMNA and the MODAC,[5] in order to claim their rights and compensation in civil and military courts.

It was in the context of these associations that the present author was able to interview 1964's former sailors regarding their memory of the 1910 Revolt more precisely. On 19 July, 2002, the former sailors Otacílio dos Anjos Santos, dubbed Tatá, UMNA's Director of Heritage and a sailor between 1954 and 1964, and Benedito Gomes da Silva, UMNA's Vice-President and a sailor between 1945 and 1964 were interviewed. The interviews took place at UMNA's headquarters downtown Rio and were attended by Raimundo Porfírio Costa, MODAC's President, and Adalberto Cândido, João Cândido's cadet son.

At the time of this collective interview, the former sailors did not make any analogies between their movement and João Cândido's. First of all, they drew attention to a difference: in 1910, there had been no traitor, whereas in 1964, one of the main leaders, Corporal Anselmo, had been one. João Cândido's history was not well-known by the sailors; according to Otacílio dos Anjos, before the publication of Edmar Morel's book:

> The problem was that João Cândido's life was not a good example. And this subject was not widespread, people did not know about it. *A Revolta da Chibata* (*The Revolt of the Whip*) by Edmar Morel, was what put it in the public eye [...] At that time, some sailors knew about it, even because they were in contact with him [João Cândido] at Praça XV. He was a public figure. But he was not a public figure ackowledged as a hero, largely because the Press did not grant him such a place. But in 1910, it did. At that time, he was the name of the moment. (Interview with Otacílio dos Santos Anjos to Capanema 2009)

It was, above all, the second editon of the book in 1963 that had had an impact on the sailors. According to Raimundo Porfírio, "It was the Sailors' Association that made the second edition of the book *A Revolta da Chibata* . This book started then to circulate on board the ships. I read it in just one day." (Interview of Raimundo Porfírio to Capanema 2009) The memory of the 1910 Revolt within the 1964 one (for the sailors of 1964 but also following repression, torture, expulsions, etc.) allows to insert

[5] UMNA stands for *Unidade de Mobilização Nacional pela Anistia* (National Mobilization Unit for Amnesty; MODAC stands for *Movimento Democrático pela Anistia e Cidadania* (Democratic Movement for Amnesty and Citizenship.)

constitutional violence—represented here by military law—into a long term and to think of ruptures and continuity within a single historical process comprehending the limits of citizenship of subordinate military in contemporary Brazil.

Conclusion

This comparative study of the two most important revolts in the Brazilian Navy in the 20th century and their issues focuses on the relationships between power and law in this particular military context at least at three levels. At first, it comes to understanding how the forms of punishment were a pragmatic option and also a way to maintain power and the submission of the Other. Next, the changes of conception of what was considered just or unjust by the officers and by their subordinate sailors have to be examined. Finally, a third aspect is about the politicisation of the memory as a way to legitimize actions towards the changing of a legal system from the sailors' point of view or to maintain order for the officers and the repression forces of the dictatorship. These two examples in parallel equally remind us of the suffering of the actors involved in these rebellions, detained and banished under the authority of the State.

Works cited

ABREU, Alzira Alves de. "A participação da imprensa na queda do governo Goulart." *1964-2004, 40 anos do Golpe: Ditadura militar e resistência no Brasil.* FICO, Carlos, Celso Castro *et al.* (eds.) Rio de Janeiro: 7 Letras, 2004, 15-25.

ALMEIDA, Anderson da Silva. *Todo Leme a bombordo: marinheiros e ditadura civil-militar no Brasil, da rebelião de 1964 à anistia.* Rio de Janeiro: Arquivo Nacional, 2012.

Artigos de Guerra. Brazil, Lisboa: Galhardo e Irmãos, 1841.

CAPANEMA P. DE ALMEIDA, Silvia. " 'Nous, marins, citoyens brésiliens et républicains': identités, modernité et mémoire de la révolte des matelots de 1910." PhD diss., Ecole des Hautes Etudes en Sciences Sociales, Paris, 2009.

—. "'Nous, marins, citoyens brésiliens et républicains': identités, modernité et mémoire de la révolte des matelots de 1910." *Nuevo Mundo Mundos Nuevos, 26 jan 2010.* Accessed 6 May, 2013. URL: http://nuevomundo.revues.org/58704; DOI: 10.4000/nuevomundo.58704.

CAPITANI, Avelino Bide. *A rebelião dos marinheiros.* Porto Alegre: Artes

e Ofícios, 1997.
CARVALHO, José Murilo de. "Os Bordados de João Cândido." In *Pontos e bordados: escritos de história e política*. CARVALHO, José Murilo de. Belo Horizonte: Ed. UFMG, 1998.
Código Penal da Armada dos Estados Unidos do Brasil. Brazil, 1891.
Diretoria do Patrimônio Histórico e Documentação da Marinha, Divisão de Documentos Especiais, Storry, Carlos Brandão, "Relatório da extraordinária viagem do navio Satélite a Santo Antônio do Rio Madeira" 6/03/1911.
Diretoria do patrimônio histórico e documentação da marinha, Hospital Nacional dos Alienados, "Ficha de João Cândido Felisberto", ofício n. 258, 04/18/1911.
GREENNHALGH, Juvenal. *Presigangas e calabouços: prisões da Marinha no século XIX*. Rio de Janeiro: Serviço de Documentação da Marinha, 1998.
FERREIRA, Jorge (dir.). *O populismo e a sua história*. Rio de Janeiro: Civilização Brasileira, 2001.
—. "O trabalhismo radical e o colapso da democracia no Brasil." In *1964-2004, 40 anos do Golpe: Ditadura militar e resistência no Brasil*. FICO, Carlos, Celso Castro et alii. (eds.).Rio de Janeiro: 7 Letras, 2004: 41-54.
Fundação Casa de Rui Barbosa, Arquivo Histórico, Correspondências recebidas, CR636/1, 7 dez., 1910.
"Memórias de João Cândido, o marinheiro," *Gazeta de Notícias*, 01/10/1913.
MENEZES, Nilza. "Os sobreviventes do barco Satélite." *Revista Primeira Versão*, ano I, n° 54, 2001.
MOREL, Edmar. *A revolta da chibata* [Organização de Marco Morel]. Rio de Janeiro: Paz e Terra, 2009 (5th ed.) [1959].
Museu da Imagem e do Som, *João Cândido, o almirante negro*. Rio de Janeiro: Gryphus, 1999.
NASCIMENTO, Álvaro Pereira do. "Do convés ao porto: a experiência dos marinheiros e a revolta de 1910." PhD diss., Instituto de Filosofia e Ciências Humanas, Universidade Estadual de Campinas, 2002.
—. *Cidadania, cor e disciplina na revolta dos marinheiros de 1910*. Rio de Janeiro: Mauad/Faperj, 2008.
—. *A ressaca da marujada: recrutamento e disciplina na Armada imperial*. Rio de Janeiro: Arquivo Nacional, 2001.
LOVE, Joseph L. *The Revolt of The Whip*. Stanford: Stanford University Press, 2012.
REIS, Daniel Arãao. *Ditadura militar, esquerdas e sociedade*. Rio de

Janeiro: Jorge Zahar Editor, 2000.
RODRIGUES, Flávio Luís. *Vozes do mar: o movimento dos marinheiros e o golpe de 64.* São Paulo: Cortez, 2004.
RODRIGUES, João Carlos. *João do Rio: uma biografia*. Rio de Janeiro: Toopbooks,1996.
SMALLMAN, S. and Shawn C. "Military terror and silence in Brazil, 1910-1945." *Canadian Journal of Latin American and Carbbean Sudies.* 24.47 (1999) 5-27.

Table 1: Sailors punished by corporal punishment at the "Board Court"[6]

Name	Date of punishment	Reason for punishment	Number of whiplashes	Observations
Cipriano Ferreira	1870	in June: absence without authorization	100	He had been a slave and joined the Army in 1868, during the conflict with Paraguay
		was the main suspect of a fire in the barracks	300	
		in October: desertion attempt	100	
	Between 1872 and 1876	indiscipline	225	
Luis de Sousa Neves	1873	a fight with the guardian	500	The commander that applied the punishment was judged himself by the War Council due to the large number
Crispiano Bernadino	1875	lack of respect towards a fellow sailor	100	He was a "pardo" [mulatto] from the Company of Apprentice Sailors. For his fourth or fifth punishments, the sailor was
	1876	insolence with the officer on duty	75	
	1878	drunkenness	75	

[6] About Laurentino Manoel da Silva, Cipriano Ferreira, Crispiano Bernadino and Afonso Rodrigues de Oliveira, see Nascimento 2001: chapter1; for José Lima, see: Nascimento 2002: 167-299. For Marcelino Rodrigues Menezes, see Morel: 57 and the sailor's interview to *O Globo,* 04/10/1952.

	1879	lack of respect towards a fellow sailor; during a public corporal punishment, used foul language before the garrison	50 (on two days) 50 (on two days, 25 per day)	transferred to another ship where the commander applied the limit of 25 whiplashes per day.
José Lima	1893	assault on a fellow sailor in the Ilha das Cobras military prison. The sailor was in the Navy's hospital for 45 days, having suffered several bruises, fractures and contusions	125	The Sailor José Lima was then equally sentenced by the War Council to 6 years of hard labour
Alfonso Rodigrues de Oliveira	before 1893	verbal assault against the officer on duty	100 (25 per day)	This sailor also committed homicide in 1893
		slept during service	25	
Marcelino Rodrigues	1910	slashed a fellow sailor with a razor	200	This is the punishment that triggered the sailors' 1910 revolt.

Figure 1: Rebels in the São Paulo battleship (November, 1910)

Photograph by Augusto Malta, *Correio da manhã*, 11/28/1910, page 1.

Figure 2: Napkins embroidered by João Cândido

Source: *Revista de História da Biblioteca Nacional* (year 1, n° 9, April 2006: 28)

Figure 3: João Cândido and Cabo Anselmo. *Última Hora,* 03/25/1964.

ÚLTIMA HORA, 27-MARÇO-1964

REVOLTA DE 1910 PRESENTE EM 64

Alerta do CGT: GREVE CONTRA PERSEGUIÇÕES

THE RIGHT TO A LAWYER: THE FIRST OF THE EUROPEANISATION OF PROCEDURAL GUARANTEES IN PRE-TRIAL DETENTION

MARIE MARTY

UNIVERSITY OF LUXEMBOURG, LUXEMBOURG

Police custody has been a burning issue for the past few years in France and Belgium and it would be difficult to find a subject more intensively discussed by the doctrine, the legislator and in case law. Indeed, in 2011, the *Salduz*[1] decision led to major reforms of the rules regulating police custody.

The definitions of police custody in the two countries are similar. A person suspected of having committed an offence may be taken into custody, which implies a deprivation of liberty, on the decision of a police officer. (Cornu 2012) The aim of the measure is to preserve the efficiency of the investigation, by preventing the suspect from destroying evidence, or contacting any person who could help him to erase the marks of his action. Police custody is a hybrid measure made up of contradictions. Firstly, it is a deprivation of liberty. Traditionally, the criminal judge is the guardian of fundamental liberties and is entitled to pronounce any deprivation of freedom, including pre-trial detention measures. However, during the first hours of the investigation, police officers have the power to deprive the suspect of his/her liberty for a limited period of time. Moreover, this measure does not lead to imprisonment as for pre-trial measures (*détention préventive* in Belgium, and *détention provisoire* in France): the suspect is kept at a police station (Merle and Vitu 448,) as he/she must remain available for any questioning or other investigative measures requiring his presence. This situation heightens the ambiguity of the measure: aimed at facilitating the investigation, police custody can be perceived as a

[1] *Salduz v. Turkey*, ECtHR, 28 November, 2008.

punishment or a degrading measure by the suspect. Finally, the status of the suspect is ambivalent. In compliance with the principle of the presumption of innocence he/she cannot be considered guilty; in practice, he/she is no longer treated as an innocent person. (*Allenet de Ribemont* 1995) It makes the suspect even more vulnerable to investigators, which is the reason why his/her rights should be strongly protected from the beginning of any procedural act.

The traditional inquisitorial legacy in France and in Belgium is still very present in the modern criminal procedure, especially during the investigation phase (Kettels 1003) characterised by secrecy and the unilateral omnipotence of authorities in their duty to discover the truth. The inquisitorial system was known for its abuses. Consequently, the necessary modernisation of the system could not go without the improvement of the position of the defendant, and so, a better access to legal advice. (Delmas-Marty & Spencer 18) However, the active participation of the lawyer during the early stages of the investigation was a difficult idea to impose. Despite the fact that the principle of the presumption of innocence requires authorities to find both exculpatory and incriminatory evidence, judicial authorities are actually inclined to find evidence of guilt, while the defence tends to challenge this evidence. The lawyer represents the interests of his client, not those of society, and so, tries to protect the suspect against the enthusiasm of judicial authorities during the investigation. Moreover, questioning is the central part of the investigation as it can quickly lead to other evidence. By advising his client to exercise his right to remain silent, the lawyer slows down the work of the investigative authorities. As a result, he may represent a major obstacle to the efficiency and rapidity of the investigation. (Berbuto and Berthe 123)

Nevertheless, the intervention of the legal advisor is essential at this stage of the proceedings. The deprivation of liberty is a police measure taken on a simple suspicion. Police officers can be influenced by the atrocity of the crime scene, the distress of the victim, the seriousness and the extent of the offence. The questioning may be skewed by this tension and the lawyer is needed to ensure that the police officer does not cross the boundaries built by the legislator. Furthermore, if police officers know the law, the same is often not true of the suspect who needs a legal professional to explain the procedure followed, what is allowed and not. Finally, the suspected person is put in a vulnerable position because of the fear and the stress caused by the proceedings; the lawyer also provides his client with psychological help often indispensable to overcome the weight of such a measure.

Until recently, the rules governing the exercise of the right to a lawyer during pre-trial detention in France and in Belgium were very significantly incomplete and different in spite of the fact that both states are parties to the European Convention on Human Rights (ECHR), ensuring the protection of defence rights, including the right to access to a lawyer. In France, the first intervention of the lawyer during police custody can be delayed until the 48th or the 72nd hour of detention due to the seriousness of the offence, and he can not be party to any questioning. In Belgium, the regime was even less protective than in France, as the lawyer was not involved during police custody. However, Article 6 of the ECHR protects the right to a fair trial and more precisely, the rights granted to the suspect or the accused such as the right to be informed promptly of the nature and the cause of the accusation, the right to be presumed innocent until proven guilty and so, the right to remain silent, or the right to legal assistance. In November 1993, the European Court of Human Rights (ECtHR) extended the scope of application of this article to the beginning of the proceedings through its decision *Imbrioscia v. Switzerland*. The Court went further three years later in the case *John Murray v. United-Kingdom* and recognised the right to access to a lawyer right from the first questioning. Despite the need for a harmonisation and a strengthening of fundamental rights during the first stages of the investigation, mainly due to the increase in cross-border criminality, these two decisions were not sufficient to persuade both states to modify their legislation. The debate had to wait ten years before seeing a significant advance, with the subsequent *Salduz* decision leading to a major change of the role of the lawyer during police custody.

The approximation of national rules governing police custody in France and in Belgium thanks to the European Court of Human Rights' impetus is therefore clear. Would it be possible to interpret this movement as a starting point towards a European harmonisation of the pre-trial detention regime through the reinforcement of procedural guarantees? Indeed, even if France was sentenced by the European Court before reforming police custody legislation, Belgium anticipated any sentence by creating an entire new regime regulating police detention. As a result, a suspect benefits from the same defence rights during police custody in France as in Belgium. This "convergence" of both national laws is part of a more general movement of harmonisation at a European level, through the strengthening of fundamental rights in the European Union. However, deep harmonisation is a laudable goal but difficult to reach: the action of the ECtHR is limited to its role of judge, and the "convergence" movement encounters the reluctance of national executive and judicial authorities in the adoption and the implementation of EU instruments.

The impetus of the European Court of Human Rights towards harmonisation

Recent developments in the jurisprudence of the ECtHR

With the *Salduz v. Turkey* decision, the ECtHR has built the foundations of a new regime regarding the right to access to a lawyer, applying this right from the very first interrogation. Subsequent decisions extended the scope of this right to the beginning of custody. In this case, Mr. Salduz was arrested by the police on the suspicion of having participated in an illegal demonstration supportive of the PKK that was considered a terrorist organisation in Turkey. During his deprivation of liberty, Mr. Salduz was interrogated without a lawyer in accordance with the legislation and he admitted his participation. In front of the prosecutor and the investigating judge, he retracted his statement, claiming that his confession was coerced. The European Court based its decision on three main ideas. (§54) First of all, the investigation stage is essential, as the evidence gathered determines "the framework in which the offence charged will be considered at the trial." During this stage, the accused is in a vulnerable situation facing complex legislation, and a stressful environment. Consequently, the assistance of a lawyer can be the only element counterbalancing this vulnerability: his mission is to ensure the rights of the defence are respected, especially the right to remain silent. The Court concludes that:

> in order for the right to a fair trial to remain sufficiently 'practical and effective', Article 6 §1 requires that, as a rule, access to a lawyer should be provided as from the first interrogation of a suspect by the police, unless it is demonstrated in the light of the particular circumstances of each case that there are compelling reasons to restrict this right. (*Salduz*, §55)

The Court goes further proclaiming that statements obtained during police custody, without access to a lawyer, irretrievably prejudice the rights of the defence.

The Court reaffirmed and clarified its position, first with the case *Dayanan v. Turkey*. In this case, the appellant exercised his right to remain silent during police custody, but he was not allowed to see his lawyer. The Court ruled there had been a violation of the right to a fair trial and detailed the different missions of the lawyer: "discussion of the case, organisation of the defence, collection of evidence favourable to the accused, preparation for questioning, support of an accused in distress and checking of the condition of detention." (§32) The impact of the interpretation given to the function of the lawyer is considerable. It indirectly confers to the lawyer a wide range of competences to achieve his goal, thus ensuring a proper defence to his client. Indeed, interpreted broadly, this mission would imply having a discussion with the suspect whenever it is needed, interrupting the questioning, and having access to the case file in order to prepare his client with full knowledge of all the relevant elements.

Among the next decisions confirming this new extensive interpretation of Article 6, one case involved France in 2010. Mr. Brusco was at first questioned as a witness by the police. During the interview, the police decided that he was more than a simple witness, and Mr. Brusco became a suspect subject to a measure of privation of liberty. However, this change of status did not go with the corresponding guarantees, and the suspect could not see a lawyer before the end of the questioning. Unsurprisingly, the Court held that there had been a violation of Article 6 §3 but it specified that the exercise of defence rights does not depend on the formal qualification given to the person suspected. From the moment the police have a doubt about the involvement of the person in the commission of the offence, he or she must benefit from the status of suspect and its inherent rights. The impact of the ECtHR's jurisprudence was substantial: France had to modify its legislation significantly and Belgium had to create an entire new regime.

The French solution

Although the European jurisprudence relating to police custody was difficult to accept for the French legislator, it became impossible to avoid it in the wake of the *Brusco* decision. Knowing that the French legislation was not in conformity with the ECtHR's new requirements regarding the presence of the lawyer during police custody, the Ministry of Justice decided to postpone any modification of the rules. Indeed, the addressee of the *Salduz* decision was Turkey, and without any decision directly addressed to France, Article 6 §3 was considered as correctly implemented in France. However, the Ministry of Justice was sufficiently worried about the potential consequences of the ECtHR's rulings to send a circular to public prosecutors in November 2009. The document reminded the prosecutors that an accusation had been founded on a body of convergent evidence, not only on the confessions given by the suspect taken into custody. Besides, the pilot study of reform of the French Code of Criminal Procedure (CPP) published in March 2010 proposed to revise the police custody system in compliance with the Strasbourg Court's jurisprudence. However, the slowness of the French legislator encountered the tenacity of defence lawyers determined to force it to apply the new interpretation of Article 6 more protective of defence rights. Through the *question prioritaire de constitutionnalité* (priority question of constitutionality) a group of defence lawyers brought this matter to the *Conseil constitutionnel* (French Constitutional Council) that had to rule on the conformity of the legislation with the Constitution. On 30 July 2010, the *Conseil constitutionnel* declared the legislation on police custody unconstitutional, but instead of striking down the law, it offered the legislator one full year to find a remedy. This position was immediately followed by the *Cour de cassation* (Court of Cassation) right after France had been sentenced in the *Brusco* case.

Finally, the parliament adopted new rules in April 2011, granting the suspect access to a lawyer as soon as he is deprived of liberty, but decided to postpone the enforcement of this measure until the deadline set by the *Conseil constitutionnel.* To conclude this painful delivery, the day after the law was adopted, the *Cour de cassation* handed down four controversial decisions through an audacious reasoning. In the first place, the court argued that the decisions of the ECtHR had to be implemented immediately by the states parties to the European Convention on Human Rights even if they were not directly involved in the decision without waiting for a conviction or a modification of the national legislation. On this premise, the court confirmed the irregularity of the custody system at stake, where the suspect could neither benefit from the assistance of a lawyer from the start of custody nor consult him before his questioning by police agents. This position forced the Ministry of Justice to issue a circular in order to implement the law of 14 April immediately, but only regarding the clauses dealing with the assistance of a lawyer, and the notification of the right to remain silent.

The current legislation represents a significant improvement of the fundamental rights that have been greatly extended with the new legislation to comply with European jurisprudence. First of all, the right to dignity is now expressed in Article 63-5 of the CCP that regulates physical searches. Even if the right to dignity was already guaranteed by the Constitution of 1958, this insertion is a strong symbol emanating from the French legislator aiming at humanising police custody, which has been greatly criticised over the past few years. Besides, the law grants a wide range of concrete rights to the suspect taken into custody. His right to remain silent has to be notified from the beginning of the police interrogation. Then, the role of the lawyer has been improved: he can consult the notification that ordered the suspect to be taken into custody, the written report of the police interrogation and the medical certificate to make sure that his client was well treated. The lawyer is also authorised to attend questionings and confrontations set up between the suspect and the witnesses, after which he can ask questions, and formulate remarks. Since 1993, he had had the right to have a 30-minute confidential interview with his client under the previous law. (Bouloc 424) Unfortunately, the exercise of the right to assistance of a lawyer is not as extensive as the ECtHR had envisaged. Indeed, the lawyer cannot access the file and check the elements already gathered by the police, which could be very useful to organise the defence properly. Moreover, he does not have the right to intervene during the auditions and confrontations although the law does not forbid it. (Pradel 14) Regarding the evidence collected without the presence of the lawyer, the *Cour de cassation* specified that no conviction could be pronounced solely on the basis of this statement. Even if defence lawyers think the system should be improved, the suspect is no longer alone with the investigator, which represents an effective improvement of the position of the defence. (Dorange and Field 168) Henceforth, Belgium presents a similar regime regarding defence rights in police custody.

The Belgian solution

In Belgium, the *Salduz* jurisprudence had a significant influence on the modification of the legislation, initiating the elaboration of a new regime with the law of 13 August 2011, known as *"loi Salduz."* Police custody was not very detailed in the previous law. It was regulated by the law of 20 July 1990 on pre-trial detention (*détention préventive.*) In case of *flagrante delicto*, police agents had the right to take a person into custody as well as any person suspected of being connected to an offence. This deprivation of liberty could not exceed 24 hours, and could not be extended by the same means as those by which it had been initiated. If the detention needed to be extended, the decision had to be made by a judge with an arrest warrant. No rules dealt with the police interrogation of the suspect who could not benefit from a special status and was not informed of his right to remain silent. Naturally, the presence of the lawyer was not tolerated. (Kettels 1001) This lack of protection for the suspect was clearly unsatisfactory and highly open to criticism. A person could be arrested on the basis of a mere suspicion and kept in the police station for an entire day, without having the opportunity to consult a legal advisor.

With the *Salduz* decision, the legislator, worried about a potential but actually inevitable conviction, decided to deeply reform the regime of police custody, in conformity with the European court's standards. A modification of the police detention legislation introduced a new article (2bis) in the CCP, giving the suspect a real opportunity to exercise his rights. From now on, the person in custody has had the right to consult a lawyer confidentially before the first police interview, but this meeting cannot exceed 30 minutes as in France. Furthermore, the lawyer is allowed to attend the police interview, in order to make sure that:

- the right against self-incrimination is enforced, and that the suspect is free to make a statement, to answer the questions of the police agents, or to remain silent;
- the suspect is well treated during the interrogation, not subject to torture or other forms of inhuman and degrading treatment;
- the suspect is informed that he has rights inherent to his status;
- the questioning is legitimate.

During the police interrogation, the legal counsellor has the right to ask for one and only 30-minute pause. His role is strictly limited to these four missions, and he is not allowed to orientate the answers of his client nor to influence him. (Franchimont, Jacobs and Masset 327-328) He does not have the right to stop the questioning or to show any documents to his client. (Leroy 854)

Regarding the admissibility of evidence collected in violation of the right to be assisted by a lawyer during police custody, the *Cour de cassation* affirmed that this evidence does not have to be excluded (*nullité*) but following the example of the French reasoning, no conviction can be reached on this sole basis. The point may be subject to a legislative modification, as the *Cour Constitutionnelle* in February 2013 declared that the term "only" makes the provision unconstitutional. As a consequence, the criminal judge is not allowed to use statements gathered in violation of the right to a lawyer even if other evidence corroborates this statement.

In spite of the criticisms coming from the doctrine regarding the insufficient improvement brought by the new legislation, the implementation of the law has been delicate for everyone as it implied structural changes. Firstly, for police officers who were not used to seeing a lawyer interfere with their work, and above all for defence lawyers, who had to organise their work in order to be available for duty. On this point, a recurrent negative remark has been expressed about the cost of the measure. Indeed, the "*permanence Salduz*" asking lawyers to be on call, was suspended for a few months in 2012 due to the lack of financial means provided by the government. France encounters the same difficulties regarding the payment of defence lawyers. (Dorange and Field 170)

However, the harmonisation of human rights in the European Union is no longer optional, but mandatory. Indeed, the increase in cross-border crime inevitably leads to an intensification of judicial cooperation between national authorities during investigation. This cooperation may lead some authorities to transfer gathered evidence such as written reports of statements collected during the police custody phase. Up to now, the emphasis has been put on the facilitation of cooperation in transnational investigations, which raises new issues regarding the protection of the suspect in custody that European Union is trying to resolve.

The need for harmonisation through the strengthening of human rights during police detention in the European Union area of freedom, security and justice

The need for a deep harmonisation of fundamental rights during police custody

Current legal instruments

Judicial cooperation within the European Union is a complex accumulation of legal instruments that can be schematically separated into two groups: the traditional system of mutual legal assistance and the modern system of mutual recognition. On the one hand, mutual legal assistance is mainly based on two instruments, both permitting direct cooperation between judicial authorities. The Council of Europe established the first set of instruments. First in 1959, with the European Convention on Mutual Assistance in Criminal Matters of the Council of Europe, which was completed with two additional protocols in 1978 and 2001. From a diplomatic discussion requiring an agreement between national Ministries of Foreign Affairs, cooperation has become a direct assistance between internal authorities through the so-called international letters rogatory. The second instrument is the Convention on mutual assistance in criminal matters between the Member States of the European Union adopted on 29 May 2000.

The second system relies on the principle of mutual recognition of judgments and other decisions of judicial authorities, which has been the basis of judicial cooperation in criminal matters since the Lisbon Treaty came into force in 2010. This principle, instituted by the Tampere

European Council in 1999 as the cornerstone of judicial cooperation in both civil and criminal matters within the European Union, is founded on mutual trust between Member States' criminal justice systems. As each Member State is supposed to ensure the same high protection of fundamental rights, a decision made by a judicial authority in one Member State should be accepted as it stands in another Member State without any condition of registration. Following this theory instruments were introduced such as the European Arrest Warrant in 2002, the Freezing Order of Property or Evidence in 2003 and the European Evidence Warrant in 2008.

In April 2010, seven Member states tabled an initiative for a directive establishing a powerful tool based on the principle of mutual recognition in criminal matters: the European Investigation Order (EIO.) This instrument is quite innovative as it would give national authorities the power to make extraterritorial decisions by establishing a common regime for gathering and sharing evidence. Indeed, a judicial decision issued by the competent authority of one Member State, in order to collect evidence, would be directly executed by the competent authority in another Member State. The scope of the EIO directive is very broad as it would cover every investigative measure. Concretely, a Belgian judge could directly order an English police officer to arrest a suspect in order to interrogate him, following the Belgian legal formalities, unless it would be contrary to fundamental principles of law in the United Kingdom. Three years after the 2010 initiative, the proposal for a directive is still under discussion. However, the tenacity of some Member States (Letters 6532-12) in the adoption of this new instrument considered as essential to facilitate cross-border investigations, could restart the adoption process.

Admissibility issues

This cooperation during investigations implies the transfer of documents, data, and elements gathered by judicial authorities in one State to another State in order to use them as evidence before a judge. But as exposed earlier, Member States do not ensure the same protection of defence rights during investigation, especially during pre-trial detention. For instance, in State A, the right of access to a lawyer implies holding a confidential 30-minute interview with a lawyer before the first questioning under penalty of nullity, but the lawyer is not allowed to attend the questioning. In State B, the right to access to a lawyer means that the lawyer cannot speak privately with his client for 30 minutes before the first questioning, but as a counterpart, he can attend the questioning and advise his client to not answer some questions. As a consequence, a statement collected in State B, without the intervention of the lawyer, does not protect the client in the same way and could be considered illegal and excluded from the case file. If a statement collected in State B is transferred to judicial authorities in State A, would it be considered illegal and excluded from the investigation file or used before a judge as evidence? Even trickier, if judicial authorities in State A fail to respect their national legislation and do not grant the person in custody access to a lawyer for 30 minutes, it should be impossible to take into account his statement, it having been collected by illegal means. But if the written report of the questioning is sent to State B before any judge can rule on the nullity of this questioning, it could be used in State B, because according to State B's legislation, the questioning would not be automatically illegal. As a consequence, the transfer of the report could clear the illegality of the evidence. How would the defence challenge this evidence and ask for its exclusion? Even if these situations are only fictional examples, they illustrate the threats to fundamental rights that intense judicial cooperation represents in a field where fundamental rights are not totally harmonised.

The strengthening of Fundamental Rights, a way towards harmonisation

If the harmonisation is a necessity, it cannot be reached without a strengthening of fundamental rights in the pre-trial phase. Indeed, common minimum standards already exist within the European Union thanks to the European Convention on Human rights, which has to be adopted by every Member State, and the Charter of Fundamentals Rights of the European Union. But the freedom given to Member States in the interpretation of those vague instruments can lead to radically different situations, which do not allow a sufficient degree of mutual trust. The example of the right to legal advice clearly illustrates the issue.

In addition with the progressive interpretation of the ECHR by the Strasbourg Court, the European Union has decided to play an active role in the strengthening of fundamental rights in criminal proceedings. In 1999, the Tampere European Council already pointed out the necessity of common minimum standards to facilitate the implementation of the principle of mutual recognition. The Hague Programme went further in 2004 and emphasised the importance of "equivalent standards of procedural rights" in criminal proceedings. In this context, the aim of the "Proposal for a Council Framework Decision on certain procedural rights in criminal proceedings throughout the European Union" was to establish a set of minimum procedural rights common to every Member State. But the proposal was too ambitious and could not reach an agreement. Therefore, a more pragmatic and specific approach was preferred, following the "Roadmap for strengthening procedural rights of suspected or accused persons in criminal proceedings" adopted by the Council in November 2009. The resolution, made part of the Stockholm Programme, focused on three main subjects, quickly followed by the corresponding legislative instrument proposals, thanks to the extended competence of the EU in criminal matters. Indeed, Article 82(2) of the Treaty on the Functioning of the European Union provides a legal basis to the harmonisation of individuals' rights in criminal proceedings by the establishment of minimum rules in order to facilitate the implementation of the principle of mutual recognition and cooperation between national authorities.

The first instrument adopted was the directive on the right to interpretation and translation, for those who do not speak or understand the language of the criminal proceedings as already enshrined by Article 6 of the European Convention on Human Rights. According to Article 2 of the directive, Member States have to provide interpretation to the suspect or the accused, without delay, the allow him to understand investigative and judicial authorities, "including during police questioning," and to communicate directly with his legal counsel. The right to understand the proceedings is extended to essential documents, which have to be translated to enable the suspect or the accused to exercise his rights of defence. The definition of the scope of "essential documents" is left to national competent authorities, except for the decision depriving the suspect of liberty. Thus, a narrow interpretation of the right to interpretation or translation and so a strict restriction of the translation of essential documents is not forbidden as long as the exercise of defence rights is guaranteed.

The second instrument adopted in May 2012 was the directive on the right to information in criminal proceedings. From the moment a person is made aware by national authorities that he is suspected or accused of having committed a criminal offence, he has the right to be informed of his rights, and the accusation against him. The rights designed by this obligation are the rights to access to a lawyer, to free legal advice, to be informed of the accusation, to interpretation and translation, and to remain silent, and they shall be given orally or in writing, possible through a "Letter of Rights." An indicative model Letter of Rights accompanied the directive, and amongst other additional rights, it mentions also the right to access the material of the case. This does not mean that the defence has to have full access to the case file during police custody. Even if this right concerns all material evidence in the possession of competent authorities, in favour or in disfavour of the suspect or the accused, it does not have to be applied immediately from the arrest. The documents have to be displayed "in due time to allow the effective exercise of the rights of the defence and at the latest upon submission of the merits of the accusation to the judgment of a court" or if the person is detained, at the "latest when a competent judicial authority is called to decide upon the lawfulness of the arrest or the detention." Furthermore, the directive provides some grounds to refuse access, for instance if the disclosure may lead to a serious threat to the life of another person or to the public interest.

The last instrument of the series has not been adopted yet since the negotiations strongly oppose two groups of Member States, those influenced by the inquisitorial tradition against the adversarial descendants. Indeed, the "proposal for a Directive on the right of access to a lawyer in criminal proceedings and on the right to communicate upon arrest" with a third party has been discussed for nearly two years, and once adopted, would force some Member States to modify their legislation, including France. According to Article 3, the scope of the instrument is very broad as it requests the Member States to ensure that the suspect or the accused has access to a lawyer "before the start of any questioning" by competent authorities, or if the person is remanded in custody, from the beginning of the deprivation of liberty. Moreover, if competent authorities need to execute any procedural or evidence-gathering act in the presence of the suspect or the accused, the presence of his lawyer should also then be required. Borrowing the words of the ECtHR, the rights of the defence have to be exercised effectively.

The directive goes even further, describing the powers of the lawyer, especially during questioning, which definitely represents a concrete improvement for defence rights. Thus, the lawyer has an active role. He shall be present at any questioning or hearing, and has "the right to ask questions, request clarification and make statements." He should also have the right to check the conditions of detention, including police custody. The possibilities to restrict the broad scope of this instrument are limited, and that might be a reason why the negotiations are so laborious. No duration or frequency of the meetings between the lawyer and his client are prescribed, only their confidentiality, but the text specifies that the limitation should not prejudice the exercise of the rights of the defence. Furthermore, derogations have to be decided by a judicial authority and subjected to a case-by-case assessment. No derogation shall be based exclusively on the seriousness of the offence or shall go beyond what is necessary. Finally, any derogation has to be justified "by compelling reasons pertaining to the urgent need to avert serious adverse consequences for the file or physical integrity of a person" and, obviously, cannot prejudice the fairness of the proceedings.

One of the most interesting points of the proposal is the remedy suggested in any case of breach of the right to access to a lawyer. In case of violation of the right to legal advice, the suspect or the accused shall be placed in "the same position in which he would have found himself had the breach not occurred." For instance, if the suspect does not have the opportunity to consult a lawyer, but remains silent throughout questioning, it may be considered that the result would have been the same if he had had the chance to consult a lawyer before the questioning. But in any case the statement of the suspect or evidence gathered in the absence of the lawyer cannot be used against him unless it does not prejudice the rights of the defence. With this provision, the European instrument interferes with national criminal laws of evidence by subjecting the admissibility of evidence to the respect of the right of access to a lawyer.

The established need for harmonisation through the strengthening of fundamental rights is no longer to be proven. However, the adoption of higher standards is not easy: the means available are limited and the negative reaction of national authorities may be discouraging.

European and national obstacles to harmonisation

The limited federative impact of the European Court of Human Rights' jurisprudence

Although it is undeniable that the ECtHR's jurisprudence influences the modification of national legislation, its federative role has to be put into perspective. Firstly, the Court does not directly strike down the laws of the State involved, but notices an infringement of the applicant's rights protected by the Convention. (Delmas-Marty & Spencer 42) The decision of the ECtHR is linked to a specific dispute, and so, to specific facts. The violation of the fairness of proceedings is appreciated as a whole, and the Court takes into account all the facts brought to its assessment. Unfair behaviour may be counterbalanced by a positive compensation: a violation of defence rights during a search for evidence may be balanced by the opportunity to challenge the collected evidence or to discuss its admissibility before the criminal judge. Furthermore, the five sections of the Court do not necessarily agree on one interpretation and sometimes, one section is not representative of the Court's overall position. Therefore, the conviction of one State does not necessarily lead to a significant change of national rules that originally founded the applicant's initiative.

However, the ECtHR's decisions do have an *interpartes* impact. Indeed, Article 46 of the Convention provides that "The High Contracting Parties undertake to abide by the final judgment of the Court in any case to which they are parties," which means that only the State prosecuted before the Court is affected by the decision. Nonetheless, the impact of this article must be attenuated. State parties may decide to modify their legislation spontaneously to comply with the interpretation given by the Court in order to avoid any conviction, as did Belgium by introducing the *loi Salduz*. In France, the *Cour de cassation* expressly affirmed in four decisions on 15 April 2011 that the State parties are required to comply with the decisions of the ECtHR, before any sentencing or any modification of the national legislation. The reaction of the Belgian legislator and the French supreme court clearly show their will to follow the ECtHR's position.

To conclude on a final negative remark, the legitimacy of the ECtHR's jurisprudence may be called into question. The role of the criminal judge is to interpret and apply the law. But as the European Convention is a living instrument, so is its interpretation by the Court. The creative work of the Court indirectly obliges the State parties to modify their legislation, in order to avoid repeated convictions. As a consequence, the legislative initiative does not come from the legislative or executive powers, but from judges, and even more questionably, from foreign judges.

Forthcoming European Union action

Even if the Stockholm programme, setting out the European Union's priorities for the period 2010-14 in the area of freedom, security and justice, focuses on the protection of human rights and fundamental freedoms, most of the instruments edited by the European Union in the criminal field over the past 15 years have indisputably emphasised the prosecution side rather than the defence side. A brief overview of EU legislative action in the criminal field reveals that Member States were more willing to adopt instruments giving their investigative agents more powers in transnational criminal proceedings in the fight against crime than protective instruments for the defence.

Several reasons may be proposed to justify this movement. Firstly, the European Union legislation appears as an "emergency solution" to a specific issue, which explains why its action is more reactive than preventive. For example, in reaction to the increase in cross-border crime within the European Union, and the rise in serious organised crime at the international level, such as terrorism, the urgency was to offer new cooperation instruments to national authorities in judicial proceedings. Significant instruments were adopted in this context of security crisis, including the Council Framework Decision of 13 June 2002 on the European arrest warrant and the surrender procedures between Member States, simplifying the extradition system, and the Council Framework Decision of 26 February 2009 on the organisation and content of the exchange of information extracted from the criminal record between Member States. A second reason is that fundamental rights are already protected at a national level through national laws, but also thanks to the European Convention on Human Rights to which all the Member States are parties. Furthermore, the 2009 Lisbon Treaty reinforced the commitment of the EU to the strengthening of fundamental rights: Article 6 of the Treaty on the EU affirms that “Fundamental rights, as guaranteed by the European Convention for the Protection of Human Rights and Fundamental Freedoms and as they result from the constitutional traditions common to the Member States, shall constitute general principles of the Union’s law.” Therefore, the adoption of harmonising instruments may not appear as a priority for the Member States, especially during the economic crisis that EU is going through.

Regarding the instruments adopted or in negotiation, a general remark may be made about their effective utility. As said before, the three directives reaffirm some rights already protected by the ECHR, to which every Member State is party. This approach is more a symbolic step than a concrete solution to protect the suspect or the accused from violation of his rights. Indeed, the minimum standards affirmed by the directives will probably not lead to the harmonisation hoped for. For instance, regarding the directive on the right to information, even if the Letter of Rights constitutes concrete progress in the strengthening of the rights of the defence, the vagueness of the time limits imposed offers the Member States the possibility to keep their current legislation as long as they provide the suspect or the accused with the right of access to evidence before the trial phase. Moreover, none of the instruments proposes any sanction at the national level in case of violation of those rights, such as the inadmissibility of the statement taken, or more radically, the discontinuation of proceedings. They do not specify if a breach of one of the protected rights constitutes an irretrievable violation of defence rights as affirmed in the ECtHR's decisions.

In addition, the choice of a directive instead of a regulation is politically wise but perhaps not the best option to achieve harmonisation, as the directive could lead to divergent national interpretations or conflicts in the transposition. The proposal for a directive on the right of access to a lawyer is very protective of the defence, which perhaps explains why an agreement is so difficult to reach. There are several issues that are source of conflict between the Member States:

- the exclusion of legal assistance for certain types of offences;
- the opportunity or obligation to consult a lawyer: Member States hesitate between a proactive position with the obligation to provide legal advice to every suspect, and a passive position where the lawyer would intervene only on request of the suspect;
- a passive or active role during the audition: will the lawyer be allowed to speak during the questioning, to advise his client to remain silent depending on the question asked, or will he just be the powerless witness of the interrogation?
- the sanction in case of violation of the right: Member States do not agree on the future of evidence gathered in breach of the right of access to a lawyer. Does the statement remain admissible or should it be excluded from the case file? What consequences for the material evidence found thanks to an irregular confession? (Flore & Honhon)

The reluctance of the States in the implementation of the right of access to a lawyer

The deficiencies of national laws

The French and Belgian modifications of legislative rules are certainly a major progress in the strengthening of fundamental rights during police custody. However, their action appears more like a "forced choice" than a real desire to improve their system. (Monville & Michiels 60) Regarding the new Belgian legal regime, the doctrine raised some criticisms, regarding its limited scope. (Leroy) The right to be assisted by a lawyer during questioning concerns only the suspect in custody. The suspect who is not deprived of his liberty is interrogated without a lawyer. He has the possibility to consult a lawyer before the first police interview, only if he is suspected of having committed a second-degree offence, or third-degree offence (offences that can give rise to an arrest warrant.) The *Cour constitutionnelle* decided in February 2013 that this part was in compliance with the Constitution and considered that the implementation of the right to a preliminary confidential interview with the lawyer would be impossible for every offence, regarding the cost and the organisation of such a measure. (Kennes)

As neither the Belgian nor the French legislation clarifies the mission of the lawyer during police custody, the total access to the case file is still a tricky subject in both States. The inquisitorial legacy is a major obstacle to the interference of the lawyer in police work. The lawyer is still perceived as an unwelcome element disturbing the investigation, the aim of the judicial authorities being the discovery of the truth while the lawyer will be preoccupied with the interests of his client. Some progress has been made, but the police still remain the masters of the investigation, and detain all the pieces of evidence while the defence only has access to some. The Belgian *Cour constitutionnelle* affirmed this position; the absence of access to the case file was not struck down, but the Court specified that the lawyer needed to understand the facts and the context that founded the police custody measure. However, according to the *Dayanan v. Turkey* decision, the lawyer has to be able to discuss the case with his client, organise the defence, find favourable evidence and prepare for questioning. As the Convention guarantees rights that are practical and effective, not theoretical or illusory (*Airey v. Ireland*,) a practical and effective implementation of the mission of the lawyer as described would imply granting the lawyer access to the case file and all the documents in the possession of the police. In addition, Article 63-4-3 of the French CCP gives investigators the opportunity to reduce the effective role of the lawyer during questioning, if they think that his intervention could be harmful to the investigation. (Matsopoulou 542)

As for legal remedies to a violation of the right to be assisted by a lawyer before and during questioning, the exclusion of the statement obtained seems to be the best solution. Indeed, it would have been too severe to punish the breach of the right with the discontinuation of proceedings. Criminal procedure law is a fair balance between the security of society and the efficiency of proceedings on the one hand, and liberty, the protection of individual rights and due process of law on the other hand. Giving priority to the rights of the defence at the cost of the security of society and other individuals' protection would lead to aberrant situations where offenders are not punished anymore if their rights are not broadly enough interpreted.

However, the solution is not perfect. Even if a confession given by the suspect in the absence of his lawyer cannot be the sole basis of a conviction, the piece of evidence gathered thanks to this confession remains admissible before a judge. The ECtHR validated this point in *Gafgen v. Germany*: the suspect gave a coerced confession to police officers, which led them to other material evidence. During the trial, the accused reiterated his confession, and so was convicted on this basis. But even if the first confession and material evidence had not been used, the irregularity committed by the police officers definitely initiated the gathering of all other evidence, and the prosecution of the suspect before a court. In addition, this clemency does not encourage a respect of the law. Putting a premature end to proceedings would send a strong message to the police and warn judicial authorities about the consequence of committing irregularities.

Abuse of process

The implementation of the legislation in France and Belgium is delicate. The confrontation of interests is easily understandable: on the one hand, judicial authorities, trying to be as efficient as possible to find evidence leading to the truth, on the other hand, the person suspected, still innocent until a final judgement is handed down by a court. During investigations, police officers can see the presence of the lawyer as an obstacle to the rapidity and the efficiency of their work. As a result, they might try to get around the law to obtain the evidence needed.

The first abuse of process is to consider the suspect as a witness. In some cases, while a witness is questioned, investigators may realise that he is more involved than they first thought, so the witness becomes a suspect and is asked to stay in order to continue the questioning. As a suspect deprived of liberty, this person has to benefit from defence rights, and so, the right of access to a lawyer. But some authorities might by tempted to delay the beginning of the measure, using this time to get statements that will be used as evidence before a judge. From the moment the authorities have some doubts about someone's involvement in the commission of an offence, this person must be considered as a suspect with inherent rights.

Another behaviour criticised by some defence lawyers, in France and in Belgium, is the use of the *audition libre* (police interview where you are free to go,) which might also represent an abuse of process. Indeed, the right to a lawyer is linked to the deprivation of liberty. In France, a person suspected of being involved in an offence can be invited to appear at a police station, in order to answer some questions about an on-going investigation, for four hours. The person who gives some statements freely, even if he is suspected of having committed an offence, does not have the right of access to a lawyer, or to be notified of the right to remain silent. The only difference is that this person is free to leave the police station anytime he wants during the police interview, and if the police officer wants to carry on the questioning, then he has to pronounce a police custody measure. The delicate point here is that most of the time, the suspect is not aware of the possibility of leaving the police interview without any consequences. Police officers may take advantage of the ignorance of the suspect who is vulnerable because he does not know the law and does not have the opportunity to consult a legal advisor.

Constitutional courts in France and in Belgium were asked to rule on this point of law. In a decision of November 2011 (decision n° 2011-191/194/195/196/197, *Mme Elise A. et autres*,) the French *Conseil Constitutionnel* affirmed that the person summoned to an interview by the police is entitled to know that he can refuse to be questioned, but does not enjoy the right to be assisted by a lawyer, as he is not deprived of liberty. In Belgium, the constitutional review of the "*loi Salduz*" was also brought to the *Cour constitutionnelle*, which recently decided in a way similar to the solution adopted in France. On 14 February 2013, the court ruled that the law was partially contrary to the Constitution: the court did not nullify the absence of the lawyer during the *audition libre* but it ruled that the absence of any notification of the right to leave at any moment is unconstitutional. Indeed, as in France, the suspect interrogated should be aware that he is not obliged to stay in the police station. (Neveu)

The solution adopted by the French and Belgian constitutional courts is not sufficient, and the presence of the lawyer should be mandatory from the moment a suspect is required to go to the police station. Indeed, the suspect will be faced with a delicate choice to make: either he agrees to answer the questions freely, or he decides to leave and risks being taken into custody. The issue here is that custody can be seen as a punishment, as the suspect is focused on the deprivation of liberty, on the degrading characteristic of the measure, instead of noticing the "package of rights" coming with the measure. The feeling is maintained by the behaviour of police officers; as their work is more easily done without the presence of the lawyer, they may influence the decision to voluntarily participate in the police interview. They might emphasise the strength of the coercive measure, the symbol that the deprivation of liberty might represent for the family, the employer that the suspect will have to inform. Alternatively, they can present custody as a waste of time, and a way to lengthen the procedure, while the importance of the police interview and the consequences for the proceedings will be minimised or even hidden.

Both situations, the abuse of the status of witness and the *audition libre* cannot comply with the ECtHR's jurisprudence and the EU directive. Regarding the jurisprudence of the Court of Strasbourg, the *Brusco* case clearly affirmed that the status of "suspect" is not to be construed formally but materially, thus independently of the terminology used. (§57) Furthermore, a circumvention of the implementation of the right of access to a lawyer with the *audition libre* system is considered a violation of

Article 6 of the Convention. In *Stojkovic v. France and Belgium*, the Court held there was a breach of fairness of proceedings when the suspect, who was not subject to a measure of deprivation of liberty, was interrogated without the presence of a lawyer, even though he had requested to see a lawyer prior to questioning. In *Grinenko v. Ukraine*, the applicant was arrested and questioned as a witness, without having access to a lawyer and under pressure, since the police reminded him that refusing to give evidence or giving false evidence was a criminal offence. The Court decided that even if the police called the suspect a witness during the first interrogation, criminal proceedings had been opened against him, so the applicant's right to a lawyer should have been applied from the first interrogation.

This situation is also incompatible with the directive on the right of access to a lawyer, still under negotiation. Indeed, Article 3 provides that the suspect or the accused is entitled to have access to legal counsel before the start of any questioning, independently of any deprivation of liberty, which makes the positions of the French and Belgian courts discordant with the directive. Furthermore, article 10 provides that if during the questioning or the hearing of any person other than a suspect of the accused, the investigating authorities realise that there are enough pieces of evidence to make him a suspect, then he must benefit from the rights of the defence. So if the witness becomes a suspect in the course of questioning, he must be notified of his rights, and the questioning may proceed only in the presence of a lawyer.

Conclusion

The coordinating power of the court of Strasbourg depends entirely on the will of the State parties. Even if the convergence of national legislations may be a positive sign of the influence of the EctHR's jurisprudence on the standardisation of procedural guarantees in the pre-trial stage, this analysis is quite limited. Indeed, the example given concerns only two Member States. In many other Member States, if national laws give the suspect the opportunity to contact a lawyer after arrest, they do not necessarily allow him to contact the lawyer immediately after arrest, in order to help him effectively from the beginning of the deprivation of liberty. (Spronken et al.)

But thinking that national differences are too important to permit the harmonisation would be overly pessimistic. It is undeniably true that the *Salduz* jurisprudence has had a strong influence in many States. The Netherlands changed its interpretation of Article 6 of the European

Convention on Human rights. By allowing the suspect to consult a lawyer before the first interrogation, the Supreme Court of the Netherlands chose to implement the European jurisprudence before being sentenced, following the example of Belgium. (Spronken et al.) Scotland had also been invited by the UK Supreme Court to modify its practice of detaining a person for six hours without a lawyer. (Dorange and Field 171) Even if the uniformity of pre-trial detention regime in Europe is still utopian, it is definitely a starting point of deeper harmonisation of fundamental rights during policy custody.

Works cited

Cases

ECtHR, 24 November, 1993. *Imbrioscia v. Switzerland*, App. n° 13972/88, Series A no. 275.

ECtHR, 10 February, 1995. *Allenet de Ribemont v. France*, Series A n° 308.

ECtHR, 8 February, 1996. *John Murray v. United Kingdom*, App. n° 18731/91, Reports 1996-I.

ECtHR, 28 November, 2008. *Salduz v. Turkey*, App. n° 36391/02, Reports of Judgments and Decisions 2008.

ECtHR, 13 October, 2009. *Dayanan v. Turkey*, App. n° 7377/03.

ECtHR, 1 June, 2010. *Gäfgen v. Germany*, App. n° 22978/05, Reports of Judgments and Decisions 2010.

ECtHR, 14 October, 2010. *Brusco v. France*, App. n° 1466/07.

ECtHR, 27 October, 2011. *Stojkovic v. France and Belgium*, App. n° 25303/08.

ECtHR, 15 November, 2012. *Grinenko v. Ukraine*, App. n° 33627/06.

Secondary Sources

BERBUTO, Sandra and Estelle Berthe. "Le point de vue des avocats. On n'en a pas fini avec Salduz." *Actualités de droit pénal*. Ann Jacos and Adrien Masset (eds). Liège: Anthemis, 2011, p. 121-153.

BOULOC, Bernard, Gaston STEFANI and Georges LEVASSEUR. *Procédure pénale.* Paris: Dalloz, 2012.

CORNU, Gérard. *Vocabulaire juridique*. Paris: Presses Universitaires de France, 2012.

DELMAS-MARTY, Mireille and J.R. Spencer (eds.). *European Criminal Procedures*. Cambridge: Cambridge University Press, 2002.

DORANGE, Aurélie and Stewart FIELD. "Reforming defence rights in French police custody: a coming together in Europe?" *The international journal of evidence & proof.* 2012, p. 153-174.

FLORE, Daniel and Amandine HONHON "Le projet de directive de l'Union européenne." Intervention at the conference "Le droit à être assisté par un avocat lors de la garde à vue : regards croisés belge, français et européen(s)", Metz (France), April 2012. http://www.statewatch.org/news/2013/mar/eu-council-eio-ms-letters-6532-13.pdf.

FRANCHIMONT, Michel, Ann JACOBS and Adrien MASSET. *Manuel de procédure pénale*. Bruxelles: Larcier, 2012.

KENNES, Laurent. "La 'loi Salduz' passée au crible de la Cour constitutionnelle : trois annulations, deux interprétations et plusieurs rejets." *Justice en ligne*. 28 February 2013. URL: http://www.justice-en-ligne.be/article533.html.

KETTELS, Aurélie. "L'assistance de l'avocat dès l'arrestation ou comment repenser la phase préparatoire du procès pénal sur un mode plus accusatoire." *Revue de droit pénal et de criminologie*. 2009, p. 989-1012.

LEROY, Antoine. "L'avocat et la loi Salduz." *Journal des tribunaux*. 2011: 851-856.

LETTERS (6532-12). Initiative from the Kingdom of Belgium, the Republic of Bulgaria, the Republic of Estonia, the Kingdom of Spain, the Republic of Austria, the Republic of Slovenia and the Kingdom of Sweden for a Directive of the European Parliament and of the Council regarding the European Investigation Order in criminal matters. Brussels, 5 March 2013.

MATSOPOULOU, Haritini. "Une réforme inachevée. – A propos de la loi du 14 avril 2011." *JCP* 19 (May 2011) 542.

MERLE, Roger and André VITU. *Procédure pénale*. Paris: Cujas, 1979.

MONVILLE, Pierre and Olivier MICHIELS. "Salduz: entre présent et futur." *Actualités de droit pénal*. Ann JACOS and Adrien MASSET (eds). Liège: Anthemis, 2011, p. 43-94.

NEVEU, Suliane. "La cour constitutionnelle belge annule partiellement la loi Salduz sur le droit à l'assistance d'un avocat en garde à vue." Lettre "Actualités droits-Libertés," CREDF, 7 March 2013.

PRADEL, Jean. "Vers une métamorphose de la garde à vue. Apres la 'décision pilote' du Conseil constitutionnel du 30 juillet 2010 et les arrêts de la chambre criminelle du 19 octobre 2010." Recueil Dalloz (2010) 2783.

SPRONKEN, Taru et al. EU Procedural Rights in Criminal Proceedings. Apeldoorn: Maklu Publishers, 2009. Report available online: http://arno.unimaas.nl/show.cgi?fid=16315.

POLICE CUSTODY IN ENGLAND AND FRANCE: A LAWFUL DEPRIVATION OF LIBERTY?

ELIZABETH GIBSON-MORGAN
UNIVERSITY OF TOURS, FRANCE

"To none will we deny or delay, right or justice" provides *Magna Carta* in its section 40. In 2015, the United Kingdom will celebrate the 800th anniversary of the Great Charter—which not only was Simon de Monfort's principal motivating force 50 years later—but which still embodies the universal values of Freedom and Justice without which there can be no democracy.

The emergence of the *Habeas Corpus*

Personal liberty is undoubtedly regarded as the most fundamental of all freedoms. A much praised provision of *Magna Carta*, section 39, drafted as a reaction to arbitrary punishment, reads: "No free man shall be taken or imprisoned [...] unless by the lawful judgment of his peers, or by the law of the land." It aimed at providing a swift and imperative remedy in cases of illegal restraint or confinement and is often considered as the very origin of the writ of *Habeas Corpus,* one of the most important writs—if not the most important—known to the Constitutional Law of England.

Defending Liberty and pursuing Justice appeared as a constant theme in England throughout the centuries and inspired constitutional reformers. The *Habeas Corpus* Act 1679 further enshrined personal liberty by allowing a detained person to challenge the legality of detention and, if successful, be quickly released. It may be sought by those detained in custody pending trial or held by the police during criminal investigations as well as by convicted prisoners. The person detained must be produced before a court and if there are no charges against them, he or she must be immediately released. *Habeas Corpus* thus became the symbol of the fight against arbitrary arrest and detention.

France, a country that prides itself as the birthplace of Human Rights, introduced its own version of the writ of *Habeas Corpus* with the Ordinance of Villers-Cotterets (1539) under Francois 1er. The 1539 ordinance made it compulsory to produce every person who had been arrested before a judge within 24 hours. It was later to be further entrenched by the Ordinance on criminal law of March 1670 initiated by Louis XIV. Its Article 12 reads: "The accused will have to be questioned by the provost in the presence of the assessor within 24 hours following the arrest." (Carbonneau 448) The country of course reaffirmed its commitment to (personal) liberty most powerfully during the Revolution of 1789. Its most famous text, the Declaration of the Rights of Man and the Citizen, enunciated amongst the "natural and inalienable rights of man" "liberty and the resistance to oppression." It was based on the belief that the more people knew their rights, the more they would cherish the laws that protected them. Its Article 7 states: "No man may be accused, arrested, or detained except in cases determined by the law and according to the forms it has prescribed." Thus, in condemning the practices of the pre-revolution *ancien regime* it proclaimed the right to be protected against arbitrary arrest and detention. It followed that people could not be deprived of those fundamental rights without injustice.

A general right to liberty

Today, the principle of *Habeas Corpus* in both countries tends to be increasingly supplanted by the right of liberty protected by Article 5 of the European Convention on Human Rights as it is thought to provide a more straightforward legal remedy. The ECHR declares in its Article 5(1) the general right to liberty and that no one shall be deprived of his liberty, except where the law allows arrest or detention. Its first paragraph provides for the lawful arrest or detention of a person in order to bring him before a competent legal authority on reasonable suspicion of having committed an offence. Under the same article, paragraph 3, which protects personal freedom after arrest, suspects should be brought "promptly" before a court and should be entitled to trial within a reasonable time or released. It is important to bear in mind that the arrested person has the right to be told of the reason for detention. Thus, the ECHR protects the rights of those who have been lawfully incarcerated clearly asserting that prisoners' convention rights cannot be violated simply on the ground of incarceration. So in principle, the right to liberty should be respected.

France and England were among the first countries to ratify the ECHR respectively in 1950 and 1951. It is well-known that lawyers from the UK even played an active role in the drafting of the Convention including Sir

David Maxwell-Fyfe, later to become a Conservative Home Secretary and Lord Chancellor. Yet it took them a long time to incorporate it into their own domestic law. France only gave legal effect to the Convention on 3 May, 1974, but did not recognize the right of individual petition until 1981, fearing that French rules on criminal procedure, especially those concerning the custody of persons arrested might be inconsistent with the Convention's standards. (Steiner 49) As for the United Kingdom, it took the country even longer to incorporate not the whole but the main bulk of the Convention via a national statute, the Human Rights Act 1998, that was finally implemented in October 2000. As the Code of Practice for the Statutory Power of Arrest by police officers, also known as Code G, introduced on 1 January, 2006, stated in its paragraph 1.2: "The right to liberty is a key principle of the Human Rights Act 1998. The exercise of the power of arrest represents an obvious and significance interference with that right." Great Britain was reluctant to recognize the supremacy of the Convention notably the jurisdiction of the European Court of Human Rights even if the latter allowed member-states a margin of appreciation in deciding whether it is necessary and appropriate to limit rights. The Convention prescribes standards of conduct and leaves the choice of implementation to the states themselves under the doctrine of proportionality which is central to the Convention's evaluation of the right of the individual and the general public interests of society. Thus, the ECHR further strengthened personal liberty and other fundamental human rights in France and England and Wales. Yet, in spite of all the legal safeguards that are now part of the French 1958 Constitution and the British Constitutional arrangements, people detained in both countries are sometimes still denied some of their fundamental rights in breach of the Rule of Law.

Indeed, France and England have both been sanctioned many times by the European Court of Human Rights for failing to comply with their obligations under the ECHR notably regarding the rights of people in custody. To take but one example that would be the catalyst for reforming custody in France: in *Brusco v. France* [14.10.2010] France was condemned for failing to tell suspects of their right to silence as well as for the inadequacies of custodial legal advice. As for the United Kingdom, in *Magee v. the UK* [06.06.2000] it was sanctioned for denying access to a lawyer to the person detained that would have been critical as he made statements that were to be central to his conviction while he was in the intimidating atmosphere of police custody. Being officially sanctioned by the European Court of Human Rights, France and England could not legally ignore the Court's decisions that they were in breach of the

Convention obligations: they are supposed to act to remedy the situation but the Court does not prescribe the remedy. Even if it is very difficult *de facto* to implement sanctions, and to force states to bring the disputed law into line with the Convention as there is no mechanism to enforce its rulings, the decisions of the Strasbourg Court do have a strong moral authority. England and France appeared as countries in breach of their treaty obligations in the international community.

The need to achieve legal certainty

As the European Court of Human Rights reaffirmed in its decision *Medvedyev v. France* [29.03.2010], Article 5 paragraph 1 of the ECHR makes it a statutory obligation for every arrest and/or detention to be lawful. National legislation must respect the rule of law that lies at the heart of the Convention. So what is really at issue in this analysis is how to better achieve not so much national security but "legal security" understood as legal certainty and predictability to make sure that rights protected by the Convention are fully applied in each member state including the rights of the people remanded in custody. Rather than examining the issue of balancing suspects' right to liberty against the need for public protection, the current analysis will focus on the urgent need in France and England for clear and accessible rules regarding police custody complying with the ECHR in the name of legal certainty and predictability and beyond that for the sake of the people who are detained—whether for just a few hours or for a few days—and for the protection of their human rights all the more since the deprivation of their liberty makes them particularly vulnerable. The first period of detention is indeed likely to have the most impact on people detained in police stations particularly if they have no warning of their arrest. What will be examined more closely are the few hours or days during which a person who allegedly committed an offence is held at the police station after having been arrested without an arrest warrant, that is custody. We will examine whether the rule of law is fully applied in police custody defined as "a measure which allows the police to hold a person who has not yet been charged with an offence but who must be kept available for investigation purposes, on non-prison premises for a time determined by the gravity of the charges which may be subsequently brought," (Cornu 439) or whether the latter tends to be a kind of lawless zone.

In this paper, what was identified by Lord Bingham as "executive detention," in other words "detention at the instance of the Executive for an indefinite period without charge and without trial" (Bingham 189) such as in cases involving terrorist suspects will not be dealt with nor exceptional arrangements. The analysis will be devoted to the so-called "normal powers of detention" understood as deprivation of liberty inflicted in accordance with the law and the procedures of the justice system.

The legal framework

In France today individual liberty constitutes one of the fundamental principles guaranteed by the laws of the Republic. It is proclaimed by the Preamble to the Constitution of 1946, which was confirmed by the Preamble to the Constitution of 1958. So defence rights are now fully part of the so-called "constitutional bloc."

From a gap in the law to the incorporation into the "constitutional bloc"

Yet, it has not always been so. Before 1958 there was a gap in the law. Police custody was not enshrined in the law. There was no legal definition of custody so it was just a police practice. Isolation of people remanded in custody and secrecy were the main characteristics of pre-arraignment custody. On 8 December, 1897 the so-called Constans Law introduced the right for the accused to have legal counsel when summoned and heard by the investigating judge in the pre-trial investigation to give him moral support and help him with his defence, but it remained silent about police custody. (Walker and Starmer 362) The latter consisted in maintaining a person at the disposal of the police for the needs of the police inquiry in the quest for the truth. Anybody could be remanded in custody including witnesses themselves. This police practice differed from the pre-trial investigation (or judicial investigation) led by a judge and based on the consent of the person involved. Originally custody emerged as a police prerogative at the very beginning of their inquiry when it was very difficult to determine the very nature of the offence allegedly committed. Before the latest reform of police custody in France introduced in 2011, it was possible to put someone in custody for a minor offence and there was only a limited access to a lawyer during custody. In other words police custody in France was not compatible with the ECHR as it clearly violated the provisions of its Article 5.

This gap in the French law left the people detained in police custody in a particularly vulnerable position, with hardly any protection against police potential unethical practices. This was all the more an anomaly since custody is not about offenders serving a jail sentence as a punishment after having been tried, convicted and sentenced by a judge. The person detained having not been convicted of an offence such detention does not amount to punishment but is mainly preventive. Thus, as Professor Lucia Zedner pointed out, this raises a key interrogation: "On what grounds can somebody be held ahead of wrong doing?" (Zedner)

Some answers are provided by what was to become a landmark law in England, PACE 1984, focusing on suspects' rights which was to inspire reformers, including French reformers many years afterwards with the 2011 reform of police custody in France.

From a better protection of suspects with PACE 1984 to the abolition of arrestable offences under the Serious Organized Crime and Police Act 2005

In England, miscarriages of justice in the 1980s due to unethical practices by the police such as premature decisions upon suspects or confessions under duress, as well as more generally speaking the unfair treatment of suspects in contradiction with Article 6(1) of the ECHR, served as a catalyst for reforming police custody. This reform aimed at laying down standards of fair treatment and fighting unethical police practices all the more as police custody is a critical stage in the criminal procedure since it is the time when the suspect is most likely to confess.

The unfair treatment of people detained by the police was hard to reconcile with Article 6(1) of the ECHR which states that "everyone is entitled to a fair and public hearing within a reasonable time by an independent and impartial tribunal" or at least with the interpretation of the European Court of Human Rights of this key provision of the European Convention. Indeed, the ECHR has implications for many areas of the criminal process from detention and questioning in the police station, the right to silence and the privilege against self-incrimination, remand decision-making to disclosure and rules of evidence. As the European Court of Human Rights upheld in its ruling *Imbrioscia v. Switzerland* [24.11.1993] "although the primary purpose of Article 6 in criminal proceedings is to ensure a fair trial by a tribunal, it does not follow that is has no application to pre-trial proceedings," ("Police arrest/ assistance of a lawyer" 1) thus implying that a fair and just trial requires a fair and just investigative stage. It once again put forward the correlation between pre-trial investigation and the trial itself, and which can include police custody in the process.

The origin of the reform of police custody in England and France

In England and Wales, if the main principles of the *Habeas Corpus* Act still apply, notably the right to be informed of the grounds for one's arrest and detention, police custody is now regulated by the Police and Criminal Evidence Act (PACE) 1984.

Police unethical behaviour at the origin of the reform of police custody in England and Wales

As Andrew Ashworth and Mike Redmayne explained "the police are the first agency to deal with all those who are arrested. They make an initial decision about whether to detain the suspect in custody pending the court appearance or to grant police bail." (Ashworth and Redmayne 228) Under section 24 and schedule 1A of PACE about arrestable and serious arrestable offences "any offence that could bring a term of imprisonment for 5 years or more was automatically arrestable." The 1984 Act was accompanied by a series of Codes of Practice which added considerable detail to the legislative provisions, explaining how certain powers and procedures were to be given effect in order to better regulate those coercive powers. The objective was to ensure that persons brought to police stations under arrest were only detained if it was necessary to do so to identify a suspect or check his address, to prevent the suspect from re-offending, to protect pieces of evidence and/or to prevent the suspect from trying to escape, and if there was sufficient evidence for a charge.

Under the law, the police are expected to ensure that those who are arrested are "treated fairly" as it was recently reasserted by the National Policing Improvement Agency in 2012. PACE 1984 established basic safeguards for those detained at police stations, including for the first time the right of access to free and independent legal advice given in private consultation. It regulated detention in the police station giving the police specific time limits within which they could detain suspects and introducing custody officers who do not take part in the police investigation. The person arrested is produced before a custody officer who is in charge of the custody record. Under Code C, the suspect must be orally informed of his or her rights; he or she must be given a written note explaining his or her rights including the right to legal counsel and the right to have a copy of his or her file as well as the right to remain silent. Besides, the suspect must have someone warned of his custody, his employer or a relative; he must be able to talk to a lawyer in private at any moment and his lawyer can attend the police questioning if the suspect wishes him to be present. Under PACE section 41(1), when detaining suspects for non-terrorist matters, the police have up to 24 hours to charge or release them although further periods of detention can be authorized, up to a maximum of 36 hours; to extend detention beyond 24 hours requires a review to be conducted by an officer of superintendent rank or above under PACE section 42(1). When the suspect is brought to the police station, the custody officer has to decide whether the suspect should be released without charge, charged or if it is thought necessary to obtain further evidence by questioning. (PACE, section 37) The general principle is that a person may only be questioned before charge and not after charge. Section 40(3) (b) and (c) requires an inspector "diligently and expeditiously" to carry out regular reviews of the time a suspect is held in custody. (Kemp and Balmer 737) Indeed, PACE Code C paragraph 1.1 requires custody sergeants to deal with all persons in custody expeditiously, and to charge suspects as soon as there is sufficient evidence to do so. In the past the police made the decision whether or not to charge the defendant. However, under the Criminal Justice Act 2003, the Crown Prosecution Service (CPS) now determines the charge in most cases, sometimes working alongside the police in a local criminal justice unit, or at other times by telephone.

If it is decided that the suspect is to be charged, the police officer must decide whether the suspect is to be bailed or remanded in police custody after charge. Once he or she is charged, PACE section 38 provides that the defendant may be bailed to appear in court or, if there are reasonable grounds for believing that detention is necessary for certain purposes, the police may keep the defendant in custody until the first court appearance. So there is a key difference between the person detained for questioning who has not been charged and the person who has already been charged and is remanded in police custody after charge. What they do have in common is the fact that they have not been tried.

Besides, a recent major change likely to have an effect on the time taken to charge suspects has been the Statutory Charging Initiative, as the prosecutors of the CPS provide guidance in pre-charge procedures. It tends to lead to delays and increases the length of time suspects are held in custody. The CPS has become more and more important as it is responsible for charging decisions in all but minor cases. In the majority of cases, the CPS only makes decisions after the investigation has been completed and all the available evidence collected. The problem, however, is that the CPS depends almost entirely on the police for the information on which it must reach a decision.

So the powers of the police to remand persons whom they have interviewed and may wish to interview again, and persons whom they have charged, pending their trial, are contained in the Police and Criminal Evidence Act 1984, undeniably a piece of legislation important to this day, as amended by the Criminal Justice and Public Order Act 1994 and by the Serious Organized Crime and Police Act 2005.

The legislation that followed PACE further increased the role of the police starting with the Criminal Justice and Public Order Act 1994 that amended the 1984 Act. Indeed, it increased the discretionary power of the police by conferring to the latter the power to grant bail with conditions. As Andrew Ashworth and Mike Redmayne observed:

> [...] previously, the police were only able to grant unconditional bail or to keep the suspect in custody overnight pending court appearance. If the introduction of conditional bail led to a small overall reduction in overnight detention of suspects by the police, it led to a significant drop in the cases of unconditional bail. (218)

In the wake of the 1994 Act, the police developed the practice of using their bail powers as a way of bargaining in their dealings with suspects. The Serious Organized Crime and Police Act 2005 that came into force on 1, January 2006 went even further as under the new section 24, the police may make an arrest for any offence provided certain conditions exist: it abolished the earlier concept of arrestable and serious arrestable offences under PACE 1984. Part 3 (sections 110, 111 and schedule 7) of the new version of PACE devoted to police powers has reshaped the basis of arrest powers for the police and abolished the notion of offences likely to justify custody. All offences now whatever their gravity can lead to custody, which means that remanding someone in custody in England can be used independently from the gravity of the offence. So the principle of proportionality no longer applies to custody in the UK. The danger is a disproportionate breach of someone's liberty which is clearly incompatible with the ECHR.

By contrast, in France, under the law (n° 2000-516) of 15 June, 2000, which strengthened the presumption of innocence and victims' rights, police custody must not only be strictly limited to the needs of criminal procedure but also be proportionate to the seriousness of the alleged offence and respectful of the person's dignity.

The case law of the European Court of Human Rights (ECtHR) as the main driver for reforming custody in France in 2011

In France, the reform of police custody was the direct result of a ruling by the Constitutional Council, relying on the case law of the ECtHR *Salduz v. Turkey* [27.11.2008]. In this case, the Court set out the importance of effective custodial legal advice as a crucial part of the accuser's right to a fair trial under Article 6(3) (c) of the ECHR. In July 2010, the French Constitutional Council (CC) ruled that the police custody regime as it existed in France was unconstitutional because a lawyer was not present: the suspect was allowed only a 30-minute consultation and was not told of his right to silence. That landmark decision (n° 2010) 14/22 QPC was made under the new reference procedure called the "priority question of constitutionality" or in French *la question prioritaire de constitutionnalité* on 30 July, 2010. It allows the French Constitutional Council to monitor the constitutionality of laws that have already been enacted. Thus, any French citizen may argue before a court that a statutory provision applicable to his case is not in agreement with the Constitution. (Accoyer)

The CC was referred to by the French Court of Cassation under the provisions of Article 61-1 on QPC regarding the rules of police custody. It refers to an injunction from the French CC to the French government. It is important to bear in mind that public authorities as well as administrative and judicial authorities are bound by the decisions of the French CC and no appeals lie against them. The CC also fixed the government a deadline, giving it one year (1 July, 2011) to reform police custody to make it compatible with the law. On Tuesday, 25 January, 2011, by 320 votes to 32, the French National Assembly voted to adopt a government reform that would extend the presence of the defence lawyer during the police detention and interrogation of criminal suspects.

The law (n° 2011-392) of 14 April, 2011 goes further than any previous reforms of police custody in France in enhancing a suspect's rights. For the first time, it provided for a clear definition of police custody—maintaining a person at the disposal of the police who has not been convicted nor charged in order no longer "to interrogate" but only "to hear" the suspect. Besides, it limits the use of police custody to offences likely to lead to one-year imprisonment. Thus, under this law, custody is a coercive measure determined by the judicial police, the equivalent of the Criminal Investigation Department, under the control of judicial authorities applied to a person against whom there is one or several reasons to believe that he/she has committed or attempted to commit a crime or misdemeanour (punishable by one-year imprisonment) and who is maintained at the disposal of officers leading the (police) investigation. So in France, unlike England, custody is linked to the gravity of the offence committed or likely to have been committed.

It also claims the fundamental principle of the dignity of the suspect, making it compulsory to notify the suspect his/her right to remain silent which had been abolished by the law of 18 March, 2003. The French prosecutor must be informed of the suspects' custody rights from its very beginning. Judicial police functions in France, which are investigative rather than preventive, are defined in the Code of Criminal Procedure, under Article 14 as "establishing the commission of offences, collecting evidence and seeking out offenders" under the direction of the prosecutor. (West 224) Under Article 62-3 the prosecutor is the one who evaluates whether maintaining a suspect in custody is necessary and proportionate to the gravity of the offence. He is also the one who makes the decision to extend the custody beyond 24 hours. After 24 hours, it is compulsory for the suspect to be taken before the prosecutor, either physically or via a video-conference.

In addition, under the 2011 law the suspect has the right to be examined by a doctor from the very beginning of custody as well as the right to have a private conversation with a lawyer. The latter has access to the custody record and can be present during the "hearing" of the suspect. So today the suspect can benefit from legal counsel throughout the time spent in custody. It is all the more essential as for the European Court of Human Rights, the importance of the police inquiry requires the presence of a lawyer during custody.

The 2011 law is undoubtedly major progress all the more since in France for a long time the lawyer was maintained at bay from the suspect to prevent defence rights from hindering the search for truth. French lawyers only played a role at the end of the criminal procedure to plead. The latest reform of police custody in France focused on the role of criminal lawyers during police custody. As the French lawyer Jean-Yves Le Borgne explained: "the main issue raised by police custody has to do with the assistance of legal counsel, which is essential to protect people who at this stage are/and should be treated as innocent."[1] Under the new law, suspects are allowed access to legal advice throughout their detention and significantly during their interrogation by the police. For the first time, the lawyer has access to any statements made by the suspect, though not to

[1] J-Y Le Borgne speaking at the Paris Maison du Barreau day conference "bilan de la garde à vue: un an après," 3 April, 2012.

any other police evidence. So the key aspect of the reform of French police custody is to allow the presence of a lawyer from the outset and throughout. Yet, a main weakness of the latest reform of police custody in France is that lawyers can only attend the hearings if the suspect asks for legal counsel and they still do not have access to the whole file.

Besides, another major source of controversy is the status of the French prosecutor, which was challenged by both the European Court of Human Rights and the French Court of cassation notably in the decision *Medvedyev v. France* [29.03.2010] as he is not a legal authority along the lines of Article 5(3) of the European Convention. So France still does not totally comply with the ECHR. Neither does England but for slightly different reasons that have more to do with the still questionable police practices and their reluctance to fully cooperate with the CPS and defence lawyers.

The shortcomings of the reform of police custody: no full access to legal advice

In the words of Andrew Ashworth and Mike Redmayne, "the European Court of Human Rights insisted that a person should have a right to legal assistance before being deprived of liberty, especially before trial." (227) One of the reasons for allowing suspects the right to consult a lawyer at a police station is to ensure that the conduct of the police towards the suspect is scrupulously fair. In the case of *Saduz v. Turkey* [27.11.2008] the ECtHR set out the importance of effective custodial legal advice as a crucial part of the accused's right to a fair trial under Article 6(3) (c) that reads:

> Everyone charged with a criminal offence has the right to defend himself in person or through legal assistance of his own choosing or, if he has not sufficient means to pay for legal assistance, to be given it free when the interests of justice so require.

In all the cases previously mentioned, France and the United Kingdom were sanctioned because they had, in some way or another, denied suspects the assistance of a lawyer thus affecting their defence rights while in custody. In each case, the ECtHR reiterated that systematic restriction of access to a lawyer pursuant to the relevant legal provisions breached Article 6 of the ECHR.

The right to legal advice applies at the investigative stage where the attitude of the suspect is decisive in any subsequent criminal proceedings.

But without going further with the analysis, it is important to recall the main tasks assigned to defence lawyers that is to protect the suspect and then represent the accused at trial, but beyond that to protect the proper functioning of the system, thus ensuring a full and wide ranging investigation. This is all the more important since the pre-trial investigation is dominated by the police in both countries as previously mentioned.

Yet, the terms under which the lawyer may assist the suspect differs depending on the legal culture. The French one is based on the importance granted to confession sometimes to the detriment of the rules of evidence and to a certain suspicion towards lawyers, especially defence lawyers seen as a necessary evil, as opposed to the English legal culture where lawyers are everywhere. Indeed, in England and Wales the suspect is entitled to legal advice at any time and lawyers are expected to engage vigorously on behalf of their clients at every stage of the process.

In the words of the experts of the Royal Commission on Criminal Procedure, the Philips Royal Commission, that was to pave the way for PACE 1984, legal counsel aims notably at "minimizing the effects of arrest and custody on the suspect." (4.77) In the wake of the implementation of PACE the courts enforced a strict reading of its section 58 guaranteeing legal advice.

In England and Wales, legal assistance is available at different stages in the process. Not only is there a right to free legal advice introduced in the 1980s at the police station, but there are duty solicitor schemes to facilitate this providing 24-hour advice across the country and to advise on representation in court. The Police Station Duty Solicitor Scheme was set up following PACE 1984 granting all suspects held at a police station the right to obtain legal advice. It is important to note that, unlike legal aid in France, there is no means or merits test and the service is free. Local solicitors operate a rota scheme so that, theoretically, there is a 24-hour service under which a solicitor can be contacted by almost every police station. Under the PACE Code of Practice, the police must tell a detained person of the scheme. Yet, suspects may choose to call their own solicitor. The provision of legal advice at the police station is generally satisfactory in the country. In some 90% of cases a defendant requesting a duty solicitor will see one within 45 minutes. But the conditions for giving and receiving legal advice are not always sufficient to satisfy the ECHR. Indeed, police officers, especially a few years after the enactment of PACE 1984, tried to prevent suspects from receiving legal advice by failing to inform them of the duty Solicitor Scheme or by not telling them it was free. Besides, when they did inform the suspect of his rights, they warned him that it would mean delay or would not be very helpful. Today, posters must be prominently displayed in custody areas of police stations and detained persons must be told their rights to legal advice orally and given in addition a written notice about the scheme.

However, as Andrew Ashworth and Mike Redmayne stated "the majority of suspects do not receive legal advice and do not have a legal adviser with them during police questioning." (88) Indeed, some suspects tend to decline legal advice if they think that having a solicitor will increase their time spent in custody. Besides, some legal advice is given over the telephone and some lawyers attend the police station only briefly giving advice but leaving before the suspect is being questioned by the police. (CPS Annual Report 43)

Unethical practices on the part of some lawyers are driven by financial considerations, arising from the structure of the legal aid system. Thus, some defence lawyers fail to protect clients in police station, sometimes out of a lack of motivation, from improper questioning. Lee Bridges and Satnam Choongh explained that:

> [S]ome do not even have the proper qualifications—as lawyers tend to delegate custodial legal advice to unqualified and untrained staff hence the introduction of a quality scheme to improve the quality of legal advice. (208)

As for legal counsel in France, which as seen previously was to be at the heart of the reform of police custody, it was considered to be far too limited, notably by French lawyers. There are numerous authorities who think that the 2011 reform does not go far enough because legal advice can be delayed by the prosecutor for 12 hours in ordinary cases, 24 hours in suspected organized crime cases and 72 hours in suspected terrorism cases. Besides, lawyers will be present but not (very) effective all the more as the police can object to questions put by the lawyer. French lawyers still have difficulties when attempting to speak to their clients while they are in police custody.

What is more, people in custody do not always know that they have the right to remain silent; there is a general lack of information about the right to remain silent in France. It is interesting to recall that it used to be compulsory. Yet, on 23 January, 2003 the French National Assembly passed the Internal Security Law notably expanding police powers. It relaxed requirements for searches and for keeping information about suspects by allowing the DNA fingerprinting of anyone "for whom there is a plausible reason to believe that they have committed an offence." Moreover, it eliminated the obligation to notify suspects of their right to remain silent. So the merit of the new 2011 law is to have re-introduced this fundamental right. Reintroducing the obligation to notify suspects of their right to silent is an important step but it is not sufficient. In fact, one has to bear in mind that the privilege against self-incrimination or the right to silence is not contained in Article 6 of the ECHR which is limited to a general right to a fair trial, Yet those fundamental rights are protected by the ECtHR which has implied them into Article 6 in various judgments on the fairness of criminal trials. In its famous decision *Funke v. France* [25.02.1993], it introduced the privilege against self-incrimination into its case law. Thus, the right to remain silent must normally be given to a suspect in a criminal case before interrogation by the police begins.

Access to a lawyer from the outset of detention and the right to confer privately with a lawyer without time limits is essential. However, there are currently in French police custody practices severe restrictions on lawyers, especially on their abilities to acquaint themselves with the investigation and charges as they are told the charges but have no access to the file itself. To protect their clients and build their case, lawyers need to have access to files.

Police custody and suspects' rights affected by cuts in legal aid

In both countries, custody takes place in a police environment. If England is based on a fairly different legal culture from France, police officers have sometimes put much pressure on suspects in order to extract confessions from them, which is not much different from duress. But the police are not the only ones open to criticism. Some lawyers do not always take their role as legal counsel as seriously as they should and are not always aware of the importance of protecting human rights during police custody. The latter point is likely to get worse by recent cuts in legal aid imposed by the Cameron government, and thus a decline in the remuneration of counsel in both countries. Legal aid funding is very poor in France. As for England and Wales, section 12 of the Legal Aid, Sentencing and Punishment of Offenders Act 2012 will subject initial advice and assistance for an individual who has been arrested and is being held in custody at a police station or other premises to an assessment of the individual's financial resources, whereas under the current provisions of the Access to Justice Act 1999, there is no such means testing. Regarding the impact of cuts in legal aid, and the fact that more and more litigants rely on conditional fee agreements, one might note that application fees can be so high that they have a deterrent effect. Besides, the number of litigants in person has recently significantly increased. More vulnerable citizens do not always understand the procedure and need assistance from the judge. This is just another illustration of the negative impact of cutting legal aid, since instead of saving time and money, those cuts might lead to longer more expensive legal proceedings. Thus, not only are such cuts likely to impact on suspects' rights in custody but might also deny individuals access to justice. As a consequence, in a country that protected individuals from arbitrary arrest and detention as early as the seventeenth century with the *Habeas Corpus* Act, the rights of suspects in custody still cannot be taken for granted.

One might wonder whether the reform of police custody in France has put an end to the culture of confessions. What seems of particular importance—and a cause of great concern at the same time—is that the 2011 law did not introduce the far-reaching reforms necessary to bring French criminal procedure into line with international Human Rights obligations. The ruling of the French CC itself was far too limited as it excluded cases involving terrorism, drug trafficking and organized crime. France and England do have now legal structures supposed to secure basic rights to people remanded in custody. But this is not enough it they are not supported by a will to apply them fully to suspects in compliance with the requirements of the ECHR. For in the words of Lord Bingham "The right to personal freedom, while it cannot be absolute, is in truth a Human Right and Fundamental Freedom, to be respected and protected as such" (Bingham 208). By this test, custody procedures in both countries must be regarded as seriously flawed.

Works cited

Cases

Funke v. France [25.02.1993].
Imbrioscia v. Switzerland [24.11.1993].
Magee v. the UK [06.06.2000].
Salduz v. Turkey [27.11.2008].
Medvedyev v. France [29.03.2010].
Brusco v. France [14.10.2010].

Primary sources

Annual Report and Resource Accounts. Crown Prosecution Service, London, 2010-2011.

BRIDGES, Lee, and Satnam Choongh. "Improving Police Station Legal

Advice." Law Society Research Study. London: Law Society 31 (1998).
"Guidance on the Safer Detention and Handling of Persons in Police Custody." National Policing Improvement Agency. London: National Policing Improvement Agency, 2nd ed., 2012.
HERSCHEL, Leigh Leonard, and Lucia Zedner. "A Report on the Administration of Criminal Justice in the pre-trial phase in France and Germany." Royal Commission on Criminal Justice. London: HMSO, 1992.
"La Garde à Vue." Les Documents de Travail du Sénat. Série Législation Comparée 204 (December 2009).
MCCONVILLE, Michael, and Jacqueline Hodgson. "Custodial Legal Advice and the Right to Silence." Royal Commission on Criminal Justice. London: HMSO, 31 December 1993.
PHILIPS, C. *et al.* "The Investigation and Prosecution of Criminal Offences in England and Wales: The Law and Procedure." London: HMSO, 1981.
"Police arrest/ assistance of a lawyer." European Court of Human Rights: Fact sheet, February 2011. Page consulted in May 2013. URL: <http://www.echr.coe.int/NR/rdonlyres/1DA09157-E81D-4DAF-A378-956F2A3BBB79/0/FICHES_Garde_%C3%A0_vue_EN.pdf>.
The Code For Crown Prosecutors: Consultation Document. The Director of Public Prosecutions. London: CPS Policy Directorate, October 2009.

Secondary sources

ACCOYER B., former President of the French National Assembly in "La QPC, Premier Bilan and Perspective." *Juris Classeur Penal* 48 (2010).
ASHWORTH, Andrew, and Mike Redmayne. *The Criminal Process*. Oxford: Oxford University Press, 3rd ed., 1998.
BEVAN, Vaughan, and Ken Lidstone. *The investigation of Crime: A Guide to Police Powers*. London: Butterworths, 1991.
BINGHAM, Thomas. *Lives of the Law.* Oxford: Oxford University Press, 2011.
CARBONNEAU, Thomas E. "The French Legal Studies Curriculum. Its History and Relevance as a Model of Reform." *McGill Law Journal* 25 (1980): 445- 477.
CLAYTON, R., and H. Tomlinson. *The Law of Human Rights*. Oxford: Oxford University Press, 2nd ed., 2009.
CORNU, Gérard. *Vocabulaire juridique.* Paris: PUF, 2nd ed., 1990.

INCHAUSPE, Dominique. *L'Habeas Corpus.* Editions confluences, collection Voix de la Cité, 1999.

JENNINGS, Jeremy. *Revolution and the Republic. A History of Political Thought in France since the 18th Century.* Oxford: Oxford University Press, 2011.

KEMP V., and N.J. Balmer. "Whose time is it anyway? Facts associated with duration in police custody." *The Criminal Law Review* 10 (2012): 735-751.

LE BORGNE, Jean-Yves. *La Garde à Vue, un résidu de barbarie.* Paris: Le Cherche Midi, 2011.

LEROY, Jacques. *La Garde à Vue après la réforme.* Paris: Lexis Nexis, 2011.

LLOYD, Jason. *An Introduction to Policing and Police Powers.* Cavendish Publishing Ltd, 2000.

PRADEL, J. *Les atteintes à la liberté avant jugement en droit pénal comparé.* Travaux de l'Institut des Sciences Criminelles. Poitiers: Cujas, 1992.

STEINER, Eva. "The Application of the ECHR by French Courts." *K.C.L.J.* 49 (1995).

WALKER, Clive, and Keir Starmer. *Miscarriages of Justice: A Review of Justice in Error.* Oxford: Oxford University Press, reprinted 2004.

WEST, Andrew. *The French Legal System.* London: Butterworths, 2nd ed., 1998.

ZEDNDER, Lucia. "Erring on the side of safety." Guest Lecture, University of Oslo, 19 May, 2011.

PRE-TRIAL DETENTION IN THE FRENCH AND ENGLISH CRIMINAL JUSTICE SYSTEMS: TOWARDS A BALANCE BETWEEN SECURITY AND LIBERTY

AKILA TALEB
SPECIAL TRIBUNAL FOR LEBANON

Effective access by the defence to the inquiry file and lack of independence of French public prosecutors

In all democracies governed by the rule of law, the overall objective of the criminal justice system is to reduce crime so as to increase security without unjustified infringement of fundamental rights. In order to maintain the necessary balance between the protection of public order, and due process of law, the legislator has to ensure that the legal framework respects both aspects of the criminal justice process. Despite national specificities in their legal traditions, England and France are both deeply involved in pursuing this goal nowadays considered as a European priority.

As such, pre-trial detention rules in both countries seem to converge, the main proof being the introduction of the defence lawyer during police interviews held at the police station. In England, the provision introduced by the Police and Criminal Evidence (PACE) Act 1984 has existed for almost 30 years (Taleb 2012) whereas in France this provision was introduced in 2011.[1] The comparison between the French and the English systems has been made possible thanks to the European Court's ruling on this very specific issue. By clarifying its position on pre-trial detention, the Strasbourg Court, in *Brusco v. France*, came to the conclusion that French legislation on police custody was not compatible with the European principles since the defence counsel was not given access to the

[1] Law n° 2011-392 of 14 April, 2011 on police custody, JO 15 April, 2011.

interrogation room at the time the suspect was being questioned. The Court also noted the absence of any provision regarding the notice of the right to silence which would benefit to the suspect. As a result, the European Court deemed that the French *garde à vue* did not meet the requirements of Article 6(1) and (3) of the Convention (right to effective legal assistance, right to remain silent and right not to incriminate oneself). The case of *Brusco v. France* thus led to a French reform that ended up with the adoption of the 14 April, 2011 Act which specifically mentions that any suspect held in custody has a right to legal advice, even during police questioning. (Art. 64, Code of Criminal Procedure (CCP)) In other words, due to the recent position of the European Court of Human rights, the police custody Act 2011 has introduced better safeguards for the suspect when being deprived of his or her freedom during police detention.

It is quite interesting, as a preliminary remark, to dwell on the legal definition of the suspect since most of pre-trial detention powers will be authorised and used unless the relevant authorities ensure that the person can be reasonably suspected of a criminal offence. As a starting point, it is thus relevant to clarify the meaning of "suspect" under French and English law. Under French criminal law, a suspect is defined as "any person against whom there exists any plausible reason or reasons to suspect that he has committed or attempted to commit an offence." (Art. 55-1 CCP)

Both the police officer of the rank of a *officier de police judiciaire* and the *procureur de la République* have the power to decide on pre-trial detention and/or on the extension of its duration. (Art. 63-1 and 2 CCP) Under English criminal law, a suspect is defined as a person against whom:

> [...] the custody officer has reasonable grounds for believing that his detention without being charged is necessary to secure or preserve evidence relating to an offence for which he is under arrest or to obtain such evidence by questioning him. If the custody officer has reasonable grounds for so believing, he may authorise the person arrested to be kept in police detention. (PACE section 37(2) and (3))

Hence, both the French and English Acts define custody as a measure of coercion towards a person against whom there is reasonable suspicion to believe that he or she has committed or is about to commit a criminal offence. Moreover, in both systems, pre-trial detention powers are held by either a member of the police or judicial authorities.

As a result, at the preliminary stage of the criminal justice process, common rules have emerged in France and in England. Hence, despite a few specificities, the powers of coercion held by the French and the English authorities, in the course of a criminal investigation, are quite similar. Of these, two will be considered herein to underline the similarities between the two systems. As for France, there have been some quite dramatic changes in the police custody regime and as for England, an intermediary public body has been introduced between the police institution (police world) and the judicial institution (judge's world) thus leading to the prosecution process being controlled by the State. A national body, namely the Crown Prosecution Service (CPS,) in charge of public prosecutions throughout England and Wales, was set up. These measures have somehow contributed to the convergence of both systems in spite of their initial divergences. Nevertheless, unless some points are improved, the converging process will only partly take place. These issues, which call for a necessary change especially in France so as to fully complete the convergence between the two systems, also reveal the difficulties to combine crime control objectives which include public order's protection and due process of law objectives which imply the protection of fundamental rights. In this paper, we will consider two topical issues that have not been resolved yet. Firstly, the question of the effective legal assistance by the defence lawyer in case counsel has limited access to the inquiry file and secondly the question of the lack of independence of the French public prosecutor.

Limited access to the inquiry file

Careful attention must be paid to this question in order to underline the differences between French and English rules, the former being less protective. If this issue were to come to the attention of the European Court, it would be interesting to wonder what the Court's position would be and as a result what the potential outcome would be with regard to the French provision.

The reluctance of French law over the access to the inquiry file

If the principle according to which suspects held in custody shall be entitled, on request, to have a lawyer (Art. 63-4-1 CCP) or a solicitor (Code of practice C 2012, para. 6.8) present when they are interviewed, has clearly and definitely been granted to detainees the question of the access to the entire inquiry file remains at stake. On that specific point, compared to English law, French law seems to have a lot to catch up. Indeed, under PACE Code of practice C, para. 2.4.:

> [...] a solicitor or appropriate adult must be permitted to inspect a detainee's custody record as soon as practicable after their arrival at the station and at any other time whilst the person is detained.

It seems that pursuant to English rules, there is no limited access to the file, which clearly is not the case in the French CCP. For this reason, E. Cape deems that English legal advisers should "keep an accurate record of their consultations with their clients and of the police interview." (Cape 5&7, Sanders, Young, Burton 243)

Under French law, the lawyer assisting the detainee is only allowed to consult some of the documents contained in the police file. These documents are the official report that notifies the suspect that he or she is from now on in custody and the rights he or she is entitled to, the official report that mentions the content of police interviews and the medical certificate, which must specifically state the fitness of the person held in custody. These are the only documents counsel can have access to. Moreover, during police questioning, lawyers cannot take copies of the evidence and can only write down notes. (Art. 63-4-1 CCP) If the police officer deems it necessary, he can prevent counsel from asking questions and decide to terminate the interview. (Art. 63-4-3 CCP) Lastly, access to other acts of investigation by lawyers such as searches is also denied and private consultations with their clients must not exceed thirty minutes. (Art. 63-4 CCP)

As most lawyers remained dissatisfied by these provisions which were severely criticized, the new regime was challenged before the French Constitutional Council (*Conseil Constitutionnel* CC) through the *question prioritaire de constitutionnalité* (QPC called the "priority question of constitutionality") procedure which provides responses to questions of constitutional importance. Consequently, lawyers claimed that the new provisions did not meet the European minimum requirements as far as pre-trial detention rights were concerned since these provisions did not enable them to provide effective legal assistance as guaranteed by the European Court. In other words, according to the applicants, unless they were granted access to all material evidence in the inquiry dossier, they would not be able to provide effective legal assistance as required by the Strasbourg Court.

Despite the applicants' relevant arguments, the French CC ruled that the new legal provisions were compatible with the French Constitution.[2] The CC recalled the police's duty to investigate crime and bring offenders

---

[2] Constitutional Council (CC), decision n° 2011-191/194/195/196/197 QPC, 18 November, 2011.

to justice by stating that pursuant to Article 14 of the CCP, the criminal police are responsible for "establishing breaches of criminal law, gathering evidence and searching for the perpetrators." The CC thus considered:

> [...] that the contested provisions do not have the objective of enabling a discussion as to the legality of investigative acts or whether the evidence gathered by the investigators is well founded if it has not resulted in a decision by the judicial authorities to prosecute and which may, depending upon the circumstances, be discussed before the examining judge or during the trial; that they no longer have the objective of enabling a discussion as to whether the decision to detain the person in police custody was well founded, which is circumscribed by the law to a period of twenty four hours and may be renewed only once. (CC 18 November, 2011 para. 28)

It further considered that any challenge to the evidence is not expected to take place at the preliminary stage where no decision to prosecute has been made but later, during the judicial inquiry, or before the court, at trial. Moreover the council noted that:

> [...] in matters relating to criminal offences and misdemeanors, no person may be convicted solely on the basis of statements which he has made if he has not previously been able to consult with and be assisted by a lawyer. (CC 18 November, 2011 para. 25)

In other words, the French provisions which limit the lawyer's access to the police file strike a balance that is not unreasonable. For these reasons, the Council ruled that:

> [...] the claims based on the fact that the contested provisions on police custody may not guarantee a fair balance between the rights of the parties and the contradictory nature of this stage in the criminal procedure are groundless. (CC 18 November, 2011 para. 28)

The same issue was further raised before the *Cour de cassation* except for the fact that the procedure required the Court to rule on the conformity of the new regime with the European Convention and not with the Constitution. In its decision, the French Supreme Court upheld the Constitutional Council's position by stating that the limited access by the defence lawyer to the police custody file did not deprive the suspect of a concrete and effective right to a fair trial as long as the access to the entire file was later granted before the investigating authority or the trial court.[3]

---

[3] Cass. Crim. 19 September, 2012, n° 11-88.111.

The decision is all the more surprising since the Supreme Court is usually expected to be less "conservative" than the Constitutional Council. Furthermore, this issue came to the attention of the *Cour de cassation* because the Court of Appeal had previously considered that an effective legal assistance required the defence lawyer to have access to the case file in its entirety. Consequently, it appears that when ruling on this issue, both the Constitutional Council and the Supreme Court undoubtedly gave priority to crime control objectives over due process of law.

Thus, the debate remains open and the issue is likely to be dealt with before the European Court. In such circumstances, the question the Court would have to answer could be formulated as follows: deprived of some material evidence of the file, can the defence lawyer still ensure an effective legal assistance to his client during pre-trial detention? It would be interesting to try to determine the plausible future outcome if this question ever came to the attention of the Strasbourg Court.

The plausible future outcome in regard to the European Court's position

If the question of limited access to the inquiry file were to come to the European Court, the Court would likely hold that there is a violation of the Convention principles with strong elements to support such a decision. Firstly, when the question of having a lawyer present during police interviews was at stake, well before the October 2010 ruling, French trial courts held that the French custody regime did not provide effective legal assistance to the suspect as required by the European Convention.[4] It is then possible to consider that the same scenario may occur since the Court of Appeal of Agen ruled that limited access to the inquiry file did not provide effective legal assistance as required by the Convention principles.[5] Therefore, although the *Cour de cassation* nullified the Court of Appeal's decision, the European Court may rule differently.

Moreover, in *Svipsta v. Latvia*, the Strasbourg Court acknowledged:

> [...] the need for criminal investigations to be conducted efficiently, which may imply that part of the information collected during them is to be kept secret in order to prevent the accused from tampering with evidence and undermining the course of justice. (para. 137)

[4] C.A Nancy, 19 January, 2010; T.G.I Paris, 12th chamber, 28 January, 2010.

[5] C.A Agen, 24 October, 2011.

Yet the Court made it clear that:

> [...] this legitimate goal cannot be pursued at the expense of substantial restrictions on the rights of the defence. Therefore, information which is essential for the assessment of the lawfulness of a person's detention should always be made available in an appropriate manner to his or her lawyer. (*Ibid.*)

More recently, in *Dayanan v. Turkey*, the Court deemed that:

> [...] the fairness of proceedings requires that an accused be able to obtain the whole range of services specifically associated with legal assistance. In this regard, counsel has to be able to secure without restriction the fundamental aspects of that person's defence: discussion of the case, organisation of the defence, collection of evidence favourable to the accused, preparation for questioning, support of an accused in distress and checking of the conditions of detention. (para. 32)

Having considered the European previous solutions in similar issues related to pre-trial detention rights, we can assert that there may be a realistic prospect of conviction if the French legislation were reviewed by the Court. But again, no absolute certainty lies as to the outcome. This reveals, here again, the difficult task that consists in keeping a balance between security requirements governed by the crime control model and freedom requirements governed by the due process of law model.

Yet, there is another issue of paramount importance that is also controversial in France and that would lead to draw a line between the French and English criminal justice systems. It tackles the French prosecutors' status and their lack of independence towards both the executive and the judicial powers.

The lack of independence of French public prosecutors

Although France and England systems both have a national service in charge of public prosecutions, the two institutions are, to some extent, different from each other especially as far as pre-trial detention rules are concerned. The main difference between the French and the English public prosecutor lies in the fact that unlike the latter, the former holds the power to deprive the suspect from his or her freedom. Yet, since the Strasbourg Court's ruling in *Moulin v. France*, the French prosecutors' power turns out to be controversial as it reveals a lack of independence from both the executive and the judicial powers.

The limits to English and French prosecution systems' similarities

Among the recommendations made by the Report of the Royal Commission on Criminal Procedure, chaired by Sir Cyril Philips and published in 1981, was the institution of a new "locally-based prosecuting service with some national features." The reason for such a change was that the Commission acknowledged it was no longer possible for the police to both investigate and prosecute crime. Hence, the Commission recommended that while the investigation powers as well as the decision whether or not to charge a person should remain within the police's jurisdiction, the decision to prosecute should be transferred and fall within the scope of a new national Prosecution Service. It also recommended the service be headed by the Director of Public Prosecutions (DPP) under the superintendence of the Attorney General; the service would not accountable to any local body (Royal Commission on Criminal Procedure 1981). The concept was embodied in the Prosecution of Offences Act 1985 that created the CPS which started to operate in 1986.

Between 1986 and 2003, the CPS was responsible for the conduct of all criminal proceedings after there had been a charge by the police or a summons. The CPS was thus competent for taking over all the proceedings initiated by the police. If it deemed the proceedings were not appropriate either because there was an obvious lack of evidence of guilt which severely weakened the case or because it was in the public interest to do so, the CPS had the power to discontinue a case. Then, in 2003, the adoption of the Criminal Justice Act introduced a new statutory charging scheme in England and Wales. Although police officers continued to play an important role in the new system, the ultimate power to decide whom and what to charge was largely removed from them and transferred to the CPS. This new charging scheme, being the direct consequence of one of the recommendations made by Lord Justice Auld in his report (Auld 41, Ashworth and Redmayne 197,) allowed English prosecutors, in relation to the majority of offences and just like their French counterparts to decide whether or not a case should enter the criminal justice system. (see Brownlee)

Consequently, in both countries prosecution authorities contribute to achieving the objective by ensuring that the perpetrators of the crimes are called to account for their actions in a legally correct and effective way. As such, the prosecutor serves as an important link in the legal chain constituted by the police, the prosecution service and the law courts since he or she is the one who, within a specific legal framework, determines whether or not a case shall enter the criminal justice process.

Nevertheless, in spite of this similarity between French and English prosecution systems, some specificities exist in the two systems. It is indeed relevant to note that the CPS is an independent body from both the police and the judiciary. As such, members of the CPS have no power to make a decision about detention at any stage of the criminal justice process. Consequently, they have no power to deprive the suspect of his or her freedom. Under English law, this competence falls within the jurisdiction of the custody officer for a period of no more than 24 hours. Any extension beyond this initial period can only be authorised by an officer of a superintendent rank or above and must not exceed 36 hours. If the detention needs to be further extended, only judges from the magistrates' courts can do so, as long as the maximum length of detention does not exceed 96 hours after the initial "relevant time." (Sanders, Young and Burton 208-211)

On the contrary, at the pre-trial stage, French prosecutors hold the power to deprive the suspect of his or her freedom during the first 48 hours of the process and this power has recently been pointed out as being quite controversial. In *Moulin v. France*, the European Court held that "a judge must be independent of the executive and of the case parties, both of which are contested in relation to the French prosecutor." (Hodgson 1361) For these reasons, the Court considered that the French *Ministère public* lacked independence and could not be a regarded as a judicial authority as required by the Convention principles. (Taleb 2011)

Alongside with the liberty and custody judge, the investigating judge and the trial judge, the French prosecutor is a *magistrat*. Indeed, it is true that the *parquet* belongs to the standing judiciary as opposed to the liberty and custody judge, the investigating judge and the trial judge who belong to the sitting judiciary. Yet, it is also true that the *parquet* and the other judges have to pass the same annual competitive examination to enter the National School for the Judiciary located in Bordeaux where they receive the same training. For this reason, the *procureur de la République* is, in accordance with Article 66 of the French Constitution, the "guardian of the freedom of the individual." But, at the same time, according to the 1958 Ordinance, the *parquet* is hierarchically accountable to the Minister of Justice and to the Executive which makes it dependent on the political power and tends to undermine its judicial functions.[6] Therefore, these two main contradictory missions, both as a *magistrat* and as an actor of the

---

[6] Ordinance n° 58-1270 of 22 December, 1958 which constitutes the organic law on the status of the judiciary Art. 5.

criminal justice policy, make the prosecutors' position in the French system difficult to define as he or she is connected both to the executive power and the judiciary. This ambiguous status creates a confusion that is, according to the European Court, prejudicial to the effective and concrete application of the Convention principles.

The non-compliance of the French provisions with the Convention principles

In *Moulin v. France*, the applicant was held in custody on 13 April and detained for more than five days without being brought before a judge. Meanwhile, she actually met a prosecutor but was not brought before the investigating judge until 18 April. According to the Court, this deprivation of her freedom was contrary to Article 5(3) of the Convention that states that "everyone arrested or detained […] shall be brought promptly before a judge or other officer authorised by law to exercise judicial power." The Court then clearly asserted that the French prosecutor was not "a judge or another officer authorised by law to exercise judicial power" as required by Article 5(3) of the Convention since he or she lacked independence from both the executive power and the parties.

On the first point, the European judges note the hierarchical accountability of prosecutors to the French Minister of Justice, the absence of security of tenure available to them (as opposed to judges who are appointed for life) and the control undertaken by the prosecutor-in-chief to direct prosecutors to initiate prosecutions. Without challenging the question of the dependence between the *parquet* and the Minister of Justice which falls within a discretionary internal debate, the Court recalls that being "a judge or other officer authorised by law to exercise judicial power" implies the fulfilment of independence requirements that French prosecutors do not meet. In other words, French prosecutors' lack of independence from the executive power prevent them from being considered as a judicial authority as required by the Convention and consequently, also prevent them from exercising detaining powers to deprive someone of his or her freedom. Yet, breaking the aforementioned hierarchical link is not conceivable since almost all the European public prosecution services provide such a link. Therefore we can catch a glimpse of the European court's position on this issue. Indeed, the court tends to lean towards the conservation of the hierarchical link between French prosecutors and their Minister of Justice in return for which any power to deprive suspects from their freedom would no longer fall within the French prosecutors' jurisdiction.

This solution is to be found in the English system since the independence of the CPS actually prevents Crown prosecutors from deciding on police detention. In England and Wales, members of the CPS are part of a hierarchy at the top of which is the Director of Public Prosecutions (DPP) appointed by the Attorney General, a non-cabinet politically neutral minister who leads the Attorney General's Office. Crown prosecutors are not members of the judiciary but civil servants who have to comply with local public action plans and policies set by their Chief Crown Prosecutor. Each Chief Crown Prosecutor is accountable before the DPP who runs the CPS at a national level. Chief Crown Prosecutors are assisted by Deputy Chief Crown Prosecutors and Branch Crown Prosecutors. Yet, none of them, neither the DPP, nor Chief Crown Prosecutors, Deputy Chief Crown Prosecutors or Branch Crown Prosecutors, hold any powers with regard to pre-trial detention.

On the second point, the European judges underline the incompatibility resulting from French prosecutors having both a monopoly on public action and taking part in the process as a prosecuting party against the accused. Indeed, according to the adage "no one may be a judge in his own cause," the European Court notes that "a judge or another officer authorised by law to exercise judicial power" cannot take part in the process as a prosecuting party. Here again, the English system seems to comply with the Court's requirement since members of the CPS are experienced lawyers, either former solicitors or barristers, but, above all, civil servants. As such, there is no incompatibility if they take part in the criminal justice process as a prosecuting party. Unlike their English counterparts, French prosecutors are members of the judiciary, "guardian of the freedom of the individual," under Article 66 of the Constitution and on that ground, the CC ruled that they were entitled to detain some powers regarding pre-trial detention. Nevertheless, the European Court recalls that, under the Convention principles, a judicial authority must be independent from the case parties, which implies, contrary to the French prosecutor, that it cannot further act against the applicant during the process. In other words, the court considers that "[t]he judicial officer must offer the requisite guarantees of independence from the executive and the parties, which precludes his subsequent intervention in criminal proceedings on behalf of the prosecuting authority." (Hodgson 1388)

Consequently, there are two possible ways for French prosecutors to comply with the court's ruling. Either, they can no longer be part of the judiciary and still be part of the process against the accused or they can remain members of the French *magistrature* (judges) but will then have to cease acting as a prosecuting party. However, as the latter option is not conceivable, the only solution that remains is that French prosecutors would no longer be members of the judiciary. Therefore, here again, it is possible to catch a glimpse of the European court's position on this issue. The court tends to lean in favour of proponents of the doctrine of the separation of French prosecutors from the body of judges. As a consequence, for the time being, French prosecutors are said to exercise "a hybrid function, half executive, half judicial and [they] have become the necessary interface between the judiciary, the state and civil society." (Dalle and Soulez-Larivière; Hodgson 1368) Thus, what would the practical options be if French prosecutors' status were reformed? Two solutions seem to have been given priority.

Without considering a full independence that may lead to what the doctrine calls a *gouvernement des procureurs*, the first solution would be, to give French prosecutors a greater autonomy from the executive power. (Pradel and Guerin 660; Ficara 509) The essential hierarchical link necessary to launch a coherent nationwide public action policy at all points in the territory would be preserved. The balance would be maintained thanks to the appointment of a "Republic or a Nation Prosecutor General" at the head of the *ministère public*. (Soulez-Larivière 112) This Prosecutor General, in charge of the coherence of the penal policy for the whole country, would replace the Minister of Justice, resulting in the separation of the Prosecution Service from the executive power. Just like in England and Wales, he would exercise the DPP's functions. (Dufour 3; Pradel and Laborde)

The second solution would lead, again just like in England and Wales, to the removal of all pre-trial detention powers from French prosecutors and the transfer these powers to a *magistrat du siège*, a French judge whose status meets the requirements set by the European Court. As things stand, this could be the custody and liberty judge. (Pradel and Laborde; Hennion-Jaquet 1390; Fourment 26) Having considered these options, there certainly exists a way forward for the Prosecution Service. Nevertheless, that is only possible if the French legislation complies with the European Convention principles.

For the moment, if the *Cour de cassation* seems to support the European Court,[7] some doubts remain as to the CC's position that seems to be reluctant to any change whatsoever. The Council still firmly asserts that prosecutors are members of the judiciary.[8] The Council, thus, does not depart from its previous position. Indeed, in its decision issued on 30 July,

[7] Cass. Crim. 15 December, 2010, n° 10-83674.

[8] CC Decision n° 2010-80 QPC, 17 December, 2010.

2010, when the Council ruled that the legal provisions regulating custody were contrary to the Constitution, it actually took the opportunity to recall that prosecutors were part of the judiciary.[9] As for Parliament, both the National Assembly and the Senate have recently expressed their will to take the European court's position into account by giving only to a sitting magistrate the power to control arrests and detentions. (*Sénat* 2010, *Assemblée Nationale* 2011)

Conclusion

There is certainly a common source of law setting rules that Members States' legislations have to respect. This source of law is the European Convention on Human Rights whose provisions are regularly interpreted by the European Court. Among these provisions lie those directly linked to pre-trial detention's minimum standards. Nevertheless, one has to acknowledge that striking a balance between crime control and due process of law is no easy task. One good example is the various and sometimes diverging comments in the literature, successive legislative reforms and the interpretations made by case authorities which all are, in a context of harmonisation of domestic laws towards the European Convention, constantly evolving. Therefore "an evolution is undoubtedly to be foreseen, the question is to what extent the unification of European Criminal Justice systems will be achieved." (Taleb and Ahlstrand)

Works cited

Cases

Svipsta v. Latvia, ECHR, n° 66820/01, 9 March, 2006.
Dayanan v. Turkey, ECHR, n° 7377/03, 13 October, 2009.
Brusco v. France, ECHR, n° 1466/07, 14 October, 2010.
Moulin v. France, ECHR, n° 37104/06, 23 November, 2010.

Secondary sources

ASHWORTH, Andrew and Mike Redmayne. *The Criminal Process.* Oxford: Oxford University Press, 2010.
Assemblée Nationale Commission des lois. December 15, 2010. *Droit pénal*, alerts 1 and 2, 2011.

[9] CC Decision n° 2010-14/22 QPC, 30 July 2010, J.O. 105.

AULD, Robin. *Review of the Criminal Courts in England and Wales.* London: The Stationery office, 2001.

BROWNLEE, Ian. "The Statutory Charging Scheme in England and Wales: Towards a Unified Prosecution System?" *Criminal Law Review* (2004): 896-907.

CAPE, Ed. *Defending suspects at police stations.* Legal Action Group, 2006.

Code of practice C. 2012. *Requirements for the detention, treatment and questioning of suspects not related to terrorism in police custody by police officers.* PACE Act. Accessed January 2013. URL: <https://www.gov.uk/government/uploads/system/uploads/attachment_data/file/117589/pace-code-c-2012.pdf>.

DALLE, Hubert and Daniel Soulez-Larivière. "Débats, Justice: à la recherche de la bonne coupure." *Le Monde.* 30 May, 2002.

DUFOUR, Olivia. "Il est urgent de clarifier la situation du parquet, rentrée solennelle de la cour d'appel de Paris."*Les Petites affiches* 15 (2011): 3-5.

FICARA, Julien. "Quelle indépendance pour le parquet? Propositions pour la constitution d'un ministère public français indépendant." *AJ pénal* (2012): 509-12.

FOURMENT, François. "Après l'affaire Moulin (CEDH, 5e sect., 23 November, 2010), encore du grain à moudre." *Receuil Dalloz* 1 (2011): 26-28.

HENNION-JAQUET, Patricia. "L'arrêt Medvedyev: un turbulent silence sur les qualités du parquet français." *Dalloz* (2010): 1390-1394.

HODGSON, Jacqueline S. "The French Prosecutor in Question." Accessed 28 March, 2013. URL: <http://ssrn.com/abstract=1743407>. (2010): 1361-1411.

PRADEL, Jean and Jean-Paul Laborde. "Du ministère public en matière pénale. A l'heure d'une éventuelle autonomie." *Dalloz.* (1997): 141-145.

PRADEL, Jean and Didier Guerin. "Les relations entre le ministère public et le ministre de la justice dans l'avant-projet de réforme de la procédure pénale." *Dalloz* (2010): 660-663.

Royal Commission on Criminal Procedure. *Report.* London: HMSO Cmnd 8092, 1981.

SANDERS, Andrew and Richard Young, and Mandy Burton. *Criminal Justice.* Oxford: Oxford University Press, 2010.

Sénat. *Rapport sur la réforme de l'enquête et de l'instruction.* 8 December, 2010.

SOULEZ-LARIVIÈRE, Daniel. "Le problème du ministère public français."

AJ pénal (2011): 112-115.

TALEB, Akila and Thomas Ahlstrand. "The Public Prosecutor, its role, duties and powers in the pre-trial stage of the criminal justice process: a comparative study of the French and the Swedish legal systems." *International Review of Penal Law* 82-2/3 (2011): 523-540.

—. "Quelles perspectives d'évolution pour le parquet français? Etude des systèmes français et anglais à la lumière de la jurisprudence européenne (à propos de l'arrêt CEDH, 23 November, 2010, *Moulin v France*)." *International Review of Penal Law* 82-1/2 (2011): 233-243.

—. "Les gardes à vue française et anglaise à la lumière de la jurisprudence européenne. Le droit à l'assistance effective d'un avocat en matière de privation de liberté: droit positif et perspectives d'évolution à l'aune de la jurisprudence de la Cour européenne" in TOURNIER, Pierre-Victor (dir.). *Enfermements: Populations, Espaces, Temps, Processus, Politiques.* Paris: L'Harmattan, coll. "Criminologie" (2012): 97-110.

THE FUNCTIONAL AMBIGUITIES OF PRE-TRIAL DETENTION IN FRANCE

SACHA RAOULT
UNIVERSITY OF AIX-MARSEILLE, FRANCE

Pre-trial detention as it is practised in France seems to be the paradigm of the "indetermination postulate" that founded the critical legal studies: changes in "words" cannot easily create changes in legal practices. While pre-trial detention has been reformed countless times since the second half of the 20th century, there is little evidence that any of these reforms has had an impact on judicial practices. Most impressively, even though the use of the *contrôle judiciaire* (judicial control of a suspect that is ordered by a judge instead of detention) has nearly quadrupled in the last three decades and even if a specialized judge was created to handle remand hearings in 2000, the ratio of detained suspects has not flinched since 1980, the first year for which the data was available. (Aubusson de Cavarlay 2006: 3) Pre-trial detention has always been an issue in the last two centuries of French political debate, (see Robert 1992) and the debacle surrounding mass acquittals in the 2005 French "satanic sex scandal" (the *Outreau* case) demonstrates the terms of this debate have not drastically changed during this period. The "law in the books," as it is called in sociology of law (Erhlich and Isaacs 1922) has considerably been amended, but there is little evidence that the "law in action" is different in any way before and after each reform.

One possibility is that we are unable to reform the institution because we do not understand its unofficial social functions. Beyond the most pragmatic remand cases, which in practice seem to be much rarer than expected, one can hypothesize that pre-trial detention fulfils other societal needs: firstly, the need for a quick punishment after the fact, thus compensating for the growing length of criminal procedures; secondly, the need for a "bargain tool" that the agents of the criminal justice system might present to the suspect in search of a confession, just as the physical tools of torture were shown to the suspect as the first step of the inquisitorial Question, the only step allowed for women and children; thirdly, the need for governing social marginality by replacing objective considerations of seriousness by subjective considerations of dangerousness and social threat, as indicated by social and personal factors.

A multi-functional model of pre-trial detention mirrors the current theories of a multi-functional system of punishment. Of course, in legal theory, punishment and pre-trial detention are two completely separate institutions defined by their completely separate aim. The aim of pre-trial detention is to protect society and the judicial investigation, whereas the aim of punishment is, tautologically enough, to punish. This oversimplification is very symptomatic of legal positivism, even though a large number of European Court of Human Rights (ECtHR) cases showed that defining punishment—mostly in contrast to post-sentence detention, another so called "non-punitive" practice—was an uneasy affair. For instance, in the latest high-profile case on this subject, *Del Rio Prada v. Spain* (July 2012) it was decided that a modality in the enforcement of sentences was "punitive" mainly because the length of prison time added by this modality was substantial. However, in the view of a minority of academics including the present author, pre-trial detention, at least as it is currently practised in France, is much closer to punishment than to other pre-trial institutions often seen as similar such as police custody. Not only does a structural analysis of the "the law in the books" show that pre-trial detention is much closer in the legal realm to prison punishment than as suggested by legal theory, but an empirical exploration of the "law in practice" also suggests that pre-trial detention is commonly consciously or unconsciously understood as a form of punishment in its daily practice, and has—not unlike contemporary punishment—several ambiguous functions.

Hidden structural similarities between the legal conditions of prison punishment and of pre-trial detention

As one can see in table 1, the oversimplified view offered by classical legal theory supposes that punishment rests solely on guilt, while pre-trial detention merely rests on safety considerations. However, if one digs deeper into the legal conditions that set out practical modalities of pre-trial and post-trial detention, those conditions are in fact much closer to each other than they seemed at first glance.

If punishment rests solely on guilt in classic positivist legal theory, this theoretical view, taught in basic criminal law classes to students alongside *mens rea* and *actus reus*, is only true of a virtual form of punishment. In

France, and in many other countries, actually enforced prison punishment requires several other conditions than guilt to be imposed. Firstly, choosing prison over other kinds of punishment; secondly, deciding that the sentence will be non-suspended; thirdly, properly enforcing this non-suspended prison sentence. These are three distinct stages in legal reasoning that each necessitates supplementary legal conditions. An assessment of guilt is obviously still necessary but is no longer sufficient, and considerations of safety are no longer irrelevant.

Similarly, if the decision to order pre-trial detention supposedly rests solely on safety considerations, although it will be demonstrated later that this is not true in practice, not all criminal procedures provide pre-trial detention in the first place. In France, the only two procedures providing pre-trial detention are the *instruction* (the inquisitorial or judicial investigation conducted for serious and/or complex crimes by a judge, in which case pre-trial detention can last years) and *comparution immédiate* that can be translated as "rapid summoning," the procedure that allows a fast-track judgment to be made, and for which the suspect will be detained until a judge is ready to see him, usually for one to three days depending on which day of the week he was arrested. These two procedures providing pre-trial detention have supplementary conditions that show that safety is of course necessary but not sufficient to detain someone before trial. Especially, those conditions are often phrased around "heavy clues of suspicion" and other considerations that reveal that an assessment of guilt is not irrelevant to pre-trial detention. The results are shown in table 2.

To sum up, prison punishment does not solely rely on guilt but on other considerations including safety considerations. Pre-trial detention does not solely rely on safety considerations but also on other factors. There are strong reasons to suspect that a personal conviction that the defendant is guilty is a key factor in many pre-trial detentions, hence a not-so-clear difference between the two institutions.

The legal conditions to order a non-suspended prison sentence

If punishment rests solely on guilt in theory, ordering a non-suspended prison sentence requires supplementary conditions, beyond guilt. Before guilt is established, one must look at the principle of legality: a prison sentence has to be allowed by law for this particular type of offence. In fact, the maximum statutory sentence for the type of offence considered will be the framework throughout this examination of post-trial and pre-trial detention. A judge's order of a non-suspended prison sentence is, in some way, related to safety. The case must satisfy at least one of three conditions. First of all, the maximum statutory sentence is longer than ten years; secondly, the convict is a repeat offender; thirdly, subjective and objective considerations related to risk, the consequences of the offence and the insertion of the convict suggest a non-suspended prison sentence be ordered. (see table 3 for legal references)

Firstly, the maximum statutory sentence is longer than ten years for what is called in France *crimes*, a category that encompasses the most heinous crimes such as murder and rape. In this case, there is no need for any supplementary condition to order a non-suspended prison sentence: guilt and legality are sufficient. What is fascinating is that until quite recently, this was also the legal regime of pre-trial detention: if the maximum statutory sentence was longer than ten years, there were no factual considerations of safety necessary to order pre-trial detention. Today, things are not radically different. In the case of *crimes* to order pre-trial detention, the judge only needs to state that the consequences of the offence are particularly serious; this is what is called *"trouble à l'ordre public,"* a vague French legal notion for which Bentham did not have kind words. (Bentham art X.) One can imagine that in the case of crimes such as murder and rape, it is not very difficult to find so-called "serious consequences." The situation has not changed much: pre-trial detention can be ordered more or less automatically if the maximum statutory sentence is longer than ten years, just like a non-suspended prison sentence can be ordered by a court without further legal motivation.

Then, recidivism is mostly a safety consideration and has been used as an indicator of dangerousness and a predictor of future offences. The invention of the suspended prison sentence in France was built around political considerations for selective incapacitation in the late 19th century since the works of positivist criminologists. Recidivism, or more loosely a criminal record, is a key factor in both enforcing a prison sentence and in ordering pre-trial detention. In fact, when the maximum statutory sentence is ten years or less, the judge who orders pre-trial detention must specify what threat the suspect poses for society. Thus, recidivism is automatically used by judges to fulfil this condition. "It is not the first time the defendant is caught driving without a license, hence there is a great risk of reiteration if he is let free before the trial" is, for instance, a representative extract from a judgment ordering pre-trial detention. (Decharron 22)

Lastly, subjective and objective considerations related to risk, the consequences of the offence and the insertion of the convict suggest a non-suspended prison sentence be ordered. This last condition, which provides for the ordering of a non-suspended prison sentence for convicts that are neither recidivists, nor guilty of the most serious offences is completely safety-oriented. The only difference between these conditions and the general conditions of pre-trial detention is that the consequences of the offence can justify a non-suspended prison sentence even though the maximum sentence is ten years or less. This used to be the case for pre-trial detention before the *Outreau* reform in 2007. Considerations of integration—Is the convict well-integrated in society?—replace considerations of representation—Can we trust the suspect to appear to court when summoned to do so? Both questions are answered using the exact same criteria: employment, marital and housing situation, etc.

However, when a non-suspended prison sentence is ordered, it does not mean the convict will actually go to jail. The non-suspended prison sentence must then be enforced, a stage that also requires supplementary conditions which highlight an ever-growing overlap between pre-trial and post-trial detention.

The legal conditions to enforce a non-suspended prison sentence

First of all, a non-suspended prison sentence is automatically enforced if the convict is placed in pre-trial detention for another case, which is a particular, but not uncommon, situation that further blurs the frontier between the two institutions.

In the simplest cases, when the convict is only tried for one offence, the legal conditions to enforce a non-suspended prison sentence depend on the length of the sentence. For a sentence of up to six months, the prison sentence is normally transformed into an alternative punishment such as community service or a fine, and without any factual motivation from the judge. This six-month threshold is the same that provides for pre-trial detention (in the case of rapid summoning) in the first place.

If the sentence is up to two years, one year in case of recidivism, transforming the prison punishment into an alternative punishment is possible, and is generally practised depending on subjective considerations that are exactly symmetrical to the safety considerations providing for a prison sentence or pre-trial detention. The result of this rule is that the key moment of most criminal trials where a prison sentence is considered is when the question to know whether the convict will be detained is asked while waiting for a second judge to enforce his sentence. Of course, this is a judgment of pre-trial detention although this second trial is only an "enforcement of sentences" trial. This moment is "mixed" with the assessment of guilt and sentencing, and all three responses are given at the same time, by the same judges and based on the same facts.

Finally, if the non-suspended prison sentence is of more than two years, the sentence is enforced with no alternative punishment considered. This two-year threshold is close to the one that provides for a long period pre-trial detention of three years.

Structural similarities

Table 3 sums up the structural similarities between an enforced, non-suspended prison sentence and pre-trial detention. The parallelism is mind-boggling, since a conscious effort to bring the two institutions that close—or even to draw such a parallel in the legal doctrine—does not seem to exist. To draw this structural parallel one had to look for the legal conditions of mechanisms that are generally taught as very separate subject matters: general theory of punishment, theory of sentencing, enforcement of sentences, rapid summoning, *instruction* and pre-trial detention *stricto sensu*.

Obviously, a last technical similarity between pre-trial and post-trial detention is the correlation between the theoretical and factual length of both forms of detention. Not only is the legal maximum length of pre-trial detention mostly (although not only) tied to the maximum sentence, but there is also the automatic fungibility of the time served in pre-trial detention, a period of time that is subtracted from the post-trial detention duration so that pre-trial detention becomes *de jure* retrospectively a part of punishment. Nevertheless, the main reason why it is here argued that pre-trial detention as it is used in France is mostly a punitive practice is not because of how the law is written, but due to the way the law is implemented.

Ambiguous functions of pre-trial detention in practice: an exploration

In 2013, a team composed of Professor Gaëtan Di Marino, David Decharron, a law student, and the present author started an exploratory empirical research of pre-trial detention in Aix-en-Provence and Marseilles, collecting a body of 118 pre-trial detention judgments through personal contacts among judges and lawyers. Thorough analysis of the corpus highlights evidence of all three ambiguous social functions of pre-trial detention mentioned above: governing social marginality, punishing guilt and bargaining with the defendant.

Social marginality and pre-trial detention

Studies of the French criminal justice system as well as the experience of practitioners all point to a simple conclusion: the same factors aggravate the situation of the suspect/convict from police custody to the enforcement of sentences.[1] Many of those factors are indicators of social marginality: a criminal record, a poor professional, housing and marital situation and a foreigner's status are all aggravating factors.

This fact is well known by statisticians and social scientists. What has been discovered here is that these factors are sometimes used expressly as a reason to order pre-trial detention. Apart from the criminal record for which examples were mentioned previously, some decisions were found that solely referred to the foreigner's or housing status as a reason to expect flight risk and thus to detain the suspect, even with severe doubts about guilt. (Decharron 47)

Guilt and pre-trial detention

Given the strong similarities between punishment and pre-trial detention, the only parameter that seems to differentiate one from the other is that pre-trial detention does not theoretically rely on an assessment of guilt, except in the rare (but nevertheless revealing) case of the criminal caught in the act for the least serious offences. However, in practice, one can strongly suspect that a personal conviction that the defendant is guilty is a leading factor in ordering many pre-trial detentions.

First of all, the law allows and even encourages the judge in charge of ordering pre-trial detention to review the evidence so that he can assess the risk and the advancement of the investigation. The judge ordering pre-trial detention has access to the exact same case file as the trial judge; (Art 144 Code of Criminal Procedure CCP) thus nothing can legally prevent the pre-trial detention judge to act factually as if he were the trial judge.

Second of all, the judge will often imply orally or even in writing that the suspect is guilty of the offence for which he is investigated as the most compelling evidence of risk. No rule forbids this practice, even though the press is forbidden to do the same. (Art 9-1 Civil Code) It should be noted that the legal conditions of pre-trial detention are notoriously easy to meet once it is suggested that the defendant will probably be convicted and sentenced to jail at the end of the investigation; risk for the investigation,

---

[1] See Aubusson de Cavarlay et al. 1995; Jobard, F. and Nevanen, S. 2005: Weltzer-Lang, D. and Castex, P. 2012; Danet, J. 2013.

risk of recidivism, risk for others, consequences of the crime are all boxes than can easily be ticked.

The analysis of the collected judgments underscores a strong proportion of decisions that are more or less overtly motivated by guilt. For instance, a type of motivation that is routinely found in pre-trial detention judgments is "the flight risk is heavy since there is large evidence of guilt and that this particular crime could be heavily punished." (Decharron annex n° 56) Projecting into the future, and contemplating the sentence that will eventually be ordered against the suspect, the judge deduces the flight risk. Hence, the root of pre-trial detention is the almost certain prison punishment looming at the horizon, and the flight risk is a way to materialize this future sentence in the present.

As explained before, both mechanisms that allow pre-trial detention require a form of legal suspicion (but not guilt) to be believable against the suspect. However, in practice, suspicion and guilt seem often confused as if they were one and the same thing. For instance, here is an extract from a pre-trial detention judgment stating that "Suspicion that Mr. X. committed the crime is heavy and results from countless clues despite his denial." (Decharron 41) The phrasing does not make a lot of logical sense, since one does not expect the concept of "suspicion" to be affected by the denial of the defendant, while of course denial will be taken into account for a definitive judgment of guilt. The phrasing "Mr. X.'s guilt results from countless clues despite his denial" makes more sense, and is probably what the judge meant in this case. Other decisions seem to equate punishment and pre-trial detention. One is particularly telling: a young man caught for aggravated theft and placed in pre-trial detention by the judge who states that "going free immediately after being caught for such a serious act could lead this young impressionable mind to believe that his crime is going to be unpunished." (Decharron annex n° 96) In other words, the difference between pre-trial detention and punishment is too subtle for a teenager to understand, so a judge should detain a teenager who expects to be punished. A self-fulfilling prophecy of sorts….

These slips of the tongue mirror the "slips of the pen" one can find in the legal conditions of pre-trial detention. Even though the CCC ensures that the suspect is presumed innocent (Preliminary art.,) the legal conditions of pre-trial detention (Art. 144) refer to "the defendant's accomplices" instead of "co-suspects" and to "the victim" instead of "the plaintiff" or "the civil party." Another condition refers to the "risk of reiteration" which implies a first iteration. Of course, any consideration related to the safety of other persons cannot logically treat the suspect as if he were innocent. Moreover, what the French legal system calls an "unjustified" pre-trial detention, which has opened a right to state compensation since 2000, is not the pre-trial detention of a person that posed no threat retrospectively. Of course, there would be no way of knowing that since a prognosis of dangerousness cannot be falsified if it is acted upon; but the pre-trial detention of an innocent *a contrario* seems to imply that the pre-trial detention of a guilty person is always justified.

Apart from these qualitative considerations, there are also strong statistical correlations between the decision "to detain" made by the pre-trial detention judge and the decision "to punish" made by the trial judge. It has been estimated by statistician and pre-trial detention specialist Aubusson de Cavarlay that people who are released before trial have a whopping 22% chance of avoiding conviction, a rate that is extremely high in France where the average acquittal rate was around 5%. (4) Drawing on professional experience, freed suspects that are convicted represent very few cases of prison re-entry. The same study reveals that the length of the sentence "decided" by the trial judge is in 95% of the cases at least equal (more or less two weeks) to the time served in pre-trial detention. (*Ibid.*) Of course, this cannot be and is not a coincidence. Judges are aware of the time served and do not want the sentence ordered to be lower. What is interesting is that this strong confirmation rate between two seemingly unrelated issues (safety detention and punishment detention) is much higher than the correlation between first instance and appeal even though they are supposed to address the same question. A 2006 report of the Aix-en-Provence Court of Appeal showed that 30% of the cases in appeal were either (rarely) an acquittal or (more commonly) a sentence lower than in first instance.

Bargaining and pre-trial detention

While plea-bargaining does not really exist in France—a loose equivalent called *comparution sur reconnaissance de culpabilité* is in place but its use is minimal—rumours that the threat of pre-trial detention was being used in a process similar to *Ancient Régime* torture to obtain a confession or information on co-suspects have always been strong among practitioners. In 1995, a respected law professor somewhat candidly titled a three-page paper "Is pre-trial detention based on the silence of the accused legal?." (Bouloc) In this paper, Professor Bouloc explains that pre-trial detention as a bargaining tool has always been a problem in France, and that detainees even have a slang term for it: "to behave like sheep" (*faire le mouton*)— because it means the suspects obeys, like every other sheep, under the judge's pressure. Professor Bouloc gives a recent example of a pre-trial detention that was expressly ordered on the sole account of the silence of the defendant, and that was annulled for contravening ECtHR ruling on torture. In the end, what the criminal justice system calls "denial," that is to say the refusal to confess in spite of evidence, is widely perceived as an aggravating factor at all stages of the procedure, although it can be illegal in some cases to refer explicitly to denial to justify either pre-trial or post-trial detention.

The empirical exploration conducted demonstrated that the same ambiguity existed with bargaining as with guilt. While few decisions to detain expressly and solely rested on the defendant's "denial," many motivations were ambiguous about it. The most obvious use of the defendant's denial as a motivation for pre-trial detention is for sex crimes. For defendants accused of sexual abuses, denial is psychologically interpreted as a sign of clinical dangerousness. This motivation—supported by criminology manuals but not by the most recent meta-analyses of recidivism studies (Hanson and Morton-Bourgon 1)—is actually recurring: several local decisions referring to "dangerousness as indicated by the defendant's denial" were found in the corpus.

For other crimes, the occurrence of "denial" used by judges as the sole sign that there might collusion between the co-suspects was found (Decharron 49)—even in case files where thousands of pages of incriminating phone wiretapping evidence made the testimonies useless—or to indicate "an obvious risk of witness intimidation." (*Ibid.* 50) Consequently, while written law does not state that pre-trial detention might be based on "denial" but only on a particular danger posed by the suspect, this danger is actually deduced from "denial."

Discomfort arises as soon as one understands that these motivations imply that were the defendant to confess to his crimes wholly, he might then be freed or bailed. This ambiguity in the text seems very close, if not identical, to classical inquisitorial torture. It is well-know practice that what is found here in the texts is reinforced orally. Some policemen will, during interrogations, repeat that confessing is good for the "image-management" of the defendant when the pre-trial detention judge will review his file. Some defence lawyers will also advise their client to do so. Just before making his decision, a pre-trial detention judge once asked a defendant if he was sure he did not want to confess. The question was reportedly perceived as a form of pressure by the defendant who lodged an appeal before the *Cour de cassation*, but the appeal was rejected. (*Ibid.* 39) In the collected judgments, there was even a case of a defendant being freed in the weeks following his confession, the court stating in writing that "after his confession and the precisions that were given on the minor role the defendant played, it is no longer needed to keep him on remand." (*Ibid*, 24)

Conclusion

Prison punishment is not solely based on guilt but also on considerations of risk and the consequences of the offence. Pre-trial detention is not merely based on risk and consequences of the offence but there are strong reasons to believe that the personal conviction of the defendant's guilt plays a major part in whether detention should be ordered or not. Thus, it is safe to assume that a substantial part of pre-trial detentions are in fact more similar to a "summary/ emergency judgment" that has to be revised ex post as it may be called a "*référé-punition*" as there is in tort law, than to police custody where most of the time spent in custody is useful for the investigation. If one sees pre-trial detention as an emergency judgment, then one must admit it may then have the same multi-functional ambiguity of the main trial. It is reductionist to assume that pre-trial detention has the sole function that was officially assigned to it.

Works cited

AUBUSSON DE CAVARLAY, B. "La détention provisoire: mise en perspective et lacune des sources statistiques." *Questions pénales* XIX.3 (2006):1-4.

AUBUSSON DE CAVARLAY, B., et al. "Arrestations, classements, déférements, jugements. Suivi d'une cohorte d'affaires pénales de la police à la justice." Guyancourt: CESDIP (1995).

BENTHAM, J. *The Works of Jeremy Bentham,* published under the Superintendence of his Executor, John Bowring. Edinburgh: William Tait, 1838-1843. 11 vols.

BOULOC, Bernard. "Le silence de la personne mis en examen peut-il justifier sa mise en détention." *Recueil Dalloz* (1995): 315-316.

DANET, J. (ed.). *Une évaluation de l'administration de la justice pénale. Les nouveaux modes traitement des délits*. PUR, 2013.

DECHARRON, David. "L'aveu dans le contentieux de la détention provisoire." Mémoire Master 2, DI MARINO, Gaëtan (ed.) and Sacha RAOULT (ed.). Aix-Marseille University, 2013.

Del Rio Prada v. Spain. ECtHR. Request n° 42750/09, 10 July, 2012.

EHLRICH, Eugen and Nathan ISAACS. "The sociology of law." *Harvard Law Review* 36.2 (1922): 130-145.

HANSON, R. Karl, and Kelly E MORTON-BOURGON. "The accuracy of recidivism risk assessments for sexual offenders: a meta-analysis of 118 prediction studies." *Psychological assessment* 21.1 (2009):1.

JOBARD, F., and S. NEVANEN. "La couleur du jugement : discriminations dans les décisions judiciaires." *Revue française de sociologie* 48.2 (2007): 243-272.

ROBERT, P. (ed.). *Entre l'ordre et la liberté : la détention provisoire ; deux siècles de débats*. Paris: l'Harmattan, 1992.

WELZER-LANG, D and P. CASTEX (ed.). *Comparutions immédiates : quelle justice ? Regards citoyens sur une justice du quotidien*. Toulouse: Erès, collection "Société", 2012.

Appendices

	Punishment	Pre-trial detention
Guilt	Necessary and sufficient	Irrelevant
Safety	Irrelevant	Necessary and sufficient

Table 1. An oversimplified but clear distinction between punishment and pre-trial detention

	Post-trial detention	Pre-trial detention
Guilt	Necessary **but not** sufficient	**Not** irrelevant
Safety	**Not** irrelevant	Necessary **but not** sufficient

Table 2. Compiling all the legal conditions that allow for a detention, pre and post trial shows a growing overlap between the two institutions

Threshold	**Enforced, non-suspended prison sentence**	**Pre-trial detention**
< 6 months	Alternative punishment possible with no motivation [132-57 CPP, for all sentences =< 6 months]	Illegal
< 1 year	Alternative punishment, except if the convict is already in detention or lacks any subjective mitigating factor (professionnal, familial, medical, efforts) [132-25 to 29 for all sentences =< 1 year]	The criminal must be caught in the act [For max. sentence =< 2years, 395 CPP]. Pre-trial detention can only be for a short period [For max. sentence =< 3years, 395 CPP, procedure of rapid summoning].
< 2 years	Same as above, except in the case of recidivism [For all sentences =< 2 years]	
<10 years	The judge needs to motivate the non-suspended sentence with the **risk** and the **consequences** of the crime [Art 132-24 CP], except in the case of recidivism.	The judge needs to motivate pre-trial detention with the **risk**, in practice recidivism is a commonly used factual evidence of such risk.
>10 years	There is no need to motivate a non-suspended sentence.	~~There is no need to motivate pre-trial detention~~ Risk can be deduced only from the **consequences** of the crime.

Table 3. Summary of the structural similarities between the legal conditions of pre-trial and post-trial detention

	Enforced, non-suspended prison sentence	**Pre-trial detention**
Heavily aggravating factors	Criminal Record **Pre-trial detention (all things being equal)** Type of the crime	Criminal record Type of crime
Mildy aggravating factors	Professionnal situation Marital situation Age Sex Denial (Although it can be illegal) Crime committed with accomplices	Professionnal situation Marital situation Age Sex Denial (Although it is illegal) Crime committed with accomplices

Table 4. Law in practice: factors that heighten one's chance of being detained

DETENTION ON REMAND AND THE PRESUMPTION OF INNOCENCE: THE FRENCH PATTERN OF A TRICKY CONCILIATION

CECILE CHASSANG
UNIVERSITY OF PARIS OUEST NANTERRE, FRANCE

Detention on remand (*détention provisoire*) raises difficulties when the presumption of innocence is examined. Indeed, in the French legal system, such a form of detention is a deprivation of liberty before the criminal verdict, resulting in the imprisonment of the person officially accused of an offence and considered legally innocent. The contradiction between detention on remand and the presumption of innocence is therefore obvious. Nevertheless, both are necessary to the French criminal procedure. The former allows the criminal justice system to fulfil its mission by making the disclosure of the truth and the research of the offender easier. The latter is an essential principle in criminal procedure. It is protected at a national level—in Article 9 of the French Declaration of Human and Citizen Rights as well as in the preliminary article of the French Code of criminal procedure (CCP)—at a European level in Article 6-2 of the European Convention on Human Rights and at an international level—Article 11-1 of the Universal Declaration of Human Rights, Article 14-2 of the International Covenant on Civil and Political Rights. The presumption of innocence, which is applied throughout the criminal procedure, covers three meanings.

At first, it involves that the burden of proof belongs to the prosecution: it is up to the prosecution, in France the public prosecutor (Pradel 320) to prove the guilt of the suspect. The defendant is presumed innocent, so he/she does not have to bring the proof of his/her innocence. The criminal division of the French *Cour de cassation* (CC) does not hesitate to quash the decisions of the courts of appeal that violate the presumption of innocence, considering that as the defendant is presumed innocent, the burden of proof belongs to the public prosecutor.1 Then, the presumption of innocence guarantees that the defendant should benefit from any doubt when the verdict is returned. It means that, if the guilt of the person is not clearly revealed, if there is not enough physical evidence or if there is any doubt about his/her guilt, the person must be discharged or acquitted by French criminal courts. (Cornu 547) Finally, the presumption of innocence also implies that the suspect must be considered legally innocent as long as his/her guilt has not been definitely established by a court. Thus, throughout the criminal procedure, the suspect (and later on the defendant) is deemed innocent, even during the judicial investigation (*instruction*): "he must be considered as not guilty and respected as such." (Cornu 547, my translation)2 The definition is the starting point of this analysis of the presumption of innocence.

Detention on remand and the presumption of innocence seem to be in conflict. The actual question raised here is more about how to conciliate them or how French law combines them. (Chassang 2009) Indeed, their articulation was derived from an idea of conciliation. The French legislator, especially through the laws of 17 July, 1970, 15 June, 2000, 5 March, 2007 and 24 November, 2009, worked in that direction. The issue of the conciliation between detention on remand and the presumption of innocence is raised at two different moments: first of all, when the decision to remand someone in custody is made, and then when the defendant is actually deprived of his/her freedom. This study mainly focuses on the decision to remand someone in custody during a preliminary judicial investigation and therefore against a person officially accused of an offence. On the one hand, if the desire of conciliation clearly appears when the decision to remand someone in custody is made, legislative inconsistencies still remain. On the other hand, due to the strict system of freedom deprivation, this conciliation does not seem to be as successful when the suspect is actually detained before trial.

An apparent conciliation when the decision to remand the suspect in custody is made

As a matter of fact, the French legislator has attempted to reconcile pre-trial detention and the presumption of innocence by making this form of detention exceptional. Additional safety was even created through the function of a specific judge: the liberty and custody judge.

[1] Criminal bulletin n° 164, CC, Criminal division, 29 May, 1980.
[2] See also Guilhermont 41-57.

Strengthening the exceptional nature of detention

To preserve the presumption of innocence, French law strictly regulates the decision to remand someone in custody. Regarding this point, the law provides that liberty remains the main rule for the person under judicial investigation who is presumed innocent. (Art. 137 CCP) However, it is not always possible to keep the person free until the end of the judicial investigation due to the given elements of this investigation. To strengthen the exceptional nature of the detention, French legislation created intermediary options between liberty and detention. Yet, when these intermediary solutions are not enough, the use of detention on remand is possible but must be rigorously justified and motivated.

The intermediary situations between liberty and detention

The first case is judicial supervision (*contrôle judiciaire*) established by the law of 17 July, 1970. Article 8 of the CCP provides that it may be imposed on a defendant who is "liable to incur a misdemeanor imprisonment penalty, or one that is more severe." The second case is house arrest with electronic monitoring, established by the law of 24 November, 2009.

Judical supervision

Judicial supervision is ordered by the investigating judge (*juge d'instruction*) or the liberty and custody judge. (Art. 138 CCP) It involves a number of obligations that can be set up for the suspect because of the judicial investigation requirements or as a safety measure. (Art. 137 CCP) These obligations are set out in Article 138 of the CCP. Some are obligations to do, others are obligations not to do and aim at different goals. Some constraints, such as the prohibition to leave home, are designed to ensure that the person remains at the disposal of the justice system and available for the purposes of the investigation. Others are financial obligations such as the requirement to provide a guarantee, real or personal securities to compensate victims; others finally depend on the specific circumstances of the case such as the prohibition to visit certain places. In case of violation of these obligations, judicial supervision can be dismissed and the person is remanded in custody. (Art. 141-2, para. 1 CCP)

Therefore, a logic of conciliation between liberty and detention underlies judicial supervision and its resulting obligations. Judicial supervision reinforces the exceptional nature of pre-trial detention by creating an additional step subject to restrictive measures while it allows the defendant to remain free. However, even if this intermediary solution is satisfactory regarding the presumption of innocence, some of its obligations seem to be ambiguous in many ways.

First of all, Article 138 of the CCP states that the person may have to provide guarantees. It means that, even though the person is presumed innocent, he/she has to pay a certain amount of money. Article 142 of the same code specifies that these guarantees are intended to ensure the representation of the person in all proceedings, the enforcement of the decision as well as the fulfilment of the enforcement of the other obligations imposed upon him. They also guarantee the payment of compensation for the damage caused by the offence, of restitution and any sum of alimony due as well as the payment of fines. The same article states that the investigating judge or the liberty and custody judge can decide that the guarantees as a whole compensate the damage caused by the offence. Thus, requiring the person to ensure the compensation of the damage caused by the offence implies a strong violation of the presumption of innocence. (Bouquet 60-62)

When studying the obligations of judicial supervision, one notices that they are essentially the same as those imposed by a probation period (*sursis avec mise à l'épreuve.*) Indeed, probation is an alternative sentence to imprisonment. Article 132-40 of the French Criminal Code (CC) states that the trial court, which imposes imprisonment, can ask for the suspension of its implementation and put the accused on probation. During this period, the convicted person has to comply with a number of obligations, including some that are very similar to those provided by judicial supervision. This is the case for the ban on driving certain vehicles, the prohibition to carry out some activities, to visit designated areas or to carry a weapon. Probation can also go along with an obligation to fix the damage caused by the offence in whole or in part, according to the ability of the person to pay, whereas, as seen above, judicial supervision may be accompanied with an obligation to provide a guarantee. This parallel is disturbing because the obligations of probation are components of the sentence while judicial supervision responds to a different objective, the needs of the judicial investigation.

It seems that the law is not fully consistent on this point. Indeed, the convicted and sentenced person and a person under judicial investigation but presumed innocent may be bound by very similar, sometimes identical, obligations whereas the goal of these obligations is different. This inconsistency seems, therefore, not to be in favor of the presumption of innocence. Nevertheless, the law of 24 November, 2009 created another intermediary option between liberty and detention, house arrest with electronic monitoring.

House arrest with electronic monitoring

The investigating judge or the liberty and custody judge can grant a placement under house arrest with electronic monitoring to a person officially accused of an offence if judicial supervision is not sufficient. (Art. 142-5 CCP) Yet, the measure can only be ordered at the request of the applicant or with his/her acceptance and if he/she incurs a sentence of more than two years' imprisonment or a harsher penalty. Article 142-7 of the CCP states that the arrest can be ordered for six months only. However, the same article specifies that this delay can be extended up to two years. This measure forces the person under judicial investigation to stay at home or in a residence determined by the investigating judge or the liberty and custody judge. He/she can leave this place only if he/she abides by the conditions set by the judge. Electronic monitoring is also a measure which allows a convicted person to avoid imprisonment, or to adjust a penalty. (Art. 132-26-1 and following CC, Art. 723-7 and following CCP) So both the convicted and sentenced person and the person under judicial investigation but presumed innocent may have to abide by the same obligation, house arrest under electronic monitoring. Once again, one can highlight a blatant similarity: the same very restrictive measure may be imposed on a convicted person and on someone presumed innocent. This legal inconsistency seems to infringe the presumption of innocence.

Judicial supervision and house arrest appear as alternatives to detention and intermediary options that are more respectful of the presumption of innocence. Nevertheless, the fact remains that in some situations, when the presumption of innocence is violated, the legislator must act. Still, despite their imperfections, these measures strengthen the exceptional nature of detention by creating additional steps. However, detention on remand is imposed in most cases. Thus, the law sets out a framework for the decision to remand someone in custody which requires the measure to be strictly justified.

Strict justifications of the use of detention on remand

Detention on remand can be imposed only when the person accused of an offence faces a prison term of three years or more or when the person intentionally evades the obligations imposed by judicial supervision or house arrest. This form of pre-trial detention has to meet one of the objectives listed in Article 144 of the CCP as well as specific requirements.

An exhaustive list of reasons for the use of detention on remand

Article 144 of the CCP exhaustively sets out the objectives targeted when someone is deprived of his/her freedom. However, the words used to describe the seven goals do not hide the fact that there are some violations of the presumption of innocence. Indeed, besides the goal of preserving clues and physical evidence and placing the suspect at the disposal of the law, (Raoult 14) other reasons presume that the accused person is guilt. (Guéry)

First of all, detention on remand can be imposed to prevent witnesses or victims and their families being put under pressure. If this reason is necessary for the preliminary investigation to be conducted properly, the person therefore appears guilty: if one assumes that the suspect can put pressure on people, he is not considered innocent. The first goal seems to presume the guilt of the person remanded in custody. Detention on remand is also meant to prevent fraudulent conspiracy between the person under judicial investigation and their accomplices. However, by trying to avoid fraudulent conspiracy so that the truth is not hidden, this goal stresses the fact that the person of interest is actually presumed guilty. Indeed, to prevent someone under investigation from meeting his accomplices indicates that this person is already an offender. (Guéry; Raoult 13)

Secondly, detention on remand may also be ordered to protect the person charged with an offence. It aims at protecting such a person from any physical harm or avoiding retaliation. But it also suggests that detention on remand, which is a form of imprisonment, is a protective measure. This goal has sometimes been very violently criticized. (Inchauspé 235-236) One may not reasonably hold a person in detention and argue it is the only way to protect him.

Next, detention on remand aims at stopping the offence or preventing the offence from being committed again. In this case, the person charged with an offence is not only presumed guilty, but also considered dangerous because of a possible repetition of the behaviour. The person has neither been tried nor found guilty of the offence for which he is prosecuted, but is already presumed to be able to repeat the offence. (Raoult 12-13) It seems that this third goal doubly infringes the presumption of innocence.

The last goal set out in Article 144 is to put an end to an exceptional disturbance of public order provoked by the seriousness of the offence, the circumstances of its commission or the extent of the damage it caused.

This is by far the "blurriest reason" (Guinchard and Buisson 1152; Inchauspé 236) and the most mysterious of those listed in Article 144. Indeed, as the article does not define the concept of public disturbance, it is not clear what the expression precisely covers, and therefore any detention could be justified by this type of disturbance. This goal appears to be a "catch-all" phrase that allows possible overindulgence in detention on remand.3 In order to avoid the abusive use of detention on remand justified by such a goal, the law of 5 March, 2007 on the prevention of delinquency restricted the possibilities to remand someone in custody. After the high-profile and controversial *Outreau* case, the law provided that the disturbance of public order could not result from the sole media coverage of the case. It also prohibited the use of public disturbance for middle-range offences, *en matière correctionnelle* in French. However, without further clarification, the justification of public order disturbance remains applicable for serious offences, *en matière criminelle* in French, whereas any crime, due to its seriousness, disturbs public order. So, this goal remains a widely undefined concept.

Thus, the list of justifications for detention on remand set out in Article 144 of the CCP allows, to some extent, to conciliate the constraints of the preliminary investigation and the preservation of the presumption of innocence by avoiding the overuse of this form of pre-trial detention. Yet, the terms used in this article are sometimes not very respectful of the presumption of innocence as they designate the person charged with an offence as already guilty. It would therefore be appropriate to rewrite these justifications so that they do not consider the suspect as guilty when he is presumed innocent. While the decision to remand someone in custody meets one of the objectives set out in Article 144 of the CCP, the law also requires the decision to be precisely motivated.

The necessity to give precise reasons to remand someone in custody

Under Article 137 of the CCP, created by the law of 15 June, 2000, the person charged with an offence is presumed innocent and remains free. Therefore, it is only because of the requirements of the investigation, or as a safety measure, that judicial examination can be ordered. Exceptionally, if judicial supervision is insufficient, house arrest can be imposed. If both judicial supervision and house arrest are ineffective, the suspect can be remanded in custody on an exceptional basis. The above law provided that

---

[3] Statements collected from a personal interview conducted on 2 April, 2009 and 12 May, 2009.

pre-trial detention could be ordered or extended if it was the only way to fulfil one of the objectives laid down in Article 144 of the CCP. The law of 5 March, 2007 reinforced the justifications for the decision to remand someone in custody. Such a decision has to point out how inadequate judicial supervision and home arrest are and how necessary detention on remand is—it is the only way to achieve one or more of the objectives defined by Article 144—based on the specific items and detailed evidence resulting from the procedure.

To strengthen the justification of detention on remand is by itself a way to prevent the abusive use of this form of pre-trial detention. However, one may wonder if this justification does not harm the presumption of innocence because it presumes the guilt of the suspect. Indeed, some authors believe that detention on remand is a "pre-judgment." (Pradel 646; Inchauspé 237; Raoult 13) If so, then the strengthening of remand justification can only reinforce this "pre-judgment." However, the European Court of Human Rights considers that "the presumption of innocence will be violated if, without the accused's having previously been proved guilty according to law (...), a judicial decision concerning him reflects an opinion that he is guilty." (*Minelli v. Switzerland* §37) French legislation seems not to be in conformity with European case-law. Thus, the will to strengthen the remand justification so as to avoid the presumption of innocence being infringed can create the opposite effect; the more the decision to remand is precisely justified, the more guilty the suspect appears to be.

Until the law of 15 June, 2000, only the investigating judge was entitled to order detention on remand. Although he/she was investigating the case even-handedly, the judge could not be truly impartial about the person under investigation when pre-trial detention had to be ordered. The law of 15 June, 2000 which reinforced the presumption of innocence tried to correct the abuses of detention on remand by establishing an additional safeguard: the liberty and custody judge. The aim is to introduce "a double-checking principle" on this type of detention by separating the authority responsible for the investigation—the investigating judge—from the one empowered to order the detention. (Vallini and Houillon 222)

The creation of a "double-checking principle": the liberty and custody judge

The law of 15 June, 2000 entrusted a specific judge with detention powers. The investigating judge no longer has the power to detain a person. If he/she considers that detention on remand is necessary, he/she drafts a reasoned remand order and transmits it to the liberty and custody judge who then decides, after adversarial debate, if the measure is justified in this case. Since 2000, under Article 145 of the CCP, he has been the only one who can decide detention on remand.

Nevertheless, in order to make this warranty effective, it is necessary for detention proceedings to be supervised by an "experienced judge." (Vallini and Houillon 258) This is why, under Article 137-1 paragraph 2, the liberty and custody judge must sit as President, deputy Vice-President or Vice-President and be appointed by the President of the French Court of First Instance (*tribunal de grande instance.*) The law of 9 March, 2004 states that, if the liberty and custody judge is unavailable, he/she can be replaced by the senior sitting judge with the highest rank. Therefore, there is a clear will to entrust pre-trial detention powers to an impartial judge experienced enough to have "the necessary distance in relation to the different stakes of the cases" and thus to "avoid hasty remand orders that are not required by the proper conduct of the preliminary investigation. (Viout 37, my translation) Under Article 137-3 paragraph 1, the liberty and custody judge rules on remand orders or on orders to extend detention or bail applications by issuing a reasoned order. Yet, as mentioned earlier, the justification requirements have been strengthened and the liberty and custody judge has to demonstrate, thanks to the specific elements and detailed evidence resulting from the procedure, that detention on remand is the only way to achieve one or more goals listed in Article 144 of CCP. He/she must also prove that these goals cannot be achieved through judicial supervision or house arrest.

However, "most of the time, when the investigating judge suggests detention, the liberty and custody judge, one of his colleagues, will go along with it." (Inchauspé 234; Matsopoulou 1496, my translation) The report drafted by the committee responsible for investigating the *Outreau* case highlights the fact that, according to the data provided by the French Department of Justice (*Chancellerie*) "the confirmation rate of remand orders reached 92 % in 2001 and 89.7 % in 2004." (Vallini and Houillon 223, my translation) It appears that this control is more a formal procedure than an actual one. Indeed, the liberty and custody judge does not know the case, "he steps in at the end" (*ibid.*, my translation) and only rules on detention on remand while the investigating judge is the one who investigate the case and is in charge of the file. Thus, the liberty and custody judge is "the worst person ever to assess if pre-trial detention is useful or not" unlike the investigating judge who knows all the elements raised in the case. (Vallini and Houillon 268, my translation)

Moreover, the liberty and custody judge is not a specialized one. While he/she is experienced indeed, he/she is not necessarily specialized in criminal law and procedure. (Le Monnier De Gouville 435-436) In some courts, including the civil court of Paris, the liberty and custody judge performs this task full time and can therefore be seen as a specialized judge. However, in some places, the same judge carries out several functions: he may work as a liberty and custody judge as well as a judge in civil law (see note supra) He is more an "odd-job" judge who does not necessarily have the time and skills to examine the remand order issued by the investigating judge. Consequently, he/she relies on the analysis and reasoning of the investigating judge by doing some kind of "copy and paste" of this reasoning. (Vallini and Houillon 268, my translation) Consequently, even if the creation of the liberty and custody judge reveals a real desire to prevent any abuse of detention on remand, it seems to be "absolutely useless" for a great majority of provincial courts. (see note supra)

Nevertheless, the conciliation between detention on remand and the presumption of innocence is obvious when the decision to remand someone in custody is made: from 2000 to 2010 remand orders declined by 38.9 % (*Annuaires statistiques de la justice*,) 4 which seems to indicate that there is a genuine will to reduce the use of detention on remand despite the numerous legislative inconsistencies previously alluded to. But the presumption of innocence must also be secured when the person is actually remanded in custody. At this stage, what is the balance struck between the presumption of innocence and detention?

Absence of conciliation during the detention period

In order to conciliate the presumption of innocence and detention on remand, a more flexible detention regime would be more appropriate. Indeed, the person remanded in custody is entitled to flexibility contrary to a prisoner who has been found guilty and is serving a jail sentence. However, during detention on remand, there seems to be no conciliation possible as the deprivation of liberty is applied quite rigorously in terms of duration and regarding the physical conditions of incarceration.

---

[4] http://www.justice.gouv.fr/budget-et-statistiques-10054/annuaires-statistiques-de-la-justice-10304/.

Excessive delays

Articles 145-1 and 145-2 of the CCP respectively limit the duration of detention on remand for middle-range and serious offences (*délits* and *crimes*.) Prior to the law of 15 June, 2000, the period of detention on remand was not much regulated. For example, when the possible prison term for a middle-range offence was ten years, the law did not limit the maximum duration of detention on remand; if the length of such detention for a crime was one year, there was no limit put on the extension of the measure. Nowadays, the duration of detention on remand is better regulated. However, in some situations, this duration is extremely long even if the person is still presumed innocent. In case of a middle-range offence, detention on remand can last up to two years and four months or, in some cases, up to three years. In case of a crime, the length of detention on remand may be up to four years and eight months.

Even if the establishment of limits reveals a will to regulate the duration of detention on remand, the extension of the measure is possible in many ways, which reduces the impact of the limits. Indeed, in case of a middle-range offence, the maximum duration of detention can be multiplied by nine, in case of a crime by almost five. Thus, the French legislator appears unable to reconcile the presumption of innocence and detention on remand because of the length of these extensions. However, under Article 145-3 of the CCP, when the detention duration exceeds one year for a crime and eight months for a middle-range offence, any extension or refusal to release the person remanded in custody should be done according to particular guidelines that justify further investigation and the expected time of completion of the procedure.

Moreover, there is some time between the order to refer the case to a court, either for middle-range offences (*tribunal correctionnel*) or for crimes (*cour d'asisses*) and the actual appearance of the suspect in court, time during which the person may be remanded in custody. As a matter of fact, when the judge and, in some cases, the judicial investigation division (*chambre de l'instruction*) consider that the facts constitute an offence, they issue an order to refer the case to the *tribunal correctionnel*, which puts an end to judicial supervision, house arrest or detention on remand under Articles 179 and 213 of the CCP. However, the decision to extend the detention on remand of the person referred to the court can be made through a reasoned order under Article 144 of the CCP. The person will be released only if the court has not begun to address the merits of the case within two months starting from the day the case was referred to the court. Furthermore, the same court can exceptionally decide to extend the detention for a period of two months when there are legal reasons or facts that prevent the case from being tried. Such a decision can be renewed once. As a consequence, in case of middle-range offences, detention on remand can last up to three years and six months.

Then, when the investigating judge and the judicial investigation division consider that the facts constitute a crime, they issue a bill of indictment (*ordonnance de mise en accusation*) to the criminal court under Articles 181 and 214 of the CCP. Nevertheless, this order does not end the detention on remand which is extended until the appearance of the person in court, but cannot exceed the period of one year starting from the day the bill of indictment was issued. However, if the court hearing cannot start within this period, the judicial investigation division may order to extend detention on remand for a period of six months. Such a decision is renewable once. In case of crimes, detention on remand can last up to six years and eight months.

Thus, such periods of detention seem all the more excessive as these delays are sometimes actually applied. For example, in the *Outreau* case, 21 months passed between the end of the preliminary investigation and the trial, and most people indicted before the criminal court were remanded in custody during the whole time (Vallini and Houillon 238.) As a consequence, in terms of detention periods, it appears that the balance between the presumption of innocence and detention on remand has not been struck. Yet, if the duration of such detention has to be reasonable, it is mainly because the measure that deprives someone of their liberty is particularly burdensome.

A minimum adjustment of the period of detention

In his treatise *Dei delitti e delle pene*, Beccaria claimed that the imprisonment of a person before his judgment should be as less rigorous as possible. (108) Indeed, the person remanded in custody is in a different situation that a convict; unlike the former who is presumed innocent, the latter has been found guilty. As such, detention on remand should be subject to more flexible rules and conditions. However, the incarceration of a person remanded in custody occurs in prison and the detention conditions are sometimes more rigorous than those applied to a convict.

The ambiguous incarceration in prison

Under article 714 of the CCP, persons remanded in custody are detained in jail. They are incarcerated in a facility that also hosts persons serving custodial sentences (Art. 724 CCP) of one year or less. (Art. 717

CCP) However, Article 716 of the same Code provides that suspected, charged and accused persons are held individually, except in three cases: if they ask to share a cell with others, if their personality requires not being alone, if they have been allowed to work or attend school or work trainings and that special organizational needs are required.

Yet, the person remanded in custody has not the same status as the one who serves a custodial sentence; the former is presumed innocent while the latter has been convicted; the first one is detained because of the requirements of preliminary investigations whereas the second one pays his debt to society. Both are incarcerated in the same institution though. Therefore, there is a risk of confusion between persons remanded in custody and convicts. It may lead to the remanded person being seen as already guilty, which does bode ill for the conciliation between detention on remand and the presumption of innocence. Thus, in 2006, European Prison Rule 18.8 advocated the separation of suspected and convicted persons in prison. The goal was to reorganize jails so as to isolate people remanded in custody from convicts. This system has been implemented in prisons since 2008. If this separation restores the presumption of innocence in jail in some way, the ambiguity of the incarceration of people presumed innocent and convicted persons within the same institution still remains.

Therefore, according to Jean Pradel, facilities especially designed for persons remanded in custody could be built. (661) Indeed, it would meet the requirements and needs of preliminary investigations while preserving the presumption of innocence. Persons sentenced to short sentences would be detained in jails and persons remanded in custody would be held in a special institution. This would put an end to the fact that persons remanded in custody are assimilated to convicts. It would also create a truly specific type of incarceration for persons remanded in custody that takes into account the purpose of such detention and is more respectful of the presumption of innocence. As a matter of fact, the issue of the prison incarceration of persons remanded in custody is all the more important since harsh conditions of detention may be imposed.

Harsh conditions of detention

Apart from a few changes, people remanded in custody are submitted to the same conditions of detention as convicts. (See Articles R. 57-5 to 57-8-23 and D. 50 to D. 521-1 CCP) More importantly, the person remanded in custody may also be put in solitary confinement, even for the whole duration of the detention on remand. Indeed, for the purpose of investigation, the investigating judge or the liberty and custody judge may order such a measure and decide to renew it in case the detention duration is extended. (Articles R. 57-5-1 to 57-5-8 CCP) Furthermore, the conditions of solitary confinement are hard. Prisoners on remand are completely isolated and therefore cannot join group walks or activities even if they keep their rights to information, visits, correspondence and religious practice, and are entitled to a daily outside walk of at least one hour. (Article R. 57-7-63 CCP) Yet, in the prison of *Hauts-de-Seine* near Paris, this walk takes place only in a small courtyard enclosed by four walls without any proper view of the outside. Therefore, the conditions of solitary confinement are particularly harsh because they further reduce the freedom and rights of the person remanded in custody. Thus, such steps taken to meet the requirements of the investigation clearly reveal the limits of any possible conciliation between detention on remand and the protection of the presumption of innocence.

Conclusion

Even if legislative inconsistencies have been highlighted, there is a genuine will to reconcile detention on remand and the presumption of innocence from the moment the decision to remand someone in custody is made via the strengthening of the exceptional nature of the detention and the creation of the liberty and custody judge. Conversely, given the strictness of the deprivation of liberty, the balance does not seem to be struck when the person remanded in custody is actually detained. Thus, even though the CCP provides that the person wrongly remanded in custody has the right to full compensation, (Art. 149 to 150 CCP) the contradiction between pre-trial detention and the presumption of innocence still remains. While the problem seems insoluble, it is not without any interest so that these two conflicting objectives should be reconciled as much as possible.

Works cited

BECCARIA, Cesare. *Des délits et des peines*. Translated by Maurice Chevallier. Paris: Flammarion, 1991.

BOUQUET, Alexandre. “Cautionnement pénal et politique criminelle: une relation à géométrie variable.” *Archives de politique criminelle* 23 (2001): 53-69.

CHASSANG, Céline. “Présomption d’innocence et détention provisoire: un exemple de contradiction en procédure pénale.” University of Paris

Ouest Nanterre la Défense, 2009.
CORNU, Gérard. *Vocabulaire juridique.* Paris: P.U.F., 2011.
GUÉRY, Christian. *Détention provisoire.* Paris: Dalloz, 2001.
GUILHERMONT, Edith. "Qu'appelle-t-on présomption d'innocence?" *Archives de politique criminelle* 29 (2007): 41-57.
GUINCHARD, Serge, and Jacques BIUSSON. *Procédure pénale.* Paris: Lexis-Nexis, 2012.
HENRION, Hervé. *La nature juridique de la présomption d'innocence, comparaison franco-allemande.* PhD diss., University of Montpellier, 2004.
INCHAUSPÉ, Dominique. *L'innocence judiciaire. Dans un procès, on n'est pas innocent, on le devient.* Paris: P.U.F., 2012.
LE MONNIER DE GOUVILLE, *Pauline. Le juge des libertés et de la détention.* PhD diss., University of Paris Panthéon-Assas, 2011.
MATSOPOULOU, Haritini. "Le juge des libertés et de la détention: un acteur de premier ou de second rôle en matière de détention provisoire?" *Recueil Dalloz* 22 (2008): 1494-1500.
Minelli v. Switzerland. ECtHR, March 25, 1983.
PRADEL, Jean. *Procédure pénale.* Paris: Cujas, 2011.
RAOULT, Sacha. "Détention provisoire: quelles pistes de QPC? *Gazette du Palais* 340 (2011): 3271-3274.
VALLINI, André, and Philippe HOUILLON. "Rapport n° 3125 fait au nom de la commission d'enquête chargée de rechercher les causes des dysfonctionnements de la justice dans l'affaire dite d'*Outreau* et de formuler des propositions pour éviter leur renouvellement." Assemblée nationale, 2006.
VIOUT, Jean-Olivier. "Rapport du groupe de travail chargé de tirer les enseignements du traitement judiciaire de l'affaire dite d'*Outreau.*" Assemblée nationale, 2005.

DETENTION CENTRES IN FRANCE AND THE UNITED KINGDOM AND THE CRIMINALISATION OF MIGRANTS: THE REALITY OF ACCESS TO JUSTICE?

GERALDINE GADBIN-GEORGE
UNIVERSITY OF PANTHEON-ASSAS PARIS II, FRANCE

Since the Treaty of Lisbon came into force in December 2009, amending the Treaty of Maastricht and the Treaty of Rome, immigration policies in Europe have been governed "by the principle of solidarity and fair division of responsibility" between the Member States including France and the United Kingdom. (European Commission 2012) The aim of the European Pact on Immigration and Asylum, launched by former French conservative President Nicolas Sarkozy in the context of the Stockholm programme (2009-2014) is to restrict illegal immigration through the stricter control of borders. The non-binding political document was unanimously accepted by 27 European States "whatever their political sensibilities or geographic situation." (Carrera & Guild) It seeks to "reject both closed door and open door policies" towards immigration. (*Ministère de l'Intérieur et de l'Immigration* 2008)

In 2009, the then conservative French government and New Labour British government published a joint Franco-British Declaration on Immigration affirming:

> their willingness to […] promote, according to the European Pact [...], a European policy of firmness and solidarity based on the […] undertaking by the states of the European Union to fight against illegal immigration […].

Since then political governance has changed but policies have not altered much.

In March 2013, French socialist President François Hollande sent all the *préfets* (who represent the government at the local *département* level) an unofficial—and unpublished—circular letter in which he required them to "fight against clandestine immigration networks." He recommended that "house arrest" be preferred to detention in a centre and confirmed the end of "quotas" of deported migrants. (Vincent 2013)

As for conservative British Prime Minister David Cameron, he endorsed his predecessor's wish to fight against unauthorised migration. He even went one step further by recently announcing the withdrawal of "legal aid […] for immigration cases" from April 2013. However, legal aid should "continue to be paid for asylum claims and criminal cases." (Jowit 2013) The UK Border Agency, an agency of the Home Office, has also announced its vision for 2015:

> To be a highly competent [...] organisation which controls migration for the benefit of the UK [...] deterring, stopping or removing those who have no right to be here [...]. ("Our agency 2015 change programme")

Both France and the United Kingdom welcome a huge number of legal migrants each year. In France and according to the *Agence France Presse*'s figures, authorised migration represented 175,000 residence permits in 2009. 99,238 residence permits were issued for the first semester of 2010 only. (Assfam 2010: 12) In the United Kingdom, "Work-related entry visas declined from 193,855 in 2005 to 113,920 in 2010." (Blinder) This is a substantial figure to which family reunion migration must be added. Conversely, unauthorised migration is targeted by the French and British governments.

Being an unauthorised migrant does not mean being deprived of rights. Illegal migrants have some rights guaranteed when they enter France or the United Kingdom. According to Article 5(1)(f) of the European Convention on Human Rights:

> No one shall be deprived of his liberty save in the following cases and in accordance with a procedure prescribed by law: […] the lawful arrest or detention of a person to prevent his effecting an unauthorised entry into the country or of a person against whom action is being taken with a view to deportation or extradition.

The right to liberty was already protected by the French Constitution of 1789 and in chapter 29 of the British *Magna Carta*. The provisions of Article 5(1)(f), which are binding on France and the United Kingdom, led to the creation of special centres now called Immigration Removal Centres in the United Kingdom and *Centres de Rétention Administrative* in France. Temporary detention will give the authorities a chance to process any application illegal migrants file (for residence, family reunion or asylum for instance) or arrange their deportation.

Detention is not a punishment. Unauthorised migration is not in itself a criminal offence. However, and just like prisoners, those detained are deprived of their freedom of movement. And just like prisoners, they have rights which should be guaranteed. These rights include the right to access legal services as and when necessary, although illegal migrants' need for legal services may differ from that of prisoners. This is what this study will focus on.

Before that, a brief but non exhaustive reminder of both countries' respective immigration policies since the early 1900s is necessary to explain the context in which the *Centres de Rétention Administrative* and the Immigration Removal Centres emerged. Comparative background information will also be given about those centres.

In this study, the terms "unauthorised" migration or "illegal" migration will be used indifferently to describe those who enter France or the United Kingdom without prior authorisation. Likewise the words "detention" and "detainee" will be used to refer to the fact of spending time in a *Centre de Rétention Administrative* or an Immigration Removal Centre. This should not be construed as a wish to criminalise migrants. All translations from French to English are the author's own. Unless otherwise stated, the provisions of French statutes mentioned below and which postdate 1990 can be found on the official governmental website <www.legifrance.gouv.fr>. All those for the United Kingdom can be found on <http://www.bailii.org/form/search_legis.html>. Likewise the provisions of the *Code d'Entrée et de Séjour des Etrangers en France* (code of entry and residence of foreigners in France or "CESEDA") can all be found on <www.legifrance.gouv.fr>. And again, unless otherwise stated, statutory provisions are those which apply in March 2013.

Historical and political background

The French *Centres de Rétention Administrative* were set up on 29 October, 1981 (by statute No. 81-973 relating to the conditions of entry and residence of foreigners in France) when socialist French President François Mitterrand was in power. The underlying idea was that unauthorised migrants should not be "retained" (hence the word "retention") in prison whilst the authorities considered their situation. In the United Kingdom, the Immigration Detention Centres were set up by the Immigration Act 1971 by then Conservative Prime Minister Edward Heath. Their name was changed to Immigration Removal Centres by the

Nationality, Immigration and Asylum Act of 2002. The aim might have been to avoid the use of the word "detention" or to place the emphasis on the need to deport migrants back to their country.

In both countries, the Industrial Revolution marked the birth of a new type of massive, initially work-related, migration. Various waves of migration then hit France and the United Kingdom in the 20th century. The legislation set out below gives some background information on how France and the United Kingdom tackled immigration before and after they joined Europe. However, it does not pretend to be exhaustive.

Migration to Britain

During the Industrial Revolution, the "workshop of the world" (Ross 28) was considered as a haven for the migrant workforce. When the economic conditions started deteriorating, Balfour's Conservative government passed the Aliens Act 1905. This statute restricted migration and implied that migrants were responsible for the emerging problems. After the Aliens Restriction Act 1914 was passed, 29,000 Germans and Austrians were deported and 32,000 other foreigners were detained in prison camps. (Holmes 94-96)

The Aliens Restriction Act 1919 was passed at a time of strong nationalism which followed the First World War. Companies in the United Kingdom lost the freedom to employ foreign workers. Migrants had to register with the police upon arrival and were subject to deportation. The 1929 financial crisis made things worse. There was little work for the native population, so foreigners were unwelcome. Jews who had hoped to escape from Hitler and seek shelter in the United Kingdom were deported to countries like Australia or Canada.

For some time following the Second World War, Britain called on migrants to work in its factories to boost its economy. (Cholewinsky 1997) But it soon became apparent that the migrant workforce was no longer prepared to return home when their presence was no longer needed in factories. At the same time, the concept of family reunion emerged. The phenomenon developed so fast that in 1947, prospective working migrants were required to sign a document in which they confirmed being unattached and with no dependent relatives. (Holmes 214) A 1949 report from the Royal Commission on Population recommended an immigration "without reserve" so long as the migrants were "of good stock and were not prevented by their race or religion from intermarrying with the host population and becoming merged into it." (Brown 2)

The Commonwealth Immigrants Act 1962 passed under former

Conservative Prime Minister Harold Wilson marked an important step in migration control. The purpose of previous legislation was to restrict non-Commonwealth migration. With the 1962 Act, former Commonwealth nationals who wished to migrate to the United Kingdom were either required to have an employment voucher from the Ministry of Labour or to be financially able to support themselves. Restrictions were even imposed on those seeking family reunion in the United Kingdom. This law was seen as a racist one. Coloured people from the former British Empire felt no longer welcome.

Many other Acts followed. They culminated in the Immigration Act 1971 creating the Immigration Detention Centres. The Nationality Act 1981 passed by the then Conservative government of Margaret Thatcher gave the authorities the right to withdraw British citizenship from former Commonwealth citizens. In 1993 the Conservatives passed the Asylum and Immigration Appeals Act. The number of asylum seekers was reduced by imposing caps on the number of possible applications. Deportation of illegal migrants was encouraged.

From 2004 the Labour government of Tony Blair briefly re-opened the borders to mass migration. 700,000 migrants from Eastern Europe came looking for work. (Winnett) Restrictions were imposed again by the UK Borders Act 2007 and the Borders, Citizenship and Immigration Act 2009. Illegal immigration continued nevertheless.

Migration to France

In France, as in the United Kingdom, the Industrial Revolution marked the increase in migration. Successive waves of workers arrived from neighbouring countries such as Germany, Switzerland or Belgium. Work migrants were soon followed by their families eager to be reunited with them. At the turn of the century, migrants were promptly blamed for the deteriorating work conditions and the reduction in salaries. During the First World War, France called on its Empire's workforce. Thousands of Algerians came to the rescue before being deported back to their country after the war.

A decree of 2 April, 1917 created the first ever 15-year residence permit. A huge number of migrants came to France between the two World Wars. Migration was encouraged by a 1927 statute making it easier to acquire French nationality. But the 1929 crisis was accompanied by a xenophobic movement affecting Polish and Jewish migrants. A law of 10 August, 1932 gave priority to employment for French workers by setting quotas for migrant workers. (Singer-Kerel) A statute of 27 September,

1940 passed by the Vichy government restricted the freedom of movement of foreigners in France, thus making it very difficult to work there. (Peschanski 21) Another statute passed on 4 October, 1940 made it lawful to detain Jewish foreign nationals in special camps. This led to the Vel d'Hiv scandal.

On 2 November, 1945, an ordinance (No. 45-2658) was passed regulating the conditions of entry and residence of foreigners in France. Most of it still applies today. The ordinance created the *Office National d'Immigration* which has the monopoly over deciding the percentage of foreigners in the workforce. As in the United Kingdom, immigration was encouraged between 1956 and 1972. The country needed migrants to help rebuild it and boost the economy after the war. Migrants were also naturally drawn to Europe as the United States had closed its borders.

Algerian migrants arrived after the War of Independence in 1962 and other Africans followed from 1964. The flow of migrants was so important and so unmanageable that the *Préfecture de police* bought an old warehouse near Marseille to detain Algerian migrants. (Morice) Two circulars (respectively called Marcellin and Fontanet after the ministers who drafted them) were passed on 23 Februaryand 15 September 15, 1972, by which only those who had a guaranteed job in France would be allowed entry. Should the migrant lose his job, he had to go back home.

The 1974 economic crisis corresponded to the election of a centre-right President, Valéry Giscard d'Estaing, and the end of the *Trente Glorieuses*, the thirty years of prosperity following the Second World War. It marked a sharp end to work-related migration. France wanted to protect its borders and reserve jobs for its own nationals. A circular of 5 July, 1974 suspended work migration into France until 1977. Family reunion migration was restored in 1975. In 1978 the authorities arranged for part of the migrant workforce—even that established for years in France—to be deported back to their countries. Algerians were particularly targeted by these measures. A law No. 80-9 (nicknamed Bonnet after the minister who initiated it) was passed on 10 January, 1980 amending the 1945 ordinance and imposing a tighter control over unauthorised migration. An illegal migrant could be detained in a prison for up to seven days if it was impossible to deport him forthwith.

In 1982 and like Tony Blair 20 years later, Socialist President François Mitterrand suspended the deportation of migrants and temporarily came back on the various previous restrictions. His aim was to satisfy his electorate amongst which he counted former migrants. Pursuant to a law No. 84-622 of 17 July, 1984, the right to a visa was not subject to the prerequisite of having a job. But the right to deport unauthorised migrants was restored by statute No. 86-1025 of 9 September, 1986 as it existed before President Mitterrand's election. It also imposed restrictions on the migrants' right of residence in France. A *Haut Conseil à l'Intégration* (Council for Integration) was set up by decree No. 89-912 of 18 December, 1989 which had the duty to help the integration of migrants. A law No. 93-1027 of 24 August, 1993 passed towards the end of President Mitterrand's term restricted the possibilities of access to residence in France.

The conditions of entry and residence were then re-defined by statute No. 98-349 of 11 May, 1998 passed under former right-wing President Jacques Chirac. For the 17 years during which President Chirac and his right-wing successor, President Sarkozy, were in power, the trend was towards a restriction of immigration in general and a willingness to fight against illegal immigration. Acts No. 2003-1119 of 26 November, 2003, No. 2006-911 of 24 July, 2006 and No. 2007-1631 20 November, 2007 were passed. As seen above and since his election in May 2012, Socialist President Hollande has not expressed the wish to carry out a reform of his predecessor's immigration policy, save for putting an end to the deportation quota.

The European approach

Even before they became European Member States, France and the United Kingdom shared similar attitudes to immigration and in particular, illegal immigration.

Firstly they faced various migration waves to which they tried to respond in similar ways. Three main waves of migration can be identified: the "primary" and "secondary" waves were forms of legal migration, work migration followed by family reunion migration. (Geddes 17) According to Geddes, the third wave was unauthorised or illegal migration of people drawn to the lifestyle and social benefits those countries had to offer. In both countries a large amount of legislation was passed, aiming at tackling this ever increasing phenomenon.

Secondly, and although France was one of Europe's founding members in 1958 whereas the United Kingdom only joined in 1973, the role played by the European legislator has an obvious influence over the French and British immigration policies. For instance, they both have to comply with the European Convention on Human Rights. However, the United Kingdom retained some independence by refusing to sign the Schengen Agreement of June 14, 1985. It also opted out of the European Council Directive 2003/86/EC on the right to family reunion. This shows that its government wanted to exercise a stricter control over its borders to prevent unauthorised migration.

Thirdly, there is a historical tendency to treat all migrants—authorised or not—as second-class citizens. It is exacerbated at times of economic crisis. There have been xenophobic movements in both countries when migrants were used as cheap labour before being deported back to their countries. Migrants, whether authorised or not, are sometimes treated as criminals. Stumpf (2006) talked about the phenomenon of "crimmigration."

After Directive 2008/115/CE of 16 December, 2008 came into force, which simplified the procedure enabling Member States to deport unauthorised migrants, the Council of Europe Commissioner for Human Rights expressed his concern over the "criminal stamp" which tends to apply to authorised and unauthorised migration alike. (Hammarberg) Talking of the "language of criminalisation" he opposed the "fairly neutral terminology" used by the Council of Europe to that of Member States for which "being an immigrant becomes associated, through the use of language, with illegal acts under the criminal law." (CECHR 2010)

Fourthly, under the influence of Europe, France and the United Kingdom now share the same concern of striking a balance between controlled migration aimed at integration (such as work-related migration, family reunion or political asylum for instance) and illegal migration. Illegal migration is the reason why the French *Centres de Rétention Administrative* and the British Immigration Detention Centres were set up. And here again, through the influence of Europe and in particular, Article 5 of the European Convention on Human Rights mentioned above, a number of rights are guaranteed to unauthorised migrants.

Before considering whether access to legal services is one of those, it is necessary to give some background information about the French and British centres, before comparing the procedures which lead to detention on both sides of the Channel.

Migration and detention in France and the United Kingdom

Tackling unauthorised migration is a complex and expensive process. In both countries, special structures have been set up where unauthorised migrants will be detained whilst the authorities consider their situation. Some background comparative information setting out how these centres are run, by whom and at what cost will help understand the context in which non-European migrants are detained. Information will also be given on the procedures which are available to detainees to dispute the detention decision made by the authorities.

Comparative information

For the UK Border Agency, the Immigration Removal Centres are:

> used for temporary detention, in situations where people have no legal right to be in the UK [...]. Those detained in any of our centres can leave at any time to return to their home country. ("Immigration Removal Centres")

Likewise in France it is possible to "retain a foreigner in an enclosed area when he is subject to a removal decision, pending his forced return." ("Rétention administrative d'un étranger en instance d'éloignement" 2013)

There seems to be three main reasons why a migrant can be detained in France or the United Kingdom: he arrived without a prior authorisation, he was granted a visa but overstayed after it expired, or he committed a criminal offence for which he was imprisoned in France or the United Kingdom and refused to leave the country after he served his prison sentence. In the latter case, the migrant is no longer a criminal and thus, should not be considered as such.

In both countries there are two types of detention which can be ordered after a migrant is arrested: the most traditional form is classic detention in a *Centre de Rétention Administrative* or an Immigration Removal Centre. Alternatively, both countries have introduced house arrest with or without an electronic tag. House arrest now seems to be the favoured option when families of migrants, including children, are arrested.

In February 2012, the United Kingdom had ten Immigration Removal Centres ("IRCs"), three residential Short Term Holding Facilities ("STHFs") near airports, 14 non-residential STHFs and 12 combined non-residential STHFs/reporting centres. In June 2011, there were 3,500 places in terms of "UK detention capacity." A total of 27,000 migrants were held in removal centres in 2011. 60% of them "were held for less than two months, fewer than 10% are held for more than one year." (Silverman & Hajela)

In France there are currently 25 *Centres de Rétention Administrative* with a total capacity of 1711 beds. In 2010, 33 600 people were held in them which is more than twice the figure of 1999. The average stay is only about ten days. (Vincent 2012)

The cost—to the French and British authorities and eventually to the taxpayer—of the *Centres de Rétention Administrative* or the Immigration Removal Centres is very difficult to assess. In 2010 the average daily overall cost of a bed in an Immigration Removal Centre was estimated at about 120 pounds i.e. about 140 euros. (Hansard 2010) For the Information Centre about Asylum and Refugees in the UK ("ICAR") the weekly cost per detainee in 2005-2006 ranged from 511 pounds (about 600 euros) at Lindholme IRC to 1,344 pounds (about 1585 euros) at Colnbrook IRC (25) so from 85 euros a day to 227 euros a day. Because details of these costs were not provided, it is impossible to know whether this cost is an inclusive one, taking into account the cost of the initial police arrest, the managements fees of the Immigration Removal Centre and the processing costs of an application for asylum or a visa, or a decision to deport. Regarding the management of the centres, most Immigration Removal Centres are run by private companies such as G4S, a leading security outsourcing group—"Accommodation Services." Therefore, bids must be regularly organised by the authorities.

In France, information is less readily available. According to a parliamentary report, the *Centres de Rétention Administrative* are run by the *gendarmes*[1] or the police and the average cost of a retention for 2008 was 2,823 euros, "excluding the cost of arrest, removal and judicial costs." (Bernard-Reymond 2009) On the basis of an average 10-day stay per retention, this amounts to about 282 euros a day.

As mentioned above, in view of the lack of detailed information given on how these figures are reached, it is difficult to draw any comparative conclusion regarding the cost of detention. However, one thing can be said for the *Centres de Rétention Administrative* and the Immigration Removal Centres, they cost a lot of money to taxpayers on both sides of the Channel.

Detention procedures

According to HM Inspectorate of Prisons and the Independent Chief Inspector of Borders and Immigration, "The decision to detain is an administrative power [...] and is not sanctioned by the judiciary." (12) Detention decisions are made by Immigration Officers and the Secretary of State for the Home Department. A similar comment can be made in France. The *préfet,* who represents the government in each *département,* takes responsibility for the detention of migrants, outside any judicial scope.

Detention in France and the United Kingdom is therefore a power of the authorities when they arrest an unauthorised migrant. However, it is not a discretionary one. The French or British authorities have to take steps against an unauthorised migrant when he is arrested. Measures have to be taken, whether it is detention in a *Centre de Rétention Administrative*

---

[1] A branch of the French Armed Forces in charge of public safety.

or an Immigration Removal Centre, or deportation.

Because the decision to detain is a purely administrative one, it should not be assimilated to a prison sentence. Detainees will be temporarily deprived of their freedom of movement outside the centre, but detention is only for a limited time, until the migrants' situation is investigated, their application processed or when they accept to return to their country of origin.

Upon being arrested, the unauthorised migrant is invited to return to his country. In case of refusal, he will be detained or alternatively, placed under house arrest (with or without an electronic tag or bracelet.) There are three advantages to house arrest. It is a good way not to disturb the migrants' family life if there are young children involved. It also means that the taxpayer's money will not be spent on accommodating someone who is bound to stay at his own home; that cost will be borne by the migrant himself. To the outside world, house arrest is less associated with imprisonment—and criminality—because the deprivation of the freedom of movement is less of a constraint. In both countries, laws have been passed to regulate detention and house arrest and ensure the protection of a number of rights.

In France

Upon arriving in France without an authorisation, the migrant may seek help from the *Office Français de l'Immigration et de l'Intégration* OFFI (French Office of Immigration and Integration.) The OFII was set up in 2009 and is headed by the *Ministère de l'Intérieur* (Interior Ministry.) It is the descendant of the above mentioned *Office National pour l'Intégration* set up in 1945 by the General de Gaulle after the Second World War. 60 years later and according to its website, the OFII has a number of missions which are delegated to it by the government:

> The management of the regular procedures next to or on behalf of *préfectures* [...]; The reception and integration of migrants allowed to reside in France on a long term basis [...]; The reception of asylum seekers; The assisted return and reintegration of foreigners in their country of origin. ("Qui sommes-nous?")

OFII officers can be found, amongst other places, in the *Centres de Rétention Administrative*.

Regarding the detention procedure itself, the rules applicable in March 2013 are set out in articles L551-1 to L555-3 and R551-1 to R553-17 of *Code de l'entrée et du séjour des étrangers et du droit d'asile* (CESEDA.)

Without any judicial input, the *préfet* only has the power to order the detention of an unauthorised migrant for a maximum of five days. His decision is written and like any other French administrative decision which adversely affects someone's rights, the *préfet* has the duty to set out the legal grounds on which he relied. This will assist the migrant in disputing the *préfet's* decision in court if he so wishes.

If retention must continue after the initial five days (for example when the migrant still refuses to return home, or pending removal or the processing of his application for a visa,) the *préfet* must lodge an application with the *juge des libertés et de la détention* (judge of freedoms and detention) of the relevant *tribunal de grande instance.* Interestingly this judicial position was created in 2000 by statute No. 2000-516 relating to the presumption of innocence. The name of this specialist judge is reminiscent of the deprivation of freedom which is associated with detention. This judge has extensive jurisdiction to decide whether someone should be detained, including in criminal custody.

The *juge des libertés et de la détention* only has 24 hours to hand down his decision further to the *préfet's* application. Non-compliance with that deadline would result in the migrant being released from the *Centre de Rétention Administrative*. The judge may refuse the renewal of the detention. Within 24 hours of the order of the *juge des libertés et de la détention*, an appeal can be lodged before the first president of the Court of appeal who must hand down his decision within 48 hours of the appeal. At the end of this period (of five plus 20 days) the *préfet* can make another application for a further 20-day retention. Therefore, 45 days is the maximum detention to which a migrant can be subjected. An exception applies to non-European terrorist suspects for whom detention can last six months.

Regarding house arrest, with or without an electronic bracelet, it is an alternative to detention in a *Centre de Rétention Administrative*. It is ordered by the *juge des libertés et de la détention,* at the detainee's request.

The *préfet's* decisions ordering detention can be disputed by the migrant before the *tribunal administratif.* This court, which is different from the *juge des libertés et de la détention,* has jurisdiction to check the legality of decisions made in the name of the government against an individual. The migrant has 48 hours to issue his action before the *tribunal administratif* running from the moment he was served with the *préfet's* decision. At the same time as attempting to have the detention decision declared null and void, the migrant can seek an order that the *obligation de quitter le territoire français* ("OQTF") asking him to quit the French territory, also be annulled. The *tribunal administratif* has 72 hours to hand down its decision.

In view of the above, two comments spring to mind. On the one hand, the procedure revolving around detention, and incidentally house arrest, is far from straightforward. Two entirely different sets of courts are involved, which are the *juge des libertés et de la détention* and the *tribunal administratif*. Both are headed by two different supreme courts which are respectively the *Cour de cassation* and the *Conseil d'Etat*. Applications before both sets of courts are subject to different rules and different limitation periods. It would be extremely complex for a non-French speaking person who is not conversant with the legal language to be successful in his applications, unless he is assisted by someone who has legal knowledge.

On the other hand, the procedure before both the *juge des libertés et de la détention* and the *tribunal administratif* is quite repetitive. As opposed to criminal litigation which revolves around very different situations, there are only a limited number of situations an unauthorised migrant might find himself in. Therefore, if it is usually important for the migrant to be able to be assisted by someone, that person does not have to be a professionally trained lawyer (*avocat*). Someone from an association working with the *Centre de Rétention Administrative,* who has some practical knowledge of immigration litigation, should be sufficient. When access to legal services is considered, the presence of relevant services is of course important.

In the United Kingdom

According to paragraphs 16 and 21 of schedule 2 to the Immigration Act 1971 and subsections 62 and 67 of the Nationality, Immigration and Asylum Act 2002, the power to detain foreign nationals belongs to the Immigration Officers and the Secretary of State for the Home Department. Unlike France where detention of non-terrorist migrants is limited to 45 days, there is no pre-determined limit in the United Kingdom as to how long the immigration authorities can detain a person pending an application for a visa or asylum being processed or whilst awaiting deportation. But in paragraphs 45ff. of *MXL and others* [2010] EWHC 2397 (Admin) the High Court held that a period of weeks is disproportionate when it leads to a parent being separated from a young child.

Just like the OFII in France, advice in the United Kingdom can always be sought from the Office of the Immigration Services Commissioner. This is an independent public body set up under the Immigration and Asylum Act 1999. Alternatively, and once a detention decision has been made, the migrant may wish to seek legal advice. The detention order is usually made by a border officer upon the migrant's arrival in the United Kingdom, or when presented to an immigration office within the country. It can also be issued once a removal decision has been made, after a prison sentence has been served or after the person has been arrested by a police officer.

In England and Wales (as opposed to the United Kingdom in general, Scotland and Northern Ireland having a different court system), there has recently been a change with the courts which have jurisdiction over immigration litigation. Since mid-February 2010, the Tribunals, Courts and Enforcement Act 2007 has transferred the work of the former Asylum and Immigration Tribunal to a First-tier Tribunal (Immigration and Asylum Chamber) and on appeal, to an Upper Tribunal (Immigration and Asylum Chamber.) The introduction of this two-tier system has made immigration litigation more complex than before, more time consuming and potentially more costly. Its aim might be to limit the number of cases heard by the higher courts.

As in France, two sets of legal actions can be issued by the migrant when a detention decision is made against him. An application for judicial review can be lodged against the detention decision with the administrative court. Unlike the French *tribunal administratif* which has a very different jurisdiction to the *tribunal de grande instance*, the British administrative court is a division of the High Court. Simultaneously and by application of paragraph 22 schedule 2 of the Immigration Act 1971 and section 36 of the Asylum and Immigration Act 2004, the migrant can apply to a Chief Immigration Officer for temporary release, temporary admission or bail, with or without an electronic bracelet. Should this application be dismissed, an appeal can be lodged to the First-tier Tribunal (Immigration and Asylum Chamber) and a further appeal before the Upper-tier Tribunal.

According to the official website of HM Courts and Tribunals Service, the migrant's appeal must be lodged within two, five or 28 days of being served with the relevant decision. These limitation periods differ depending on whether the appeal is in connection with a fast-track case, an application made within or outside the United Kingdom. (HM Courts & Tribunals Service 2013)

Just like France, the detention procedure is not straightforward but repetitive. Services have been made available to migrants. Here again, the services might be difficult to use without the assistance of someone, whether or not professionally qualified as a lawyer.

Access to legal services

Saying that the authorities—in particular the French ones—are not keen on detailing the detainees' conditions of access to law is an understatement. This may be because they do not want to disclose too much information or simply that there is not much to say about their need to access legal services. A few preliminary comments must be made.

Firstly, the concept of legal services must be defined. Although unauthorised migrants tend to be assimilated to criminals, the fact of being an unauthorised migrant is not, in itself, an offence. Being sent to a *Centre de Rétention Administrative* or an Immigration Removal Centre is not a punishment. The detainee does not have to defend himself against a criminal charge. He just wants to avoid deportation and have his application (for a visa, etc.) speedily processed by the authorities. The scope of the legal services needed is therefore limited.

Secondly, another issue is when the detainee needs access to legal services. There are two crucial points: when he is arrested and sent to a *Centre de Rétention Administrative* or an Immigration Removal Centre and subsequently, once detained, if he feels his application is not processed quickly enough by the authorities. Thirdly, do the authorities respond to those needs. In other words, are the rights of unauthorised migrants less protected than those of criminals?

In France

By decision No. 86-216 of 3September, 1986, the *Conseil Constitutionnel* held that detention, which should only apply when it is impossible to deport the migrant immediately, should comply with the individual's rights to a proper defence and be limited in its duration and scope.

The CESEDA grants detainees a right to legal information and assistance. After his arrest and upon detention being ordered by the *préfet,* the migrant must be informed, in a language he can understand, of his rights. In particular, he must be informed of his right to apply for legal aid for any actions he might want to bring before the *juge des libertés et de la détention* or the *tribunal administratif.* Like any other person in France and for any type of legal action, legal aid is not granted automatically but is subject to compliance with certain financial and merits criteria. The migrant should be told that during the whole detention, he can benefit from an interpretor, counsel and a doctor.

The OFII officers who work in each *Centre de Rétention Administrative* must stress that the migrant only has five days to make an asylum application from the moment he is informed of his rights. Entries are made on a special register, confirming that the relevant information has been given and when. If the *préfet* seeks the renewal of the initial five-day retention, the *juge des libertés et de la détention* is under a duty to remind the detainee of his rights once more and ensure that he was not only informed of his rights but capable of exercising them. Likewise the *tribunal administratif* exercises control over the compliance with the migrant's rights, if and when a legal action is brought before the relevant judges.

Statute No. 2007-1545 of 30 October, 2007 created a *Contrôleur général des lieux de privation de liberté* who visits the various places where people are held, to ensure that their fundamental rights are guaranteed. This controller not only visits *Centres de Rétention Administrative* but also prisons. He must make sure that the *Centres de Rétention Administrative* have a specific room for *avocats*, one for the OFII and one with a telephone to ensure that the detainee's rights to a defence can be exercised.

Avocats are of course likely to assist migrants and give them legal advice and representation in court. Recent cuts in the legal aid budget mean that the legal profession is less available. However, this does not affect the migrants' access to legal services. As explained before, the procedure before the *juge des libertés et de la détention* or the *tribunal administratif* is complex if done on a one-off basis, but it is repetitive. Specialised charity organizations Cimade, Ordre de Malte, Forum Réfugiés, France Terre d'Asile and Assfam which enter into contracts with the French state to help detainees provide good quality legal advice as well as, incidentally, psychological advice. The associations receive funding. The figure put forward for the first ten months in 2013 was 4.2 million euros which, due to the economic crisis, would represent a 20 to 50% reduction for some centres. (Tassel "Centres de rétention: Valls rend la parole aux associations" 2012)

An interesting incident must be mentioned, which casts some light on the attitude taken by the authorities to illegal immigration. The contracts passed with Cimade, Ordre de Malte, Forum Réfugiés, France Terre d'Asile and Assfam expired on 31 January, 2013. A public bid requiring other charities to step in was supposed to be made. However, information was leaked which revealed that the draft bid would have imposed a 500-euro fine on the charities in case of "non-compliance with the duty of reserve and obligation of discretion." (Tassel "Immigration: les associations sommées de se taire?" 2012) The underlying message was that any charity allowed in the *Centres de Rétention Administrative* should refrain from disclosing any negative information to the outside world. After this was revealed to the media, the said clause was removed from the draft bid. (Tassel "Centres de rétention: Valls rend la parole aux associations" 2012)

The above incident does not necessarily mean that there are breaches of human rights in the *Centres de Rétention Administrative*. But it shows that the government is not keen on spending too much time—and too much taxpayers' money—discussing the rights of illegal migrants.

A recent law No. 2012-1560 of 31 December, 2012 amended the provisions of article L611-1-1 of the CESEDA by confirming that a foreigner who is unable to provide evidence of his right to be in France can be "retained" by a police officer or a *gendarme* whilst his identity and situation are investigated. The emphasis was placed once more on the fact that an illegal migrant is not a criminal. This followed the *cour de cassation*'s order No. 11-19.250 of 5 July, 2012 by which the French supreme court held that the *garde à vue* (police custody) could not apply whilst a foreigner's identity or right of residence were being checked.

In the United Kingdom

As mentioned above, Conservative Prime Minister David Cameron has announced his intention to withdraw legal aid for immigration cases from April 2013. (Jowit) This is not just directed at unauthorised migration as most legal fields have recently sustained drastic cuts. However, the actual withdrawal of legal aid can mean two things. On the one hand, the court dispute of a detention decision is not of sufficient interest to justify granting migrants a loan of taxpayers' money. On the other hand, the court procedure before the administrative court and the First-tier Tribunal (Immigration and Asylum Chamber) may be complex if dealt with on a one-off basis. But unlike a criminal trial which requires substantial work for the defendant, it is also repetitive.

Unlike French *Centres de Rétention Administrative* and according to the UK Border Agency, the structure of the Immigration Removal Centres is much more open, at least apparently. For instance and if we look at the information provided online about Brook House, solicitors are amongst the many visitors who can go to an Immigration Removal Centre. (2012) A list of recommended solicitors is provided on the Legal Services Commission's website. (2012) For most if not all, Immigration Removal Centres,[2] legal visits can take place throughout the working week by prior

[2] See UK Border Agency's website on Morton Hall.

appointment. Some centres (like Dover) even have legal surgeries.

Moreover and unlike the French authorities who tend to be cagey about the conditions in which detainees can access legal services, there are reports published in the United Kingdom by HM Chief Inspector of Prisons. Incidentally and like the *Contrôleur général des lieux de privation de liberté,* HM Chief Inspector of Prisons not only controls Immigration Removal Centres but also prisons. For Tinsley House for instance, and according to paragraph 3.1 of a 2011 report, "detainees" have access to legal services:

> Detainees could access legal advice through the twice-weekly duty advice surgeries, but it was more difficult for detainees to find a solicitor to represent them. Significantly fewer non-English speaking detainees had a solicitor. Detainees could communicate with their solicitors easily. Word and PDF files could not be opened in the IT suite which prevented detainees from obtaining information from important legal websites. Detainees had access to up-to-date legal text books, but country of origin information reports were not available electronically or in hard copy. There were sufficient facilities for solicitors to meet their clients. There was insufficient information available to detainees who wished to complain about their solicitors. (25)

For Yarl's Wood, paragraph 3.1 of the 2011 report states:

> Most detainees had a lawyer but the detention duty advice scheme was oversubscribed. There were few notices in the centre providing up-to-date relevant information on legal advice. Detainees could easily contact their lawyers but fewer detainees than at other centres had had a visit from their lawyer. The library lacked sufficient relevant material. Good internet access to legal resources was hampered by excessive printing restrictions. Legal visits facilities were good. Bail for Immigration Detainees provided valuable workshops. (27)

In paragraph 1.12 of their general report, HM Inspectorate of Prisons and the Independent Chief Inspector of Borders and Immigration concluded that:

> Detainees reported difficulties with obtaining good quality legal advice and around a quarter […] told us they did not have legal representation. A fifth of those held for more than six months [...] said they had not made a bail application. (6, 8)

A number of conclusions can be drawn from the above. On the one hand, HM Chief Inspector of Prisons reaches the view that being computer literate is important. Online legal information is sufficient for the migrant to know his rights but in the centres mentioned above, online access was insufficient or too restricted. On the other hand, should a solicitor be instructed, the "facilities" are available for detainees to meet with him. HM Chief Inspector of Prisons is of the view that the British government has provided enough funding to grant the migrants access to legal services. However, non-English detainees have difficulties getting hold of a solicitor. If they find one, visits from solicitors are rare and little information is available on how to sue a solicitor if he is negligent. In a nutshell, the authorities have done a lot for detainees and only minor improvements can be made by the authorities. However, the legal profession is either not available or not interested in illegal migrants.

The objectivity of HM Chief Inspector of Prisons is disputable here. Generally speaking, a profession cannot be expected to work for free. By withdrawing legal aid from immigration law, the authorities deprive detainees of the possibility to instruct a solicitor. HM Inspectorate of Prisons and the Independent Chief Inspector of Borders and Immigration are aware of that problem. According to paragraph 1.12 of their report, "More restrictive Legal Service Commission (LSC) funding rules mean that there are now fewer providers in a position to take on detainees' cases." (12) HM Chief Inspector of Prisons fails to mention the Immigration Law Practitioners' Association ("ILPA") whose members provide free advice to detainees and act as a lobbying group.

Just like in France, the repetitive nature of the legal problems faced by illegal migrants means that people with a limited legal background should be sufficient to advise them. If HM Chief Inspector of Prisons criticises the legal profession, he praises associations, such as the Association of Visitors to Immigration Detainees (AVID) and Bail for Immigration Detainees (BID), which help detainees with their legal and sometimes psychological issues.

Conclusion

The background information given above shows that even before they joined Europe, France and the United Kingdom adopted a policy of border control, filtering migration according to their needs or their wish to allow family reunion. Both countries have shown, through the number of residence permits granted each year, their willingness to welcome authorised migration. Since they respectively joined Europe in 1958 and 1973, both countries have had to abide by European legislation. The current European policy aims at tackling unauthorised migration. Article

5(1)(f) of the ECHR allows the limited detention of migrants until they are deported or extradited.

Detention is purely administrative. It is ordered pending the investigation of the migrant's situation or his deportation. Detention should not be construed as a punishment although illegal immigrants are often considered as criminals on the grounds that their entry into a country was unauthorised. Because the migrant does not have to defend himself against a criminal accusation made against him, the opportunities he has to go to court are limited. They mostly involve disputing a detention decision, applying for bail or asylum. The limited scope of legal problems which a migrant may come across means that he does not need a wide access to legal services. Both countries seem to provide adequate ways of accessing law. In France and in the United Kingdom, migrants can instruct a lawyer. They have until now been able to apply for legal aid although in the United Kingdom this right was partially withdrawn on 1 April, 2013 after the Legal Aid, Sentencing and Punishment of Offenders Act 2002 came into force. Due to major cuts in the public funding of justice, legal aid is no longer available to migrants not detained They can seek the advice, including legal or psychological, of volunteers working for specialised charities, they can access the internet to look for legal information and documentation.

Conversely, the relevant procedures applicable before the French and British courts are complex and subject to strict deadlines. In France and depending on the type of action sought, two entirely different courts have jurisdiction. In the United Kingdom, a recent reform introduced a two-tier system which makes access to law more complex. If, due to the administrative nature of immigration detention, migrants cannot be sent to prison, the outcome of any court action is important. Should an application against a detention decision not be issued in time, or should it fail to succeed, the migrant will be deported. In France, Assfam and four other charities working in the centres denounced the French "deportation machine." They criticised the fact that a quarter of those detained "from July 2011 were deported before the fifth day of detention, i.e. without having a chance to see the judge [...]." (2012) In the United Kingdom and unlike France where a statutory 45-day limit applies, the absence of a maximum detention limit led to 40 migrants being detained in 2012 for more than two years. (Travis) This shows that in some cases, the human rights of migrants may occasionally be breached. In *Lamari v. Secretary of State for the Home Department* [2012] EWHC 1630 (Admin) rendered on 18 June, 2012, the High Court held that Mr Lamari who suffered from a mental illness and was subjected to continuing detention, should be released and granted damages.

There does not seem to be an ideal solution to the problem of unauthorised migration. European Member States must obviously strike a balance between the rights guaranteed to any human being in a democracy and their national interests. On the one hand, freedom of movement should be restricted as little as possible. On the other hand dealing with illegal immigration should not place too heavy a financial burden on the taxpayer. Unauthorised migration should be tightly controlled.

Works Cited

Assfam. *Immigration: le nombre de titres de séjour délivrés est en hausse*, 24 August, 2010. Accessed 25 October, 2012. URL: <http://www.assfam.org/spip.php?article968>.

Assfam, Forum Réfugiés, France terre d'asile, La Cimade and Ordre de Malte. *Rapport 2011 sur les Centres et Locaux de Rétention*, 2012. Accessed 20 March, 2013. URL: <http://www.france-terre-asile.org/component/flexicontent/item/7817-cprapport-2011-sur-les-centres-et-locaux-de-retention-administrative>.

BERNARD-REYMOND, Pierre. *La gestion des centres de rétention administrative peut encore être améliorée; rapport d'information n° 516 (2008-2009)*. 3 July, 2009. Accessed 29 October, 2012. URL: <http://www.senat.fr/rap/r08-516/r08-51623.html>.

BLINDER, Scott. *Non-European Labour Migration to the UK*. Oxford: University of Oxford. The Migration Observatory. 30 January, 2012. Accessed 11 December, 2012. URL: <http://migrationobservatory.ox.ac.uk/briefings/non-european-labour-migration-uk>.

BROWN, Ruth. "Racism and immigration in Britain." *International Socialism* 68 (Fall 1995). Accessed 28 November, 2012. URL: <http://www.marxists.org/history/etol//newspape/isj2/1995/isj2-068/brown.htm>.

CARRERA, Sergio, and Guild ELSPETH. *The French Presidency's European Pact on Immigration and Asylum: Intergovernmentalism vs. Europeanisation? Security vs. Rights?* Centre for European Policy Studies. September 2008. Accessed 30 October, 2012. URL: <http://www.ceps.eu/files/book/1706.pdf>.

CHOLEWINSKI, R. *Migrant Workers in International Human Rights Law.* 1997. Oxford: Oxford University Press.

Council of Europe Commissioner for Human Rights. February 2010. CommDH/IssuePaper(2010)1. *Criminalisation of Migration in*

Europe: Human Rights Implications. Accessed 19 October, 2012. URL: <https://wcd.coe.int/ViewDoc.jsp?id=1579605#P88_9354>.

European Commission. *Immigration policy*. January 2012. Accessed 12 October, 2012. URL: <http://www.europarl.europa.eu/ftu/pdf/en/FTU_4.12.3.pdf>.

Franco-British Declaration on immigration of July 2009. Accessed 23 October, 2012. URL: <http://ukinfrance.fco.gov.uk/en/about-us/working-with-france/justice-home-affairs/migration/>.

G4S. *Accomodation Services*. 2013. Accessed 23 February, 2013. URL: <http://www.g4s.uk.com/en-GB/What%20we%20do/Services/Care%20and%20justice%20services/Immigration%20and%20Borders/Accommodation%20services/>.

GEDDES, Andrew. *The Politics of Migration and Immigration in Europe*. London: Sage Publications, 2003.

HAMMARBERG, Thomas. *It is wrong to criminalize migration*. Council of Europe Commissioner for Human Rights, 2008. Accessed 20 November, 2012. URL: <http://www.coe.int/t/commissioner/Viewpoints/080929_en.asp>.

Hansard. "Immigration: Detention Centres Questions by Baroness Warsi." Lord Hansard text for 4 February, 2010 (pt 0002.) London: House of Commons, 2010.

HM Chief Inspector of Prisons. *Report on an announced inspection of Yarl's Wood Immigration Removal Centre*. London: HM Inspectorate of Prisons. July 2011. Accessed 13 January, 2013. URL: <http://www.justice.gov.uk/downloads/publications/inspectorate-reports/hmipris/immigration-removal-centre-inspections/yarls-wood/yarls-wood-2011.pdf>.

—. *Report on an announced inspection of Tinsley House Immigration Removal Centre*. London: HM Inspectorate of Prisons, February 2011. Accessed 30 October, 2012. URL: <http://www.gdwg.org.uk/downloads/hmip2011report.pdf>.

HM Inspectorate of Prisons and the Independent Chief Inspector of Borders and Immigration. *The effectiveness and impact of immigration detention casework*. London: HM Inspectorate of Prisons, December 2012. Accessed 15 February, 2013. URL: <http://www.justice.gov.uk/downloads/publications/inspectorate-reports/hmipris/thematic-reports-and-research-publications/immigration-detention-casework-2012.pdf>.

HM Courts & Tribunals Service. *Immigration and Asylum Tribunal – Appeals*. Last modified 10 January, 2013. URL: <http://www.justice.gov.uk/tribunals/immigration-asylum/appeals>.

HM Prison Service. *Regime information for Dover Immigration Removal Centre*. Last updated 5 March, 2012. URL: <http://www.justice.gov.uk/contacts/prison-finder/dover-immigration-removal-centre/regime>.

HOLMES, Colin. *John Bull's Island: Immigration and British Society 1871-1971*. London: Macmillan, 1988.

Information Centre about Asylum and Refugees in the UK. *Detention of Asylum Seekers in the UK. Thematic Briefing prepared for the Independent Asylum Commission.* London: Runnymede Trust, 2007.

JOWIT, Juliette. "Immigrants too often taking advantage of UK public services, says Cameron." *The Guardian*. 14 February, 2013. Accessed 16 February, 2013. URL: <http://www.guardian.co.uk/politics/2013/feb/14/immigrants-taking-advantage-cameron>.

Legal Services Commission. *November 2012: Update on Legal Services for Clients Detained at Immigration Removal Centres (IRCs)*. Last modified November, 2012. URL: <http://www.justice.gov.uk/downloads/legal-aid/civil-categories-of-law/irc-provider-list-november-2012.pdf>.

Ministère de l'Intérieur et de l'Immigration. *The European Pact on Immigration and Asylum*. 2008. Accessed 15 October, 2012. URL: <http://www.immigration.gouv.fr/IMG/pdf/Plaquette_EN.pdf>.

MORICE, Alain. "Violences expérimentales à l'abri des regards?". *Vacarme* 44 (Summer 2008.) Accessed 8 December, 2012. URL: <http://www.vacarme.org/article1623.html>.

OFII. *Qui sommes-nous?*. Accessed 13 January, 2013. URL: <http://www.ofii.fr/qui_sommes-nous_46/index.html?sub_menu=1>.

PESCHANSKI, Denis. "Le régime de Vichy a existé. Gouvernants et gouvernés dans la France de Vichy: juillet 1940–avril 1942" in PESCHANSKI, Denis. *Vichy 1040-1944: Archives de guerre d'Angelo Tasca*. Milano: Feltrinelli, 1986: 3-36.

"Rétention administrative d'un étranger en instance d'éloignement." Last modified 11 February, 2013. URL: <http://vosdroits.service-public.fr/F2780.xhtml>.

ROSS, Stewart. *The Industrial Revolution*. London: Evans Brothers Ltd, 2008.

SILVERMAN, Stephanie J. and Ruchi HAJELA. *Immigration Detention in the UK*. Oxford: University of Oxford, Migration Observatory, 2012: 3-7.

SINGER-KEREL, Jeanne. "Protection de la main d'oeuvre nationale en temps de crise; le précédent des années trente." *Revue européenne de migrations internationales* 5/5-2 (1989): 7-27.

STUMPF, Juliet P. "The Crimmigration Crisis: Immigrants, Crime, and Sovereign Power." *American University Law Review* 56 (2006): 367-419.

TASSEL, Fabrice. "Immigration: les associations sommées de se taire?" *Libération*. 11 December, 2012. Accessed 13 January, 2013. URL: <http://www.liberation.fr/societe/2012/12/11/immigration-les-associations-sommees-de-se-taire_866761>.

—. "Centres de rétention: Valls rend la parole aux associations." *Libération*. 20 December, 2012. Accessed 27 January, 2013. URL: <http://www.liberation.fr/societe/2012/12/20/centres-de-retention-valls-rend-la-parole-aux-associations_869054>.

TRAVIS, Alan. "Service Commission (LSC) funding rules mean that there are now fewer providers in a position to take on detainees' cases." *The Guardian*. 12 December, 2012. Accessed 29 December, 2012. URL: <http://www.guardian.co.uk/uk/2012/dec/12/deportees-detained-over-two-years>.

UK Border Agency. *Our agency 2015 change programme*. Accessed 19 March, 2013. URL: <http://www.ukba.homeoffice.gov.uk/aboutus/organisation/agency/>.

—. *Immigration Removal Centres*. Accessed 7 December, 2012. URL: <www.ukba.homeoffice.gov.uk/aboutus/organisation/immigrationremovalcentres/>.

—. *Morton Hall immigration removal centre*. Accessed 11 December, 2012. URL: <http://www.ukba.homeoffice.gov.uk/aboutus/organisation/immigrationremovalcentres/morton-hall>.

—. *Brook House immigration removal centre*. Accessed 7 March, 2013. URL: <http://www.ukba.homeoffice.gov.uk/aboutus/organisation/immigrationremovalcentres/brookhouse>.

VINCENT, Elise. "Les centres de rétention, polémiques depuis leur création." *Le Monde*. 3 May, 2012. Accessed 25 October, 2012. URL: <http://www.lemonde.fr/election-presidentielle-2012/article/2012/05/03/ce-que-l-on-sait-des-centres-de-retention_1695076_1471069.html>.

—. "Immigration illégale, le grand écart de Manuel Valls." *Le Monde*. 13 March, 2013. Accessed 25 March, 2013. URL: <http://www.lemonde.fr/societe/article/2013/03/13/immigration-illegale-le-grand-ecart-de-m-valls_1847264_3224.html>.

WINNETT, Robert. "Tony Blair: I don't regret opening UK borders to

European immigrants." *The Telegraph*. 24 June, 2012. Accessed 17 October, 2012. URL: <http://www.telegraph.co.uk/news/uknews/immigration/9352335/Tony-Blair-I-dont-regret-opening-UK-borders-to-European-immigrants.html>.

IMMIGRATION DETENTION IN THE UK: THE ROLE OF OVERSIGHT MECHANISMS AND CONSTRICTING RULES TO RAISE STANDARDS

CATHERINE PUZZO
UNIVERSITY OF TOULOUSE II, FRANCE

The detention of rejected, unauthorized migrants who are held in prison-like facilities, often for long periods and sometimes without legal review has developed on a large scale in many democratic countries. Over the last 30 years the growing trend has been to use detention as a technique of migration control to ensure border controls. Governments have often argued that the security of the state and the fight against unauthorized migrants have legitimized detention powers. Increasingly immigration detention has become a bureaucratic, administrative process in the hands of the executive and not always within the courts' jurisdiction. Such situation reveals the predominance of political considerations over the respect of fundamental liberties of specific categories of populations who are in a particularly vulnerable situation.

In Britain although asylum applications are at a twenty-year low, the country has built one of the largest detention estate in Europe to confine migrants whose asylum application is being processed or who are waiting to be deported. Preventive detention is said to limit the risk of absconding but there is no maximum time limit and some migrants spend prolonged periods in detention. It is an administrative process not automatically reviewed by courts that interferes with migrants' most fundamental right: the right to liberty. It is the expression of state power and has a discretionary and arbitrary character. Immigration detention also raises the question of the state's responsibility to protect rights and freedoms.

This article begins with a presentation of the evolution of immigration detention; it then examines the role of oversight mechanisms over the ways migrants are detained and the gradual implementation of standard regulations. Finally the last section attempts to assess the effectiveness of these mechanisms in the light of the latest developments in the field of immigration detention.

Evolution of immigration detention in the UK

The historical development of immigration detention sheds light on the specificity of this form of detention which has gradually criminalized migrants and has justified the development of increasingly out of proportion state powers over non-citizens. The 1971 Immigration Act (paragraphs 16 to 21, schedule 2) gave immigration officers the right to put in jail anyone found without the travel documents necessary to enter the UK. The text introduced administrative detention since immigration authorities were conferred a discretionary power, permitting detention, but as Wilscher notes "not requiring detention." The period of detention was meant to be as short as possible before sending back the irregular migrant. Hence detention was the exception until the 1980s: 95 in 1973, 138 in 1974, 188 in 1975 and 1,034 in 1980. (Wilscher 88) Towards the mid-1980s the rule became applicable to failed asylum seekers in the absence of any specific provision for that category of migrants. The Conservative governments argued that detention would prevent irregular migrants and failed refugees from absconding. Detention was then claimed to be necessary because of the absence of transit zones and random identity checks as those existing in France for example. Gradually, detention became a normalized tool of immigration control and its duration increased. By the time New Labour came to power, although it was still regulated by primary legislation it was administered by executive instructions issued by the Home Office to its staff.

Tony Blair's first government set to devise a "comprehensive and long-term strategy to modernize immigration controls."[1] Their first reforms implemented via primary legislation included the right to bail hearings with the Immigration and Asylum Act 1999 which granted in its Part III the right to automatic bail hearings after eight days in detention and then again after 36 days. It thus gave immigration detainees rights closer to that of criminal suspects and introduced clear rules in the judicial process to consider the case of immigration detainees. However, that provision was soon amended by the Nationality, Immigration and Asylum Act 2002 which still provides migrant detainees with some right to bail hearing, but leaves the onus to make a bail application on the detainee's representative.

---

[1] 1998 White Paper on immigration and asylum *Fairer, Faster, Firmer.*

The 2002 text also introduced the Fast Track procedure, an accelerated process for considering asylum claims. While their case is 'fast-tracked' migrants are confined in specific facilities for a period that could be described as "pre-decision" detention. This procedure is used for the cases deemed straightforward and according to British authorities unfounded. The provision had already been announced in the 1998 White Paper *'Fairer, Faster, Firmer'* which forecast the progressive extension of detention. It is meant to limit the risks linked to temporary admission but the systematic use of "pre-decision" detention raises the question of the proportionality of the use and continuation of detention. To what extent can immigration officers assess the likelihood of the offence? How imminent is the risk of absconding to legitimize detention?

The decision to detain migrants preventively is made by an immigration officer and such decision is not automatically reviewed by a judicial authority. The examination of the application takes about ten to 12 days, during which migrants might be detained even if the Home Office is keen to stress that other solutions than detention may be proposed. The very tight time scale is always against migrants' rights: most migrants struggle to understand the complex and unfamiliar procedure and clear information is not always available. Many do not have access to legal advice and meet their solicitor just before their interview. Lawyers do not have the right time to gather legal evidence to defend their clients. As a result in 2011 out of 2,118 cases which were fast-tracked only 66 were granted refugee status (3%) and seven humanitarian protection or discretionary leave to remain. The delay to submit an appeal against refusal being very short, only 5% were successful.[2]

Although detention should be as short as possible, Detention Action's research (2011) suggests that in 2010-2011 migrants were detained for an average of two weeks before their application was processed and that before being removed migrants had spent in total 58 days in detention.

The current coalition government has not modified most of the guiding principles regarding detention that were laid by their predecessors. The Fast Track procedure is still operating in Harmondsworth Immigration Removal Centre (IRC) for men and Yarl's Wood IRC for women. The detention estate has further developed and the UK Border Agency (UKBA) continues to argue that detention measures are meant to protect the public against re-offence and absconding. They have not abolished one of the most controversial provisions of the system: the absence of a maximum length of detention. Parliament has not yet approved the 2008

[2] <http://www.refugeecouncil.org.uk/assests/0002/5610/Asylym_Briefing_2013. pdf>.

European directive which provides for the harmonization of European systems to expel irregular migrants and for a maximum duration of 18 months for any irregular detained.[3]

However, a long-awaited reform was finally adopted by the Coalition government under the initiative of its Liberal Democrat Deputy Prime Minister. In December 2010, Nick Clegg announced that the UK was eliminating its policy of long-term detention of migrant children. Families with an irregular status are dealt with by special case workers for families and their cases are looked at by an Independent Family Returns Panel. The government has sought to expand the range of non-custodial facilities designated to "host" migrant families due to be deported. Nevertheless, the opening of the pre-departure accommodation centre located in Pease Pottage (near Gatwick) for those non-compliant families has raised numerous criticisms. It has been observed that this family-friendly accommodation merely amounts to disguised detention. So far the Coalition has not improved the situation of unaccompanied minors whose age is in dispute and who are often detained with other adults as there is a widespread culture of disbelief among immigration officers as to the trustworthiness of their claim. Once again such practices reveal that the state is more concerned with the maintenance of controls, whatever the psychological costs for detainees and the economic and financial costs for the government.

Detention has become a central piece of immigration and asylum policies and even an aspiration for the Home Office.[4] It has been used as a regulatory tool of asylum right and the 2005 White Paper recommended that about 30% of applications for asylum should be examined within the fast-track procedure. Currently the latest figures reveal that 11% of asylum applications go into the Detained Fast Track procedure. Hence, although not mandatory, the growth of detention over the past 30 years has entailed an expansion of the range of groups confined and the enlargement of the detention estate. The growing use of detention "reflects decisions consciously made by governments about how to deal with particular social issues." (Burnett and Chebe 96)

---

[3] Directive 2008/115/EC of the European Parliament and of the Council of 16 December, 2008 on common standards and procedures in Member states for returning illegally staying third-country nationals.

[4] See "*The five year strategy for asylum and immigration,*" Governmental report, February 7, 2005, and "*Controlling our Borders: making migration work,*" White Paper, 28 February, 2005.

Specificity of immigration detention in the UK

Michael Flynn (2011) defines the phenomenon of immigration detention as "the deprivation of liberty of non-citizens because of their status". This definition has the merit to be simple and comprehensive as it views foreigners detained in IRCs as a single cohort even though the reality is far more complex. IRCs detain various categories of non-citizens, male and female as well as minors despite the recent reform. The main categories include asylum seekers pending examination of their claim within the Fast-Track procedure, asylum seekers pending a decision whether to remove, failed asylum seekers due to be rapidly removed to their country of origin, foreigners with an irregular status (irregular leave to remain, absence of working permit, unauthorized immigrants with forged or fake documents used to enter the UK, overstayers) and foreign prisoners. The latter, since 2006 and the scandal over foreign prisoners, are transferred into these centres just before their deportation to their country. It is the only example of a mandatory detention (UK Border Act 2007) for a group of foreigners, whether they have been convicted of a wide range of crimes or sentenced to more than one year. Despite the multiplicity of situations and the existence of many categories of migrants detained, the most common is of people who have sought asylum at some point in their immigration adjudication process. (Silverman and Hajela 2012) In 2010, 17,790 were held in detention and 57,085 were either deported or left voluntarily. (Global Detention Project 2011)

In the absence of a maximum period of detention in IRCs, courts have been led to clarify the notion of a "reasonable" period to hold someone in detention. As early as 1983 the British courts defined the lawfulness of immigration detention with the leading case *Hardial Singh (R (Hardial Singh) v. Governor of Durham Prison* [1983] EWHC 1 (QB) which first established what later became known as the *Hardial Singh* principles: there must be intention of deporting the person and powers to detain must be used for that purpose; the period of detention must be reasonable in all circumstances; if deportation cannot be effected within a reasonable period, then the Secretary of State should not exercise his power of detention; removal should be enforced rapidly and with diligence by the Secretary of State. Such principles have been further confirmed in more recent cases *Wahamba Lumba & Kadian Migthy v. Secretary of State for the Home Department* [2011] UKSC 12 and *Sheperd Masimba Kambadzi v. Secretary of State for the Home Department* [2011] UKSC 23. The Supreme Court has held that these principles apply to the UK Border Agency when detaining foreign nationals for immigration purposes and has reasserted the need to consider the "reasonableness" of detaining someone. Hence it was stated that the migrant's refusal to make a voluntary departure may have little or no relevance to the use of detention. The Supreme Court also made clear that policies on the use of immigration detention should be made public. Secret policies used by the UKBA such as the non-publication of regular reviews of detention make detention unlawful. The criteria defining a "reasonable" duration to detain somebody raise the principle of proportionality "which provides that any decision to deprive a person of his or her liberty must be proportionate to specific ends established in law." (Flynn 2011: 3) The conditions of detention contradict this principle of proportionality: a number of official bodies (domestic and international) as well as field charity organizations have repeatedly pointed out that the UK's practice of detention has resulted in serious mental, physical health deterioration of detainees (self-harming, attempted suicide) and in violence leading to riots and protests.

Over the past decades the UK detention estate has expanded to adapt to decision-makers' policies to exclude a growing number of foreign individuals. In the 1970s the first immigration detention centres were prisons aisles, juvenile centres for young delinquents or military buildings refurbished and transformed into centres. Following numerous campaigns organized by pressure groups and charities in charge of migrants' rights, it became clear for governments of the day that prisons were inadequate places to detain migrants, even if temporarily. A programme to refurbish or build specific sites dedicated to the incarceration of migrants began in the mid-1980s and the number of places increased rapidly during the Labour decade. That had become all the more necessary since the number of asylum seekers, irregulars and failed asylum seekers, had grown substantially from about 26,205 applications in 1990 to 80,000 applications in 2000. As of February 2013 Britain has a total capacity of 3,408 beds with a variety of immigration detention centres to be defined as "the facilities used to confine non-citizens until they can be deported or their claims assessed." (Flynn 2011) Britain has 11 long-term IRCs, three short-term residential centres, one semi-secured "family-friendly" centre. In addition there are 36 short-term hold facilities (STHFs) for very short detention periods (a few hours, up to a night) and specific facilities in various prisons and police stations. Oakington IRC closed in November 2010 and a new short-term detention centre (25 beds) opened in Northern Ireland. (AVID) The detention estate is vast with differing levels of security; some places built according to prison norms whereas others look like ultra-safe residence.

IRCs are under the supervision of the UK Border Agency (UKBA), the delivery agency of the Home Office responsible for immigration and asylum operations. Since their creation the private sector has been closely involved in their management and although some IRCs are operated directly by the UKBA and the Prison Services the majority is managed by private organizations contracted out by the UKBA. The implications of the private sector and the paradox represented by private providers have been explored by Bigo and Bacon. Contracts awarded to private firms concern the custodial services, but also catering, cleaning and healthcare services. Currently, seven of the IRCs are run by private providers who subcontract with private healthcare agencies for primary healthcare services. The British custodial market is currently dominated by multinationals such as Group4Securicor, The GEO Group, Serco and Reliance. The predominance of financial and economic considerations is unambiguous: methods to recruit staff, salaries, professional skills, staff training, and quality of the services proposed. Despite their assertions to deliver public services in the best interests of consumers and in the most ethical manner, profits are clearly a priority over migrants' rights.

> Serco is a values-led company with a culture and ethos that is at the heart of everything we do. We give our people real responsibility, allowing them to put their ideas into practice and to truly make a difference for our customers and the public. Our approach has made us one of the world's leading service companies and our vision is to be the world's greatest. Our service ethos means that our customers come back to us again and again. These long-term relationships help us to meet their changing needs and to do what we do best […] bringing service to life.[5]

In the words of GEO Group they are unrivalled as regards the quality and price they can offer (management of the IRCs of Dungavel and Harmondsworth):

> GEO UK can develop new facilities 30-50 per cent **faster** than the typical government project, with cost **savings** of up to 40 per cent and management cost efficiencies of 10-20 per cent throughout the lifespan of the facility.[6] (My emphasis)

The daily average cost of keeping detainees constitutes an essential aspect in the management of these facilities and the work of Burnett and Chebe sheds light on detention conditions for a new exploitable workforce whose

---

[5] <http://www.serco.com>. Consulted May 2011.

[6] <http://www.Geo.com>. Consulted May 2011.

labour in the IRCs should contribute to the upkeep of their detention.

The management of IRCs by private providers does not preclude the presence of UKBA staff (permanent staff like managers, temporary staff and interim personnel) but inspections regularly point out dysfunctions due to the poor collaboration between UKBA staff and staff working for the custodial firms. The lack of clear instructions and the bad knowledge of the role and responsibility of each category are the most common criticisms raised at the managers of these centres. This is evident in centres where the UKBA staff is insufficient and has not been correctly trained to fulfil its mission, hence the incapability to give the necessary instructions correctly to private providers. In the past, such mismanagement has had significant repercussions on the fragile status of migrants whose files were lost during their transfer from one IRC to another. (HMIP report on Oakington 2010) The situation has improved since 2007 though. Before that date, although there was always a permanent member of the Home Office in any IRC to control the way private providers were accomplishing their mission, it seems that the UKBA staff was merely making a record of detainees' complaints without any further action. Since 2007 and the creation of the UKBA the presence of personnel from the Home Office has been more systematic and their role and interaction with subcontractors have been reinforced. There are still two management systems and two categories of personnel in IRCs but the latest regulations define how tasks should not overlap and how both categories of personnel are supposed to cooperate in the best way so as to guarantee optimal detention conditions.

Constraints on detention practices: oversight mechanisms and regulations

In his book on the British and American immigration detention systems, Daniel Wilscher asks whether detention camps can be "an exceptional political space beyond law." (299) Independent oversight mechanisms over any detention estate are a necessity to make sure that the range of coercive powers in the hands of the custodial institutions are used fairly, reasonably in accordance with the rule of law. Such mechanisms are required by international conventions (Council of Europe's Convention against Torture and Inhuman and Degrading Treatment for example) and domestic legislation (see below for the British case) giving monitoring bodies an absolute right of entry to all places of detention and the publication of reports on all its findings. In the UK since the opening of the first detention centres in the 1970s, the performance of privately and publicly run detention centres has been closely monitored by independent observers, like field charities, which have had many occasions to challenge the executive detention policy, and institutional oversight bodies such as Her Majesty's Inspectorate of Prisons (HMIP) and the Independent Monitoring Boards (IMBs.)

The gap between what is set out in policy, prescribed in the legal texts and the reality of detention has to be constantly monitored, as Ann Owers, former Chief Inspector of Prisons recalls:

> One crucial element is a regular programme of actual inspection visits, communicating directly with detainees. It is not possible to inspect places of detention simply by looking at policies, processes or alleged outcomes.[7]

Over the last decade the tightening of controls operated in IRCs and the consequent adoption of constricting rules have been designed to detect and prevent abuses but also to promote best practice. The rules have been reminding immigration staff that migrants have rights and that detention conditions must be suitable not to breach these rights. Such boundaries derive from the criminalization of immigration and asylum law where migrants are considered as a "threat" to the nation, as criminal foreigners to exclude and expel from the territory.

These boundaries have been shaped by the distinctiveness of immigration detention in the UK and also been modelled by the specificity of the legal instruments regulating migration and asylum. The current legislation on immigration and asylum results from the stacking up of different texts since the foundation act, the Immigration Act 1971. Primary legislation only defines principles which are supplemented by immigration rules, and the Home Office has had to issue a large number of administrative guidelines to give "flesh" to the legislative skeleton. Primary legislation has provided rules to control the admission and expulsion of non-nationals but rules on the daily treatment of detainees have been issued on an *ad hoc* basis by the UKBA: the most important being the Detention Centre Rules 2001 and subsequently the many Detention Service Orders, which provide for the standards to be met in IRCs. The regulatory norms and the controls to monitor the system are meant to address some fundamental flaws in the system. The norms impose a positive duty of compliance of standards by private organizations and UKBA staff in their treatment of detainees; they set limits to arbitrariness and discretionary powers. The UK detention estate is vast, operated under a mixed management system and the standards have been

---

[7] IPCC Chair Dame Ann Owers, Speech to the London School of Economics, 20 February, 2013.

developed to achieve a level of consistency progressively across the detention facilities. They have also permitted the Home Office to monitor the performance and compliance of its private providers and in the case of repeated failure, contracts have not been renewed and tenders have been awarded to other contractors.[8] The gradual development of regulatory tools has gone alongside the reinforcement of operational controls in the detention estate. For clarity's sake norms regulating detention practices are presented first before looking at the role of institutional bodies in charge of assessing conditions at detention sites.

Regulatory tools

The 2001 Detention Centre Rules (secondary legislation) which regulate detention practice in IRCs are based on rules for the prison system. Their adoption has meant a considerable forward step at a time when the management of IRCs by private providers had led to terrible incidents in the absence of norms.[9] The 2001 text details admission conditions, release, criteria to respect to ensure detainees can communicate with the external world, notably access to legal information. But it also specifies material and sanitary conditions to be implemented in any centre. It draws the attention of the management team to the specific care due to women and children. However the rules only provide indicators to private organizations who are then free to interpret them. Such broad interpretation has resulted in differential treatment observed in the immigration detention sector. Reports on detention conditions, either produced by the HMIP or field associations have repeatedly pointed out the poor performance of some private providers and the ensuing devastating consequences for detainees.

> We were disturbed to find one of the least safe immigration detention facilities we have inspected, with deeply frustrated detainees and demoralized staff, some of whom lacked the necessary confidence to manage those in their care. Brook House was an unsafe place. (HMIP report on Brook House 2010)

The Detention Service Orders (DSO) have been issued progressively to further spell out the role of contractors when implementing the 2001 text. They aim at improving performance and compliance of UKBA private

---

[8] Kalyx Services which was running Harmondsworth was replaced by GEO Gp in July 2009.

[9] See Teresa Hayter, *Open Borders. The Case against Immigration Controls* for one of the first study denouncing detention practices in the 1990s.

contractors and deal with daily detention conditions in IRCs: protection of children, health controls, freedom of movement within the centre, rules to respect by visitors, rules to regulate complaints against the UKBA. These public documents bind the subcontractor to the UKBA and specify the obligations, procedures and standard norms that private firms must respect. They are meant to raise standards and make transparent the way the UKBA expects detainees to be treated. More recently, to regulate the escort process the UKBA has issued its first consolidated version of the *Detention Services Operating Standards Manual* which brings together all the standards that have been introduced since December 2002.

Another important text which has constrained immigration staff working in IRCs is the *Physical Control in Care (PCC) Manual* (2005) issued by the Justice Secretary. The manual was classified secret up to 2010 but had to be published in the wake of campaigns run by associations defending freedom of information. The campaigns were organized after the death of a teenager in a youth centre, death due to the use of constraint techniques. Initially these constraint techniques should only have been used for underage prisoners convicted of a criminal offence to restrain them by inflicting some kind of pain (a distracting technique). In reality female and underage migrants have also been suffering from these constraining techniques, either in detention centres or during the repatriation process. The manual stipulates that any staff of the Home Office or working for the Home Office, who is making usage of force while carrying out their duty must have been correctly formed and must have obtained an official certificate to be able to use them. A five-day initial training is organized by the The National Offender Management Service (NOMS, Ministry of Justice) and regular annual updates are necessary so that the certificates can still be valid. The text also regulates in part, the training of personnel working for private subcontractors who make use of violent techniques while escorting unwilling foreign detainees. The publication of the text did not lead to its cancellation and the British authorities have been arguing that the use of violence must remain an exceptional factor in repatriation procedures, only to be used when necessary. The text details the limits not to be crossed but it has nonetheless legitimized violent practices and has institutionalized the training of staff to the use of violence even though they belong neither to the police nor the army.

Watchdogs

Before looking at the function of the HMIP and the IMBs, it is essential to mention the very significant role played by field charities in defending immigrants' rights. The first very active watchdogs were created towards the mid-1980s and developed rapidly throughout the 1990s to challenge the governmental policies which had been using detention as a deterrence tool to curb immigration and asylum. Some of these charities work within specific professional sectors: medicine (*Medical Justice Network*, *Médecins sans frontières*, *The Medical* Foundation,) law (*Bail for Immigration Detainees*, *Immigration Law Practitionners*,) psychology, education, social support (*Association of Visitors in Detention*,) religious support (religious communities, in particular the Jesuits.) Their activities have been organized in three main directions: first and foremost, by visiting, helping and supporting detainees on a daily basis; secondly, they have also sought to communicate and campaign to inform the general public of the fate of immigrants in detention and they have been promoting discussion to raise awareness in denouncing the plights of the UK immigration system; thirdly, they have also been quite active in lobbying MPs, politicians and testifying in parliamentary committees to persuade Government to reform the system, offering their insight into the experiences of detained migrants. Thanks to the expertise and experience gained over the years, these charities have managed to represent refugees' concerns to the government, the media and the general public. The empirical dimension of their daily activities has given them a legitimacy to interact with the government to let refugees be heard and they also interact frequently with statutory control bodies.[10]

Institutional watchdogs depending on the Ministry of Justice (MOJ) should provide an independent oversight of detention facilities. Their duty is to ensure that detainees are cared for humanely and decently and live in safe, healthy conditions. They have also to make sure that the Home Office contractors comply fully with the requirements set out in the Detention Centre Rules 2001 and the Detention Service Orders issued by the UKBA. Her Majesty's Inspectorate of Prisons has been in charge of controlling prisons, youth centres and IRCs since the Immigration and

---

[10] The lobbying function of these charities and their role in the elaboration and implementation of measures regarding the detention of migrants was explored in a former article. See Catherine Puzzo. "Femmes réfugiées dans les centres de rétention administrative en Grande Bretagne: déni de parole." *Anglophonia/ Caliban French Journal of English Studies, special issue on Women, Conflict and Power* (2010) 27.

Asylum Act 1999 and the Detention Centre Rules 2001. The current body of inspectors with Nick Hardwick as Chief Inspector is composed of lawyers, doctors and social workers nominated for a five-year period. These inspectors are not part of the detention estate, which should guarantee their independence. Their announced or unannounced visits are done on a regular basis to assess conditions at detention centres and to make recommendations to improve the way IRCs and short-term facilities are operated. These inspections which can last over a week, lead to a preliminary report, which can be amended by the private firm managing the centre. A final official report is then published within four months following the inspection. In the wake of the reports produced by the HMIP the service provider in charge of managing the centre has to produce an action plan taking into account the recommendations made by the inspectorate and/or producing documentary evidence of compliance with procedures. The IRC is then inspected again during an unplanned visit to make sure that the recommendations have been followed. A follow-up report is then produced. All these documents are then gathered in the annual report that is transmitted to the Home Office. For their visits, the HMIP has been using and adapting a protocol, initially created for inspecting prisons. The concept of "healthy prison" was introduced by the HMIP following its report "Suicide is Everyone's Concern. A thematic review by HM Chief Inspector of Prisons for England and Wales" in May 1999. The "healthy prison" criteria have been adapted to IRCs to check several aspects: if detainees are held in safe conditions; if they are respected and proposed purposeful activities that will benefit them; if they are prepared for their release into the community. The "healthy establishment assessment" allows the HMIP to issue a final judgment on the overall performance of the centre inspected: good, reasonably good, not sufficiently good or poor.

Recently the HMIP has produced a consultative report on its new expectations as regards immigration detention. From October 2011 the legal services market has been changing and new outcomes-focused regulations (OFR) have been adopted. Such approach means that services for consumers should be driven by outcomes rather than by detailed and prescriptive rules to follow. With respect to detention and inspection performed by the HMIP, the inspectorate has had to modify its standards against which inspections take place, focusing more on outcomes to be achieved by contractors rather than strict process to be followed. Critics of the new approach stress that it will give a greater flexibility to private providers who, even though they are operating within the broader framework of the 2001 Detention Rules and the Detention Service Orders may nonetheless interpret the operating standards differently .

Another series of controls are carried out by the Independent Monitoring Boards created in the 1950s (Prison Act 1952, section 6) to visit prisons and youth centres. The competence of IMBs was extended by the Immigration and Asylum Act 1999 to reflect the commitment the general public should have to life in jail. IMBs are composed of ten to 12 volunteers who are independent and unpaid members of the public. They monitor detention places with a view to check safety conditions and living standards to make sure that "proper standards of care and decency are maintained."[11] The 1999 text defined their missions quite strictly and imposed the same procedural rules to be observed during these visits: detention conditions must be humane and fair; if some failure is observed the IMB can refer to the Justice Secretary or any administrative authority in charge of the centre; the committee has to write an annual report for the Home Secretary. The report establishes the degree of compatibility between the application of norms and what has been observed in the centres. To fulfil their mission, IMBs have an unlimited and unconditional access to IRCs, in particular internal documentation. They can talk freely to inmates, staff and managers of the centres to discuss of any problem inside the establishment. Their annual reports are submitted to the local administration and local politicians of the region and to the Home Secretary and contain their observations and recommendations to the attention of the Justice Secretary. If their role looks like those of the HMIP, their creation and the significance of their reports differ quite considerably. Their local situation makes them closer to the centres located in the region they are in charge of monitoring but they have a more fragmented vision of the detention practices compared to the HMIP. These committees perform an essential role of observation, since like the HMIP they systematically point out the failure to observe the regulation and the lack of care due to detainees, medical and psychological care, quality of meals and services for example. With the setting-up of these committees the general public can enter the confined world of prisons and IRCs; they represent the external eye of civil society. However, the shortness of the answer provided by the Justice Secretary to these reports is emblematic of their relatively secondary role. These letters signed by the Justice Secretary often amount to no more than a formal acknowledgement of the reception of the report. The report is not always followed by an action plan from the UKBA to redress the failure observed.

More recently, the Independent Police Complaints Commission (IPCC)

---

[11] IMB website <http://www.imb.gov.uk>. Accessed May 2010.

created by the Police Reform Act 2002 to investigate complaints against police services, has also been handling complaints against the UKBA services and since 2010 against subcontractors of the UKBA, in particular private firms in charge of running IRCs. The creation of the commission and the development of its role to include cases in IRCS were born out of famous affairs where the dysfunctioning of police services came to the light —Menezes case, summer 2005 and Manuel Bravo's suicide the same year in an IRC. Several degrees of complaints exist according to the seriousness of the complaint. Initially all the complaints are addressed to the same service, which then will transmit the most serious ones to the IPCC. Certainly the intention behind the creation of the IPCC was to restore trust and confidence in the system. Nevertheless, is the independence of such a commission granted when it can only examine the cases that are referred by the same service that has been accused of failing its duties? It is yet too early to know about the direct and indirect effects of the work of this commission over the administrative practice inside these centres.

Appraisal of the "boundaries" around immigration detention

Immigration detention in the UK appears as a complex reality where detention practices can be pictured as a fast-moving field. Assessing the effectiveness of the rules in force and the role of the various watchdogs suggests three comments. Firstly, the independence of the various bodies in charge of controlling the detention estate, the variety of these bodies and the publicity of their reports should guarantee that some form of democratic accountability exist for the Home Office services and their staff. It is all the more necessary as people detained are the most vulnerable and detention centres should not be "lawless environments where detainees are at the mercy of both their guards and their government masters." (Wilscher 301)

Secondly, The Home Office policies and the consequent regulations have tried to impose a standardized mode of operation in all IRCs. But as Pierre Bourdieu noted the implementation or the failure to implement regulations depend on the willingness and the interests of those who have the monopoly of implementing them.[12] There has been no uniform

[12] See Pierre Bourdieu. "Droit et passe-droit. Le champ des pouvoirs territoriaux et la mise en œuvre des règlements." *Acte de la Recherche en Sciences Sociales*. 1990: 81-82. Quoted in Fischer and Spire, 14.

implementation of the rules in IRCS, instead there has been an array of practices and various detention regimes. The reading of the many reports produced by the HMIP, the IMBs and those of field charities draws our attention to such disparity. The proclamation of detailed regulations and published instructions has been meant to introduce some form of uniformity and safeguard migrants' rights. Undeniably, detention conditions and practices have globally improved over the past 15 years: the specificity of immigration detention and the special attention due to some categories of detainees have been acknowledged; improvements have resulted from more directive interventions from the UKBA with a better coordination between UKBA staff and private providers; the Home Office has imposed regular professional training to its subcontractors and has set up a regulatory frame to delimit the range of actions and practice that are acceptable.

Thirdly, there is still room for improvement and there are at least two essential dimensions which have yet to be addressed more clearly. As regards the accountability of the private providers, it has been stressed that complaints procedures should be clarified to better define the providers' responsibilities, to make the complaint more automatic in certain cases. It is also about making sure that effective disciplinary action and corresponding sanctions are given in case of management failure. It is a question of restoring the trust migrants can have in a protocol which is yet too bureaucratic, too detailed before any complaint can be lodged in an effective, rapid and fair way. For instance it means that a service of professional interpreters should be used more systematically to make sure that language is not a further barrier to bureaucratic hurdles. Regarding the use of force to constrain migrants, the necessity, proportionality and the legality of the use of force in certain circumstances should be carefully and dutifully assessed before resorting to it.

Conclusion

A few remarks can be made on the specificity of immigration detention in the UK. First of all, immigration detention is specific in so far as it is non-mandatory and not punitive. It is a purely administrative sanction which should be used as a last resort and sparingly. However, as Daniel Wilscher notes, it is a "formally discretionary power" of the executive and there is no automatic judicial review of the administrative decision to detain somebody. It means that detainees must challenge the lawfulness of the decision to detain them, especially when considering the absence of any clear time limit to detention.

Secondly, successive governments have gradually "criminalized" immigration and asylum. The progressive convergence of criminal law and immigration law has been explored by Julie Stumpf who described this process under the term "crimmigration." As such detention, which is one of the tools to characterize criminal law, has taken a central role in UK migration policy and law. The range of groups likely to be detained either preventively or before their deportation has expanded and so has the detention estate. Over the years the British state apparatus has evolved and adapted to the new constraints: from less than a hundred detainees in the early 1980s to around 25,000 at the end of 2010. (Home Office 2010) It has had recourse to external actors whose position and status in the detention system has led to highly criticized dysfunctioning. Despite the executive's efforts to promote clear standards, to impose protocols and to improve transparency, a secretive culture and a "culture of disbelief" are still prevailing.

Finally, we cannot but agree with Michael Flynn (2012) who argues that a too narrow focus on the improvement of treatment of detainees helps to rationalize the practice of immigration detention by the executive and let us forget the proportionality of immigration detention to the aims of immigration policy.

Works cited

AVID, Association of Visitors to Immigration Detainees. URL: <http://www.aviddetention.org.uk/images/uk%20residential%20spaces%20feb%202013.pdf>.

BACON, Cristina. *The Evolution of Immigration Detention in the UK: The Involvement of Private Prison Companies*. Working Paper Series. Refugee Studies Centre, Department of International Development, Queen Elizabeth House, University of Oxford. Working Paper n° 27. September 2005.

BIGO, Didier. "Les entreprises de coercition paraprivées: de nouveaux mercenaires?" in OLSSON, Christian (dir.). *Les entreprises paraprivées de coercition : de nouveaux mercenaires? Cultures & Conflits* 52 (Winter 2003): 5-10.

BIRNBERG, Peirce & Partners, Medical Justice and the National Coalition of Anti-Deportation Campaigns. *Outsourcing abuse. The use and misuse of state-sanctioned force during the detention and removal of asylum seekers*. 2008. URL: <http://www.libertysecurity.org/IMG/pdf_outsourcing_abuse.pdf>. Accessed May 2011.

BURNETT, Jon and Fidelis CHEBE. "Captive Labour: asylum seekers, migrants and employment in UK immigration removal centres." *Race & Class* 51.4 (2010): 95-103.

CPT – Report to the government of the UK on the visit to the UK carried out by the European Committee for the prevention of Torture and Inhuman or Degrading Treatment of Punishment (CPT) from November 18 to December 1, 2009. Published December 12, 2009.

Detention Action. *Fast Track to despair. The unnecessary detention of asylum seekers*. May 2011.

FISCHER, Nicolas, and Alexis SPIRE. "L'état face aux illégalismes." *Politix* 3.87 (2009): 7-20.

FLYNN, Michael. *Immigration detention and proportionality*. Global Detention Project Working Paper No.4. February 2011.

—. On the Unintended consequences of Human Rights Promotion on Immigration Detention. Global Detention Project Discussion Paper, March 2012.

Global Detention Project, *UK Detention Profile 2011.* URL: <http://www.globaldetentionproject.org/countries/europe/united-kingdom/introduction.html>.

HAYTER, Teresa. *Open Borders. The Case against Immigration Controls*. London, Pluto Press, 2004.

HMIP–Report on a full announced inspection of Brook House Immigration Removal Centre, 15-19 March, 2010 by HM Chief Inspector of Prisons.

HMIP–Report on an unannounced short follow-up inspection of Oakington Immigration Reception Centre, 2-5 August, 2010 by HM Chief Inspector of Prisons.

HMIP–Report "Suicide is Everyone's Concern" May 1999 by HM Chief Inspector of Prisons for England and Wales. URL: <http://www.justice.gov.uk/downloads/publications/inspectorate-reports/hmipris/thematic-reports-and-research-publications/suicide-is-everyones-concern-1999-rps.pdf>.

SILVERMAN, Stephanie and Ruchi HAJELA. *Immigration Detention in the UK*. 22 May, 2012. URL: <http://www.migrationobservatory.ox.ac.uk/sites/files/migobs/Immigration%20Detention%20Briefing.pdf>.

STUMPF, Juliet P. "The Crimmigration Crisis: Immigrants, Crime, and Sovereign Power." *American University Law Review* 56 (2006): 367-419.

TYLER, Imogen."'Welcome to Britain'. The Cultural politics of asylum." *European Journal of Cultural Studies* 9.2 (2006): 185-202.

WILSHER, Daniel. *Immigration Detention. Law, History, Politics*. Cambridge University Press, 2012.
WEBBER, Frances. "UK: the real immigration debate." *Race & Class*. 53.3 (January-March 2012): 91-98.

TRANSLATING LAWS OF EXCEPTION: THE CASE OF CONTROL ORDERS

GEORGE FOURNIER
UNIVERSITY OF LYON 3, FRANCE

The specificities of the measures taken by the British governments to counter terrorism have made it difficult for translators to convey them into a foreign language.[1] As *ad hoc* measures, they were designed to confront exceptional circumstances, which accounts for the arduous task of transferring them into foreign legal systems. The notion of Control Order, namely the arrest and detention of alleged terrorists, is a very recent one in Great-Britain. It was widely popularized with articles published in the press about the arrest of suspects following the 9/11 attacks and the 2005 London bombings. More recently, Peter Kosminsky's *Blitz,*[2] a well-documented fiction film on the jihad in Great-Britain helped complete the popularization of this issue. In this fiction film, the director aptly dramatized a case of Control Order imposed on a second generation Muslim young woman. It was the opportunity for the filmmaker to inform the British population about some of the features of this law of exception:

> She [Nassima, the protagonist] is on trial, the charge against her cannot be disclosed, she is not allowed to be present and neither is her lawyer and she is represented by someone she has never met and who is not even working for her.

As always with films, it is the scariest aspect of the law, the most dramatic one that is highlighted, and it needs to be qualified even though the narrative includes situations some people have been confronted with since 2001.[3] As is often the case with laws of exception, the interest

---

[1] One of the most famous examples being *Vigipirate* as a French equivalent to the UK threat levels.

[2] *Britz* was broadcast in 2007 on Channel4.

[3] "At their most stringent, control orders could have allowed for detention without

Control Order has aroused abroad has led to translations which, for the lack of exact equivalence, have had to make do with approximating notions and borrowings from neighbouring legal fields.

The diachronic approach adopted in this study is inspired by the extended period covered by the Control Order legislation. The main evolution that can be traced between the Prevention of Terrorism Act 2005 and the Terrorism Prevention and Investigation Measures Act 2011 is linguistic. When translating these idiosyncratic structures, should translators opt for equivalents or should they keep the words in the source language with footnotes? A study of some of the most controversial notions related to Control Order should try and bring answers to this issue and more generally to the translation of laws of exception.

Communicating on Control Order

The exceptional nature of the Control Order measures springs from the decisions that were made by the British government in the wake of the US Patriot Act 2001—the UK Anti-terrorism, Crime and Security Act 2001—and later modified in the aftermath of the 2005 London wave of attacks. Politicians felt the need to respond with legal measures to the general outcry of the population and to menaces that, by then, had spread globally. The 2005 London bombings represented a watershed in the politicians' perception of terrorism with a sudden move from attacks on foreign land—which usually arouse sympathy towards the victims—to terrorism on mainland—which at the time aroused awe and terror, not to mention the endangering of the citizens' safety and the economy of the nation. The heated debates that raged over the passing of this string of measures of exception, and one in particular—namely the preventive and indefinite detention of supposed terrorists without prior appearance before a judge or any legal representative—testify to their controversial nature. It should be kept in mind that Control Order was brought in after the Law Lords declared, in 2004, that indefinite detention in Belmarsh prison without charge for foreign terror suspects went against the European Convention on Human Rights.

> The highest court in the UK, the law lords, declare by a majority of 8-1 the indefinite detention of foreign "terrorist suspects" incompatible with the Human Rights Act and hence the European Convention on Human Rights.[4]

---

trial control orders." (Fenwick & Phillipson 312)

[4] *House of Lords ruling on the Belmarsh detainees*, 16 December, 2004.

The opposition to the 2005 Prevention of Terrorism Act was violent in spite of tragic, though favourable, circumstances. It was all the more so as the measures taken contravened the *Habeas Corpus*, which is a cornerstone of the English legal system. On the contrary, for advocates of the legislation, the notion of *Habeas Corpus* was not relevant because of the extremely unusual circumstances, which explained the enforcement of measures of exception, as explained by Lord Hoffmann:

> The liberty of the subject and the right to *Habeas Corpus* are too precious to be sacrificed for any reason other than to safeguard the survival of the state. But one can only maintain this position if one confines the concept of deprivation of liberty to actual imprisonment or something which is for practical purposes little different from imprisonment. Otherwise the law would place too great a restriction on the powers of the state to deal with serious terrorist threats to the lives of its citizens.[5]

As mentioned above, these measures were designed to target nationals but also foreigners: Control Order measures are the last actions that can be taken by governments when they address threats from foreigners who cannot be prosecuted because of international conventions which forbid the deportation of people who can be either tortured or executed in their country of origin. The difficulty in approaching Control Order as a series of measures of exception is increased for foreigners in so far as defendants, in this particular case, have to prove that they are innocent (of the accusations) while conversely there lies at the core of other legal systems, the French one among others, the establishing of the truth. But how can innocence be proved when those who are accused of crimes do not even know the nature of these supposed crimes? That is what is aptly summed up in Peter Kosminsky's film which fictionalises a case of intralingual translation[6] in which a legal expert explains in simple terms to a layperson, a young Muslim woman, the charges levelled at her:

> Nassima: "The hearing is in two weeks and you can get the Control Order lifted up by hearing".
>
> Lawyer: "Theoretically, it could be lifted up at the hearing. But I won't be doing it. […] The control order is a very unusual piece of legislation. It is designed to prevent you committing a crime in the future rather than punishing you for the one you committed in the past. They can issue it

---

[5] *Secretary of State for the Home Department (Appellant) v. JJ and others (FC) (Respondents).*

[6] "Intralingual translation or rewording is an interpretation of verbal signs by means of other signs of the same language." (Jakobson 548)

without revealing the ground to you or your legal representative. In this case the Home Office haven't revealed the ground."
Nassima: "But they'll be revealing it at the hearing."
Lawyer: "Probably not in fact. They're not required to do so, usually they don't. And the hearings are almost always closed."
Nassima: "What is that mean?"
Lawyer: "They take place without the subjects of the order or their lawyer attending."
Sabia Iqbal: "You mean, they're examining my case but I can't be present."
Lawyer: "That's right."
Sabia Iqbal: "Why?"
Lawyer: "Because sensitive matters may need to be discussed … classified matters."
Nassima: "Surely if Sabia is on trial she has the right to be represented."
Lawyer: "But she will be represented by … Richard Craig Q.C."
Nassima: "Who is he?"
Lawyer: "He is a special advocate. They are appointed by the attorney general to represent defendants in closed proceedings."
Nassima: "So when does she meet him?"
Lawyer: "She doesn't, I'm afraid. He isn't working for Miss Iqbal, he is working for the State."
Nassima: "Oh, this is insane."
Lawyer: "You're actually quite lucky. In some cases of Control Order, defendants are not represented at all."

The dismay that is felt by the supposed terrorist and her friend echoes the general outcry of those who in the UK at the time worked to safeguard the rights of citizens. The linguistic changes between the Anti-terrorism, Crime and Security Act 2001 and the Terrorism Prevention and Investigation Measures Act 2011 testify to the political controversies that were unfolding among politicians. They bear the traces of the several antagonistic debates that stirred the British governments in those days. Should governments counter terrorism by stepping up the measures? Should they abide by the decisions made at both national and international levels and designed not to antagonize pressure groups?[7] Should they try to

---

[7] An example of these pressure groups is the Working Group on Arbitrary Detention. It "was established by resolution 1991/42 of the former Commission on Human Rights […]
(a) To investigate cases of deprivation of liberty imposed arbitrarily or otherwise inconsistently with the relevant international standards set forth in the Universal Declaration of Human Rights or in the relevant international legal instruments accepted by the States concerned."
<http://www.ohchr.org/EN/Issues/Detention/Pages/WGADIndex.aspx>. Website accessed in January 2013.

avoid criticisms from those willing to see legislation evolve towards more respect of human rights at the expense of what was the priority for the governments of the time: national security?[8] This difference in the political approach of the subject is found in the evolution of the terminology with as most obvious example, the repetition of Control Order 132 times in the Prevention of Terrorism Act 2005 against only nine times in the Terrorism Prevention and Investigation Measures Act 2011.[9] A further quantitative analysis of the documents confirms the evolution from a straightforward approach of the issue, as adopted soon after the bombings, to a subtle one designed to shun criticisms, a point to be discussed at a later stage.

A closer linguistic analysis provides instructive pieces of information: about the lengths of the texts, the 2011 Act corresponds to increased inflation in words as compared to the 2005 Act: from 992 word-types and 12525 word tokens to 1447 word-types and 22142 word tokens. The use of roundabout phrases and structures meant to avoid controversy and opposition partly lies at the origin of it. The passage, in the title, from the notion of Terrorism Act, dating back to 1939, to Terrorism Prevention and Investigation Measures Act as introduced in 2011 is an apt illustration of this inflationary move. This evolution is also traceable in the disappearance of the word "detention" and its replacement by "residence," the increased use of the latter bespeaking both a loosening of control but also the carefulness of the legislator. The sharp decrease in the repetition of Control Order between 2005 and 2011—first used 146 times then only 18 times six years later—also bespeaks the governments' will to correct the position about the way measures were first presented to the population rather than the measures themselves. Was there a softening of the measures in the meantime or did the legislators anticipate the problems linked to this type of law by deciding to avoid antagonism and to exclude terms likely to attract the fierce criticisms of potential opponents? Both explanations are relevant as illustrated by the rebranding, in 2011, of the 2005 text: "control order light."

Few were the real changes and as far as the rights of the suspects were concerned, only the conditions of the detention were revised over the period spanning from 2005 to 2011. For instance, neither the suspects nor

[8] In November 2001, following the attacks on the United States on September 11, the UK declared a public state of emergency and derogated from (restricted) Article 5 of the European Convention to put into place an indefinite detention policy. It was the only European country to do so. Article 5 of the convention guarantees the right to liberty and security of the person and protects individuals against arbitrary detention.

[9] Research carried out on *AntConc*, a software tool for lexical analysis.

their legal representatives were at any time allowed to have information about the nature of the offences. In most cases it was claimed that the accusations were based on sensitive intelligence which precluded their presentation to a court and made both release and deportation impossible.

Between calques and equivalences

The main difficulty when translating laws of exception from English into French does not only rest with the passage from concepts inherited from the common law into concepts from the civil law system—an exercise legal translators are regularly confronted with and which has been widely documented[10]—but with finding corresponding and meaningful structures. The notion of Control Order appeared in 2005 even though terrorism on mainland Britain was a threat previous governments had had to face too. The main challenge that crops up when dealing with measures of exception is the constant uncertainty as to whether the terminology applies to the judicial or administrative domain, keeping in mind that, under normal circumstances, measures designed to restrict freedom result from a judiciary and not an administrative decision.

The key concept in the passage from the source language to the target language is the one of equivalence. It is meant to facilitate adjustments to foreign legal systems and it serves to avoid coining words and phrases which would be meaningless in the target language. The notion of custody in England and Wales[11], for instance, does not correspond to the same reality in France: the length of detention, the conditions, and the decision-makers are not the same, hence the need either to keep the word in the source language with explanatory footnotes or to opt for equivalences or even for hybrid structures or paraphrases. The major constraint lies with the need to strive for a translation that takes into account the procedure in the source language without either going into detail or being confusing. An apt example is Article 5, paragraph 3 of the European Commission of European Rights, one of the international regulations contravened by Control Order:

---

[10] One of the most recent examples of comparative study of legal models from a linguistic point of view is *The Oxford Handbook of Language and Law*. (Tiersma & Solan 664)

[11] For the sake of explicitness, the scope of this study is restricted to England and Wales which have identical legal systems.

> Everyone arrested or detained in accordance with the provisions of paragraph 1.c of this article shall be brought promptly before a judge or other officer authorised by law to exercise judicial power.

The reference to "other officer authorised by law" was added to comply with the requirements of the British authorities who were apprehensive about the notion of "judge": if "or other officer authorised by law" had been omitted, British defendants might have argued for the strict respect of the terms of the law. If "judge" had been the only word to appear in the text, legal officers might have been excluded since, in England and Wales, they have prerogatives which, on the continent, are given to judges only. A strict interpretation of the law, as it was originally couched in French, may have excluded from the procedure all the members of the legal profession but the British judges. The text in French was modified to match the English version though it was not necessary since, in France, only the professionals called *juges* have these prerogatives. A related controversy recently appeared when Julian Assange, the founder of *Wikileaks*, appealed to the British Supreme Court to avoid extradition to Sweden on account of the fact that, according to British law, he could not be extradited to Sweden because the order was issued by a Swedish public prosecutor, while in England, to be valid, this procedure has to be carried out by a judge.[12]

---

[12] "She is trying to establish that the judicial authority referred to is "a judge or other officer authorised by law to exercise judicial power".

[…]

11.25am: Rose turns to the *Schiesser v Switzerland* case. The court found that there were limits to the inclusion of prosecutors in the definition of judicial authorities if the prosecutor was not independent, Rose says.

11.30am: Rose now turns to *Skoogstrom v Sweden* (1984), a decision of the European Commission on Human Rights, in which, she says, it was expressly held that a Swedish prosecutor could not be "a judge or other officer authorised by law to exercise judicial power" for the purpose of Article 5(3) of the European convention on human rights, because she lacked the essential quality of independence.

11.41am: Montgomery's case, for Sweden, gives no definition of judicial authority, Rose says.

The most recent relevant European court of human rights decision is *Medvedyev v France*, Rose says. In this decision the court held that the investigating magistrate fulfilled the role of a "judge or other officer authorised by law to exercise judicial power." Julian Assange extradition appeal at supreme court. *The Guardian online.* Wednesday, February 1.

The impossibility to find exact equivalences results in the choice of hyperonyms, explanatory statements or even periphrastic structures designed to avoid mistakes. The range of possibilities then becomes wide and translators have to go for the most relevant option, the one corresponding to the sociolinguistic environment.[13] For specialists of legal matters, the borrowing of English words suffices since thorough knowledge of law helps make sense of the circumstances and draw the relevant conclusions. Yet, as proved by the Julian Assange example aforementioned, such may not always be the case and standard obligations and prerogatives do not exactly match.

Yet, to some extent, the way laws of exception are designed helps make comparisons easy since the need to protect civilians leads Western countries to adopt identical measures. A juxtaposition of the English and French systems shows that identical restrictions have been imposed upon suspects: house arrest, restrictions on visits and on the use of means of communication, among others. The main problem that lies at the core of *contrôle judiciaire*, as a possible translation in French of Control Order, is that, in French, the corresponding set of measures refers to the judicial authority, while, until 2005, Control Order was issued in the UK by the Home Secretary only, making it impossible for translators to resort to this notion. Originally, the decision to impose Control Order upon suspected terrorists lay with the Home Secretary and its enforcement and its follow-up fell within the realm of the police which were in charge of these assignments. The intention to give the police forces not only the duty of protecting public interests, but also of taking preventive measures and the fact that the Home Secretary was responsible for it all, once oriented the terminological research in French towards "*mesures de police*."

While in France orders related to control have been monitored by the investigating judge (*juge d'instruction*), and issued by the judge for freedom and detention (*juge des libertés et de la détention*), in England these measures, up until 2005, were issued by the Home Secretary hence the incongruity of a translation by *contrôle judiciaire* even though in terms of their semantic contents, the realities these two terms refer to are very close.

Figures are hardly ever mentioned in translation studies on account of their apparent transparency. Yet, figures can be treacherous and they hide

[13] "Sociolinguistic competence refers to the knowledge of the sociolinguistic conventions for performing language functions appropriately in a given context and the mastery of appropriate language in different sociolinguistic contexts with emphasis on appropriateness of meaning and appropriateness of form with regard to two language and culture contexts." (Cao 43)

huge complexities translators need to deal with, if the spirit of the law is to be understood in all its complexity. They represent the major source of supplementation[14] with adaptations and footnotes. Teresa May's announcement, in January 2011, that "detention without charge [was] reduced from 28 to 14 days, but with the Home Secretary retaining the option of 28 days in an emergency," revealed the fact that charges had to be formed within a maximum of 28 days but hid the fact that suspects were not necessarily informed of the nature of the charges even during their detention. While the implications of this measure are crystal-clear for British experts, such may not be the case with lay people or foreigners. As a result, should translators provide explanations of one sort or another? That is what happens very often, even at an official level and, for instance, some form of explanation was afforded by the Council of Europe itself when translating "pre-charge detention" by *détention 'pré-inculpation' de 42 jours*[15] which partly solves the problem of misunderstandings about the duration since it indicates the differences in the period of detention in the UK as opposed to the periods of detention in the other European countries.

Translating "pre" and "post" structures

"Pre-trial" is one of the most recurring words when dealing with detention, as borne out by the lexicalization of the collocation "pre-trial detention." Among the few definitions of "pre-trial" available, the following one, found in a law case,[16] states that it is: "to detain defendant without bail pending trial." As exemplified by this definition, "pre-trial," whether under its amalgamated form or hyphenated form, has gradually tended to overshadow "pending." It is also borne out by the Final Report of the Independent Reviewer on the Prevention of Terrorism Act 2005 in which structures using the "pre" preposition abound. The wide usage of the "pre" prefix in American English also accounts for the popularity of "pre-trial" as underpinned by results on the main search engines, the first pages returning answers connected to the US legislation.

Regarding "pre-trial detention," the structure itself does not appear as such in official documents but mostly in texts dealing with detention related to Control Order. Most of the occurrences come from opponents to

[14] Supplementation as a translation of "étoffement". (Vinay & Darbelnet 350)

[15] Council of Europe, <http://assembly.coe.int/ASP/XRef/X2H-DW-XSL.asp?fileid=17680&lang=FR>. Website accessed in January 2013.

[16] Bifford Detention Motion - Department of Justice, <http://www.justice.gov/usao/mow/news2011/bifford-detention.pdf>. Website of the US Department of Justice, accessed in November 2012.

these measures who highlight its repressive nature. They stress the point that pre-trial detention is intended to be preventive though in effect it is repressive.[17] *Détention avant jugement* is the most common translation of "pre-trial detention." It corresponds to Eugene Nida's definition of formal equivalence, or "gloss translation" (Bassenett 176) in which the translator "attempts to reproduce as literally and meaningfully as possible the form and contents of the original" (Nida 159) preserving grammatical units, consistency in word usage, and meaning in terms of the source context." (Sin-Wai & Pollard 1154)[18] Though *détention avant jugement* is found in many texts dealing with foreign legal decisions, it is not the syntagm French lawyers and legal experts would favour, *détention provisoire* being the term that is spontaneously referred to. This tendency, in the literature about legal matters, to use calques corresponds to two main features. The first one arises from the fact that legal matters from abroad are reported by people who are not necessarily legal experts. More often than not they are experts in the field of communication and, in their effort to communicate, they opt for idioms modelled on the structure from the source language and which native experts in the target language would not use. Secondly, by departing from the expected structure in the target language, commentators underline, with calques, the foreign dimension of laws which require to be explained from a different perspective; they afford readers an insight into a singular way of approaching legal matters. The use of the corresponding French term would conversely erase the cultural differences. The main advantage of this kind of coined structure, patterned on the source language, is the fact that though not appropriate from a terminological point of view, it corresponds, in the case of Control Orders, to foreign realities like the detention without charges of suspected terrorists and their release without trial or judgment by the legislative authorities.

"Pre-charge" and "pre-trial" have met with much success following the laws of exception recently passed and the changes they have brought about. The duration of the detention—whether it is custody or any other form of detention—is not identical on either side of the Channel and since the different stages leading to the termination or the extension of the detention do not correspond either, new locutions have appeared to

[17] "The purely preventative aim of the control order system, its separation from the criminal justice process, its application to home citizens and the length of time for which an individual could be subject to it however placed it towards the more repressive end of the spectrum of measures operated by comparable western democracies." (Anderson 130).

[18] Vladimir Ivir, *Formal Correspondence*, in Sin-Wai & Pollard.

account for these new realities. "Pre-charge detention", a related concept, is the structure chosen by Klaas de Vries, the European Parliament Rapporteur for the Dutch Socialist Party when dealing with British laws on terrorism. This locution corresponds to the period when a person, after being arrested is detained so as to determine the nature of the offences and the characterization of the charges. As mentioned earlier, the translation into French that the Council of Europe suggested for pre-charge detention was *détention pré-inculpation de 42 jours.* This structure raises the question of why this neologism was preferred over *détention pré-inculpatoire de 42 jours* or even better, because more idiomatic, *détention avant inculpation de 42 jours*, the latter being the most commonly used form in French. *Détention pré-inculpatoire* is actually a calque resulting from the influence of the English language among international institutions, while *détention avant inculpation* is the term used in French. "Pre" is undeniably one of the most widely used prefixes even though "post" has lately been in favour with commentators. Being flexible, easy to understand and widespread, these structures are bound to thrive and lately, in English, has appeared the syntagm "post-charge questioning" referring to cases when the police are allowed to carry on the questioning of a person who has already been charged. Paratactic structures being fewer in French, in the legal sphere at least, the translations of sentences which combine "post" have up until now been idiomatic, as proved by *permettre l'interrogatoire des individus soupçonnés de terrorisme après leur mise en accusation* as a translation of "to enable post-charge questioning of terrorist suspects".[19]

Formal equivalence is part of a more general phenomenon that has lately appeared, both in French and English, and which consists in the generalization of hyperonyms—generic words—at the expense of a wide variety of existing terms. This phenomenon consists in imposing words that are less precise and less technical but easier to understand because they are more general. Their repetition gradually leads to acculturation and their appropriation as the relevant terms, though they are not the original ones. Because of the transparency of these structures, they gradually overshadow the original technical terms so that "pre-trial detention" becomes the relevant word at the expenses of "held in custody." This phenomenon is the sign of a need for more transparency about legal matters targeted at non professionals. Indeed, "pre-trial detention" is easier

---

[19] Official Document System of the United Nations, <http://daccess-ods.un.org/access.nsf/Get?Open&DS=A/63/173&Lang=F>. Website accessed in November 2012.

to understand than "held in custody" and so are all the collocations associated with "custody" such as "to be remanded in custody." The popularisation of legal topics through articles in the press or on TV, through news reports and series, requires that some sort of facilitation be found. "Pre-trial" represents a form of explanation meant to generate transparency which, nevertheless, can be misleading since, in the case of Control Order, trials are hardly ever part of the procedure.

Translating detention in the case of Control Orders

One of the recurring features when examining texts related to Control Order is the repetition of "detention" which vies for prominence with "custody" as exemplified by the following excerpt extracted from the Prevention of terrorism Act 2005:

> An individual detained under this section—
> (a) shall be deemed to be in legal custody throughout the period of his detention

From a terminological point of view, the most relevant French equivalent is found in the field of criminal law and the translations that come to mind immediately is *détention provisoire* or *garde à vue*.

> Toute personne détenue en vertu du présent article
> (a) sera considérée comme étant en détention provisoire / en garde à vue durant tout le temps de sa détention

The analysis of usage is essential to highlight the differences that exist between "custody" and "detention." Up until 2005 the need for governments to curtail the suspects' rights to enjoy freedom was guaranteed by imprisonment, that is to say detention in prison, while from 2005 onwards control, rather than custody, was resorted to through electronic monitoring devices or, in more severe cases, house arrest. For advocates of Control Orders, the measures imposed on terrorist suspects were not harsh enough, a contention that would later been borne out by the fact that by 2006 many had absconded.[20]

What strikes the attention of the reader in the English text is the use of

---

[20] "In 2010 a study by the Centre for Social Cohesion found that under the control-order system introduced by the Labour government, one in six controlees (16%) had absconded." "Terror suspect's disappearance sparks criticism of control-order regime."

"legal custody" since it is a notion that is most commonly used for child support, child care and the lawful entitlement for a person to make decisions on behalf of someone else. The emphasis is on the curtailment of the people's capacity to uphold their rights rather than on the infringement on their capacity to enjoy freedom. While the notion of custody was not mentioned in the Anti-terrorism, Crime and Security Act 2001, it was found once in the The Prevention of Terrorism Act 2005. The emphasis on detention, which was a priority in the 2005 Act, with nine occurrences, was later abandoned and the Terrorism Prevention & Investigation Measures Act 2011 made no reference to it.

The translation into French raises several issues, the first one having to do with the possible repetition of the word *détention*. *Détention*, in French, needs to be qualified and, as a collocation, it is always associated with adjectives and in particular *provisoire—détention provisoire*—though when the Control Order law was first enacted, the corresponding adjective in French was *préventive—détention preventive*. At the time in England and in France, the emphasis was for the authorities on the protection of the population and that is the meaning conveyed by the adjective *préventive* in *détention préventive*. Yet, in the meantime, pressure groups defending the interests of the defendants[21] required that the emphasis be put on the duration of the detention which was considered, in some cases, too long. Replacing *préventive* by *provisoire* was a way to enshrine in words the fact that the detention could not exceed a reasonable time. Moreover, *préventive* presupposes that the person under this sanction is either guilty or dangerous while *provisoire* merely insists on the fact that the detention is not meant to last, which dispels doubts about whether or not the person is guilty. This terminological debate is a reminder of the controversy that raged over the Control Order measures and in particular over the notion related to "the interfering proactively with the liberty of suspects before any offences have been committed." (Fenwick 1724)·

As far as spoken French is concerned, and before *préventive* was substituted with *provisoire*, *préventive* had become such a common stock phrase in French, a metonymic version of *détention préventive* so commonly used even in the population, that the word *détention* was totally superfluous. In crime series, for instance, *en préventive* was used to give a realistic overtone to fiction.

Though, from a linguistic point of view, *détention provisoire* is the most relevant translation, the context makes it impossible to use it since it

[21] Liberty (The National Council for Civil Liberties) is one of the most prominent organisations.

implies detention in prison and at the time, and following the Law Lords's decision, it was not permitted. It is by a near antonym that "detention" can be translated, that is to say by *liberté* and more precisely by *liberté provisoire*, a translation which incidentally was borne out by the release from the Belmarsh prison of ten suspects after the passing of the 2005 law against terrorism and their subjection to Control Order. Yet, the obligations imposed on terrorist suspects by the anti-terrorism measures were such that the notion of *liberté* was not appropriate either, not to say paradoxical. More specifically, suspects were forced to reside in places decided upon by the authorities and they were to respect strict obligations about the number of visitors and their identity, plus the need to apply for prior authorization. Hence, the need for translators to stay close to the notion of detention and to choose from either *détention*, *rétention* or *assignation à residence*.

As regards *rétention*, the word has a special status since it is part of the French administrative arsenal and it is used for foreigners, which was the case for some suspects in 2005. Yet, *rétention* in French involves the notion of deportation which is not what happened to any of the foreign suspects subjected to Control Order. Moreover, *rétention* implies that foreigners should reside in specially designated places. That was the case for some controlees in the early years of Control Order and some were subjected to relocations to different parts of the country so as to stop communication with potential accomplices.

Theoretically, "detention" can lead to two separate procedures, namely the legal custody of supposed terrorists with either as prospect a future court hearing and a judgment or deportation to their country of origin bearing in mind the fact that, under international law, no one can be sent back to a country where torture or death can be suffered.[22] These two separate procedures have corresponding terminologies which for the first one corresponds to *détention* while the latter corresponds to *rétention* or more exactly to *rétention administrative* which, as indicated by the term itself, is an administrative procedure and is applied to foreigners only who are detained pending deportation.

In the case of Control Order, *détention* is the exact translation for "legal custody," though *détention* requires to be qualified. The intention to protect public interests, to take preventive measures and the fact that the

[22] Article 3 of the United Nations Convention Against Torture (UNCAT) prohibits extraditions to places where torture is still in use: "No State Party shall expel, return ("*refouler*") or extradite a person to another State where there are substantial grounds for believing that he would be in danger of being subjected to torture." <http://www.hrweb.org/legal/cat.html>. Website accessed in January 2013.

Home Secretary should be responsible for it, once oriented the terminological research towards "*mesures de police*." Nevertheless, this notion was not adapted for cases of terrorism and *détention provisoire* seemed better suited. Yet, because of the history of some cases of detention which lasted over five years, *detention préventive* proved even more adequate, the idea contained in it being to isolate people to stop them from being harmful rather than to keep them waiting. From a chronological point of view, *détention* is the word that was relevant until 2005 since until then terrorist suspects were held in prison, in particular at Belmarsh prison: after 2005 most of the suspected terrorists under the 2001 Act were released from prisons and their condition from then on was close to "house arrest", "detention" being then to be translated by *assigné à residence*.[23]

As for the translation of "Control Order," it raises many issues due to procedures which are different on either side of the Channel even though the purpose—to protect the population—is the same. Since judges have also been allowed to decide on measures of Control Order from 2005 onwards, *contrôle judiciaire* seems to provide the right translation, the one most adequate in so far as it falls within the terminology of the judiciary. *Tutelle pénale* a term which existed in France until 1970 and which was the equivalent of *rétention de sécurité*—which the former French Home Secretary under Nicolas Sarkozy's presidency, Rachida Dati, had wanted to reintroduce in the French legal system—was also possible though it applied only to measures following the serving of a sentence, which is not the case here. A realistic alternative to *contrôle judiciaire* seems *être soumis à / faire l'objet de mesures de sûreté*. While in 2011 *contrôle judiciaire* was the relevant translation considering the lifting of many previous measures designed to restrict the freedom of people, in 2005 *mesure de sûreté* was more adapted in the absence of cases of imprisonment. Once again, this example proves the need to take into account the period at which a text is issued particularly when it comes to the translation of legal measures evolving over a period of several years.

Ordre de contrôle can occasionally be found in commentaries about the English Control Order[24]. Yet, it is a neologism; it is no lexicalized legal

---

[23] In Québec French, there is the locution "*sous garde*", which can be translated literally by "under guard" but in both Québec French and English this notion is most commonly used for minors and under 18s.

[24] "La nouvelle loi permet au *Home Secretary* d'adopter un ordre de contrôle contre un individu s'il 'a des motifs raisonnables de suspecter que l'individu en question est, ou a été, impliqué dans des activités liées aux terrorisme' et qu'il juge l'adoption d'un ordre de contrôle imposant des obligations à cet individu

French and it cannot be found in official texts. The closest notion in French is *contrôle judiciaire* which corresponds to many of the obligations related to Control Order, like "house arrest" and also the restrictions about meeting people or taking part in activities, among which the most obvious ones being political, like propaganda and proselytism. In France the list of these obligations number 17[25] and can be modified at any time by the judge for liberties and detention with a modifying order. The translation that is most recurrent in the press on the subject is *ordonnance de contrôle* though it should be borne in mind that in the French legal system the notion of *ordonnance de contrôle* does not exist. The widespread usage of *ordonnance de contrôle* when it comes to anti-terrorism measures, whether in the press or on the websites of international organisations of human rights, has succeeded in imposing a structure which is both a neologism and a calque. One of the few advantages of this translation is its transparency which accounts for its popularity. Though not linguistically satisfactory, it seems to fulfil its function which is to communicate on the issue. Though it is not legally accurate, the context in which it is used often suffices to provide the necessary explanations. Yet, for linguists and legal experts with purist views, *contrôle judiciaire* remains the only acceptable translation.

Conclusion

A diachronic approach of legal matters allows for a closer look at the evolution of language which bespeaks the evolution of mentalities and the way legislators must adjust the formulation of the law to the sensibility of the several social groups which try and make themselves heard. This task is all the more arduous as the laws under examination were designed to cope with exceptional circumstances. The measures taken in the wake of the 9/11 attacks were conceived with a view to protecting the population and to satisfying the general outcry of the British population. Some of them, regarding the detention of suspects and the circulation of information, went against national and international regulations and even though the UK suffered the tragedy of attack on its mainland four years later, the then government had to back down on measures like the conditions of detention.

Accommodating opposite views embodied, on the one hand, by the

---

nécessaire pour des raisons liées à la protection des membres du public contre un risque de terrorisme". (Elliott)

[25] *Code de procédure pénale sur le contrôle judiciaire.*

international institutions asking for the strict respect of human rights and, on the other hand, by the population demanding tougher measures designed to ensure its safety requested linguistic prowess. "Custody", "detention" referred to radically different realities in 2001, in 2005 and in 2011. Translating them meant adjusting to what was going on at the time and to the evolution of justice: the police being gradually endowed with duties and responsibilities exclusively in the hands of the Home Secretary up until 2005, terminology had to change accordingly. Control Order has provided an adequate illustration of the tug-of-war at the heart of the translation process between the respect of accuracy and the need to communicate. Should translators opt for calques, equivalents or should they try to find inventive structures likely to help the foreign readers understand the situations without being deceived about the exact nature of this notion? Although *ordonnances de contrôle* is a neologism, it has partly solved the problem by providing people, who are interested in the way laws of exception tackle the issue of terrorism in the UK, with a meaningful though not really adequate answer.

Works cited

ANDERSON, David. *Control Orders in 2011. Final Report of the Independent Reviewer on the Prevention of Terrorism Act 2005.* Independent Reviewer of Terrorism Legislation. London: the Stationary Office, 2012.

BASSENETT, Susan. *Translation Studies.* London: Routledge, 2002.

BOCQUET, Claude. *La Traduction juridique. Fondement et méthode.* Bruxelles: De Boeck, 2008.

Code de procédure pénale sur le contrôle judiciaire. URL: <http://www.lexinter.net/PROCPEN/controle_judicaire.htm>. Website accessed in November 2012.

Convention européenne des droits de l'homme. Strasbourg: Les Éditions du Conseil de l'Europe, 1995.

CAO, Deborah. *Translating Law*. Clevedon, Buffalo, Toronto: Multilingual Matters Ltd, 2007.

CORNU, Gérard. *Vocabulaire juridique* . Paris: PUF, 2011.

FENWICK, Helen. *Civil Liberties and Human Rights*. London: Routledge, 2012.

FENWICK, Helen and Gavin PHILLIPSON. *Constitutional & Administrative Law*. London: Routledge, 2013.

GREENSTEIN, Rosalind (dir.). *La Langue, le discours et la culture en anglais du droit*. Paris : Publications de la Sorbonne, 2005.

GREER, Steve. *The European Convention on Human Rights. Achievements, Problems and Prospects*. Cambridge: Cambridge University Press, 2006.

House of Lords ruling on the Belmarsh detainees. 16 December, 2004. URL: <http://www.libertysecurity.org/article973>. Website accessed in December 2012.

ELLIOTT, Mark. "La 'Guerre' contre le Terrorisme et la Constitution du Royaume-Uni." *European Journal of Legal Studies* 1.1. Website accessed in December 2012. URL: <http://www.ejls.eu/>.

IVIR, Vladimir. "Formal Correspondence," in SIN-WAI, Chan and David E. POLLARD. *An Encyclopedia of Translation*. Hong Kong: The Chinese University Press, 2001.

JAKOBSON, Roman. *Langage in Literature*. Cambridge, MA: Harvard University Press, 1987.

"Julian Assange extradition appeal at supreme court". *The Guardian online.* Wednesday, February 1. Website accessed on April 2013. URL: <http://www.guardian.co.uk/media/blog/2012/feb01/julian-assange-extradition-appeal-at-supreme-court-live-blog>.

NIDA, Eugene. *Toward a Science of Translating: With Special Reference to Principles and Procedures Involved in Bible Translating*. Leiden: Brill Archie, 1964.

Secretary of State for the Home Department (Appellant) v. JJ and others (FC) (Respondents). Website accessed in December 2013. URL: <http://www.piblications.parliament.uk/pa/1d200607/1djudgmt/jd071031/homejj3.htm>.

Les Droits de l'homme. Repères juridiques européens. Strasbourg: Les Éditions du Conseil de l'Europe, 1999.

OLOHAN, Maeve. *Introducing Corpora in Translation Studies*. Londres: Routledge, 2004.

"Terror suspect's disappearance sparks criticism of control-order regime." *The Guardian online.* Website accessed on January 2013. URL: <http://www.theguardian.com/uk/2013/jan/01/terror-suspects-disappearance-control-order>.

TIERSMA, Peter and Lawrence SOLAN. *The Oxford Handbook of Language and Law*. Oxford: Oxford University Press, 2012.

TOURY, Gideon. *Descriptive Translation Studies: And Beyond.* Amsterdam: John Benjamins Publishing, 1995.

VINAY, Jean-Paul and Jean Louis Darbelnet. *Comparative Stylistics of French and English: a Methodology for Translation.* Amsterdam: John Benjamins Publishing, 1995.

CONTRIBUTORS

Sivila Capanema is a Senior Lecturer in Brazilian studies at the University of Paris Nord, Campus Condorcet where she is a member of the research center Pleiade (former CRESC.) In 2009, she completed a thesis entitled "We, sailors, Brazilian citizens and Republicans: identity, modernity and memory of the sailors' revolt in 1910" under the supervision of Mr. Juan Carlos Garavaglia. Her research interests are the social and cultural history of modern Brazil.

Roy Carpenter is a Lecturer (Professeur Agrégé) at Jean Moulin University where he teaches American legal and political institutions. He is a Doctor in American studies from the University of Versailles Saint Quentin-en-Yvelines where he completed a thesis entitled "Jonathan Edwards: the crisis of authority in 18th America" under the supervision of Pr. Bernard Cottret. He is the author of several articles about the Great Awakening.

Marion Charret-Del Bove is a Lecturer at the law faculty of Jean Moulin University Lyon 3 where she teaches advanced courses in legal English. Her main fields of research are the comparison of criminal procedures in England, the USA and France as well as issues of legal translation.

Céline Chassang is a PhD researcher at the University Paris Ouest Nanterre La Défense, under the supervision of Pr. Elisabeth Fortis. Her thesis subject is "*L'étranger en droit pénal français.*" She is a member of the Research Centre of Criminal Law and Criminology of the same university where she also teaches criminal business law and special criminal law.

George Fournier is a Senior Lecturer at the Department of English of Jean Moulin University Lyon 3. He is Head of the Master's degree in Translation Studies and teaches advanced courses in theoretical and practical translation. His main fields of research are contemporary British civilization and the comparative translation of French and Anglo-Saxon institutional systems.

Géraldine Gadbin-George is an Associate Professor at University Panthéon-Assas (Paris.) Prior to entering higher education, she practised as a French *avocat* and an English solicitor. Her research work deals with access to justice in England and Wales, as well as comparative law. She recently published in *Revista Critica Penal y Poder* (Barcelona) and *Comparative Law Review* (North America.)

Elizabeth Gibson-Morgan is a Doctor in public law. She graduated from Political Sciences in Bordeaux. She has been teaching common law and legal English at the University of Montesquieu-Bordeaux IV as well at the French national school for judges for 16 years. For the past six years, she has been a Senior Lecturer at the department of law and languages at the University of Tours where she is a member of the Institute of Criminal Sciences and Justice. She is also a Visiting Senior Research Fellow at King's College in London.

Neil Jarman is Director of the Institute for Conflict Research where he has carried out research on such issues as street violence, disputes over parades, management of public order, police reform, racist and homophobic violence and human rights in a number of countries including Northern Ireland, South Africa, USA, Israel/Palestine, Kosova, and Nepal. He is currently working with the Office of Democratic Institutions and Human Rights (ODIHR) at the Organisation of Security and Co-operation in Europe (OSCE) as a member of an international panel tasked with drafting guidelines relating to law and practice on freedom of assembly.

Kenneth O. Morgan is Visiting Professor in the Institute of Contemporary British History at King's College, London. He was formerly Fellow and Praelector in Modern History and Politics at Queen's College, Oxford, and Vice-Chancellor at the University of Wales, Aberystwyth. He has written many books on contemporary British political history, such as *Labour in Power 1945-1951*, *The People's Peace*, and *Ages of Reform*, as well as biographies of Lloyd George, Keir Hardie , James Callaghan, and Michael Foot. He has been a working peer in the House of Lords since 2000, where he serves on the Select Committee on the Constitution.

Marie Marty is a PhD researcher at the University of Luxembourg, under the supervision of Pr. Stefan Braum. Her research interests are comparative criminal law, EU criminal law and protection of fundamental rights in criminal proceedings. Her thesis subject is about admissibility of evidence in cross-border criminal matters: the research addresses the question whether the national laws of evidence are similar enough to allow the free movement and free admissibility of evidence between EU Member States.

Fabrice Mourlon is a Lecturer at the University of Paris 13 where he teaches students in continuing education. His research focuses on the legacy of the conflict in Northern Ireland, which includes the study of dealing with the past in a post-conflict society, assistance to victims and survivors and the role of their testimonies in reconciliation.

Catherine Puzzo is a Senior Lecturer in the department of English Studies (University Toulouse II le Mirail) and member of the research group *Cultures Anglo-Saxonnes* (EA 801.) Her most recent publications include a paper on migrants' rights in the UK, "International migrants' rights in the UK fom the 1998 Human Rights Act to the Big Society concept: a review article" *Lisa e-journal, Equal rights: myth or reality in contemporary English speaking societies?* (1st semester 2014). She is currently involved in the international project SoMI (Securitization of Migrant Integration,) a UK-US comparison on the typology of collective mobilization of migrants and minorities of recent migrant origins (Paris III–Rutgers, State University of New Jersey.)

Sacha Raoult is an Assistant Professor at the University of Aix-Marseille, where he is a member of the research centre of private law and criminal sciences within the Institute of criminological and criminal sciences. He teaches in particular in the field of judicial supervision (*contrôle judiciaire*,) house arrest and detention on remand. He is Visiting Professor at McGill University and the University of Chicago. He is also a member of the Regional Observatory of crime and social contexts.

Akila Taleb currently holds the position as a legal consultant at the Pre-Trial Chamber of the Special Tribunal for Lebanon. She is a Doctor in law and has completed a PhD in criminal Law and criminal Justice alongside which she has worked for seven years as a temporary lecturer and a research assistant at the Universities of Lyon 3, Lyon 2 and Lyon I and, for four years, as a caseworker at the prosecution department of the Court of Appeal of Lyon. Her articles published in various legal journals particularly focus on comparative criminal law and criminal justice in light of the European Court of Human Rights' case-law.